THE MESSAGE IN THE MUSIC

STUDYING CONTEMPORARY PRAISE AND WORSHIP

EDITED BY

ROBERT WOODS

AND

BRIAN WALRATH

FOREWORD BY RICHARD J. MOUW

Abingdon Press
NASHVILLE

THE MESSAGE IN THE MUSIC
STUDYING CONTEMPORARY PRAISE AND WORSHIP

9-23-21

Copyright © 2007 by Abingdon Press

This book is printed on acid-free paper.

Library of Congress Cataloging-in-Publication Data

The message in the music : studying contemporary praise and worship / edited by Robert Woods and Brian Walrath ; foreword by Richard Mouw.
  p. cm.
  Includes indexes.
ISBN 978-0-687-64564-0 (pbk. : alk. paper)
1. Contemporary Christian music—History and criticism. I. Woods, Robert, 1970– II. Walrath, Brian.

ML3187.5.M47   2007
264'.23—dc22

2007030340

07 08 09 10 11 12 13 14 15 16—10 9 8 7 6 5 4 3 2 1

MANUFACTURED IN THE UNITED STATES OF AMERICA

CONTENTS

FOREWORD

Richard J. Mouw

WHat are you folks at Fuller doing to help us get rid of all of this repetitious 'praise music' we are having to sing in our congregation these days?" The person posing that question to me was a longtime supporter of Fuller Seminary, and I knew him to be a great admirer of our founder, Charles E. Fuller. So instead of giving a detailed answer, I just sang the song that Dr. Fuller led his audience in singing every week on his pioneering radio broadcast, "The Old Fashioned Revival Hour":

> Heavenly sunshine, heavenly sunshine,
> Flooding my soul with glory di-vine.
> Heavenly sunshine, heavenly sunshine,
> Hallelujah, Jesus is mine.

Eighteen words there, with one two-word phrase repeated four times.

Fortunately, my questioner took my point in good humor. Repetitious singing is nothing new in the evangelical world. And if you are not an evangelical? Well, then you have to be sure in making your complaint that you are willing to level the same criticism at your favorite group of Catholic monks, who probably manage to repeat "kyrie eleison" quite a bit when they sing.

Praise music often gets a bad rap. (No pun intended!) And that is why we should be grateful for this book. In these pages people who know the traditions of Christian hymnody take a careful look at the actual content of contemporary worship music, and treat it respectfully. Better yet, they treat it with theological care.

I am a switch-hitter when it comes to worship music. I love the old hymns, but I also like praise music. The greatest liturgical innovation of the past half-century is the screen, and it has accomplished much good. People can worship with their hands freed up to move around. Their eyes are lifted upward rather than staring down at a hymnbook. These are good things.

But there is a downside also. As I write this I have just returned from a gathering where about 200 students on Fuller's campus sang some praise songs. At the end of the time of singing, though, they launched into an oldie: "What can wash away my sin? Nothing but the blood of Jesus." That was great—except for one thing. There was no harmony. For once I wished they could be looking at a hymnbook as they sang—and without two guitars and the drums.

But the instincts that made for the "blending" of old and new were good ones. Now we have to get beyond instincts, however. We need some solid theological guidance.

Throughout the history of the Christian church vital and faithful music has come forth when an enthusiasm for the gospel has been intertwined with deep biblical and theological reflection—Luther and the Wesleys provide us with obvious cases in point.

This book gives us the kind of theological guidance that we need for our own day. More than that, it is a sign of hope that the hunger for spiritual renewal that we see in our new patterns of worship can also motivate us to think new theological thoughts about the life and mission of the church. I find that so encouraging that I am inclined to raise an old-fashioned "Ebenezer!" in gratitude. And I am even willing to follow that up with the singing of a repetitious praise song!

Richard J. Mouw
President, Fuller Theological Seminary
Spring 2007

CONTRIBUTORS

DIANE BADZINSKI is Associate Professor of Communication at Colorado Christian University in Lakewood, Colorado. Her research program has centered on mapping behaviors/attributes to communication outcomes. She has coauthored a textbook in statistics and has published in a variety of research journals, including *Journal of Applied Communication, Communication Research, Human Communication Research, Western Journal of Communication*, and *Journal of Advertising*.

MARGARET BRADY is Director of Worship Arts at North Park Theological Seminary. She has worked with the Evangelical Covenant denomination in developing resources in global worship, intergenerational worship, and current worship music; conducted extensive surveys on the use of worship music in undergraduate and graduate educational institutions; and consulted on the use of current worship music at colleges in Australia, Hong Kong, and Singapore. Dr. Brady is convener for the Contemporary and Alternative Worship group of the North American Academy of Liturgy.

KEITH DRURY is Associate Professor of Religion at Indiana Wesleyan University in Marion, Indiana, where he teaches practical ministry courses. He writes a weekly column for ministers that has been published on the Internet since 1995 and is the founder of Indiana Wesleyan University's Christian Worship major. He is the author of numerous books and articles, including *The Wonder of Worship: Why We Worship the Way We Do*.

JAY HOWARD earned his Ph.D. from University of Notre Dame (1992) and currently is Professor of Sociology and Vice Chancellor and Dean at Indiana University–Purdue University Columbus in Columbus, Indiana. He is coauthor with John M. Streck of *Apostles of Rock: The Splintered World of Contemporary Christian Music* and has published related research in *Popular Music* and the *Journal of Popular Culture*. Dr. Howard's research interests range from religion and popular culture to the scholarship of teaching and learning. He is a Fellow of the P. A. Mack Center at Indiana University for Inquiry on Teaching and Learning and serves as Deputy Editor of the American Sociological Association journal, *Teaching Sociology*.

GUY JANSEN is a well-known church music leader in his native New Zealand. He has been music director for many national church assemblies and conferences in New Zealand and Australia. He is currently Director of the Choir at St Johns-in-the-City Presbyterian Church, Wellington, where he also is part of the contemporary music team. Jansen coedited *Servant Songs*, a major international song collection, and has been producer/session pianist for five recordings.

JENELL WILLIAMS PARIS is Professor of Sociology and Anthropology at Messiah College in Grantham, Pennsylvania. She is the author of *Urban Disciples: A Beginner's Guide to Serving God in the City* and *Birth Control for Christians: Making Wise Choices.*

DAVID PASS ministers under the auspices of PassWord International, a faith-based music and missions organization. He has published over two hundred songs, many of which have been recorded by his wife, Liz, and other gospel artists. Dave and Liz currently minister and teach on music and worship in South Africa, Zimbabwe, Mozambique, Brazil, the USA, and the UK. He is also author of the books *Music and the Church* and *Faith Development in Context.*

BERT POLMAN is Professor and Chair of Music at Calvin College in Grand Rapids, Michigan, and a Senior Research Fellow for the Calvin Institute of Christian Worship. Primarily a musicologist, with specific interests in church music, hymnology, and worship, Polman has been a church organist since age fifteen. He has done editorial work on five hymnals, authored most of the *Psalter Hymnal Handbook,* is coauthor of a forthcoming commentary on praise and worship songs, and is writing a book on the history of musical settings of the "Magnificat."

WENDY J. PORTER is Director of Music and Worship at McMaster Divinity College in Hamilton, Ontario, where she leads chapels and teaches classes and seminars on music and worship, including a favorite, "I Can't Worship to *That* Music!" Wendy has led worship since she was a teen, has sung in churches throughout North America, and has held several church worship positions. She has recorded two CDs and has written many worship songs and published articles on the contemporary worship phenomena.

LESTER RUTH is the Lily May Jarvis Professor of Christian Worship at Asbury Theological Seminary. He also teaches in the Robert E. Webber Institute for Worship Studies in Orange Park, Florida. Trained as a historian of worship, he has done most of his work in American Evangelicalism or the ancient church. He spent six years as a Methodist pastor before teaching full time at Yale Divinity School.

BRIAN WALRATH is Associate Professor of Music and Worship Arts at Spring Arbor University in Spring Arbor, Michigan. As lead professor in the Worship Arts major program, he teaches courses in music, music ministry, and worship studies. He has served on local and national worship planning committees in the Free Methodist church for the past twenty years and has used contemporary worship music since the early 1980s in church and parachurch ministry with Youth for Christ, where he was a full-time staff member for twelve years.

JOHN D. WITVLIET is Director of the Calvin Institute of Christian Worship and serves as Associate Professor of Worship, Theology, and Music at Calvin College and Calvin Theological Seminary. He is the author of *The Biblical Psalms in Christian Worship* and *Worship Seeking Understanding*, and coeditor of *Worship in Medieval and Early Modern Europe*.

ROBERT WOODS is Associate Professor in the Department of Communication and Media at Spring Arbor University in Spring Arbor, Michigan, where he teaches courses in research and ethics. His scholarly articles have appeared in many publications and spanned wide-ranging topics such as online learning, reality TV, and Free Methodist worship. He is coauthor of the recent *Media Ethics: Cases and Moral Reasoning* (7th ed).

ACKNOWLEDGMENTS

In any project of this magnitude there are many individuals to thank. First, we thank God for sustaining us through this project during the last two years. We are mindful of His perfect timing, endless patience, and marvelous grace. Each time we experienced a setback or fell behind in schedule, something was provided that quickly caught us back up and in most cases put us ahead of where we had been.

Many Spring Arbor University (SAU) students were instrumental in helping to bring this project to completion. Rob Vischer's passion for worship music helped the project get off the ground at the earliest stages. Jennifer Timm served as the index coordinator who supervised the work of Jonathan R. Dibbern, Carmelle Novak, Archie Woods, Frank Meely, and Sarah Shirlen. Sarah Shirlen spent additional time formatting each chapter and cleaning up the references. Megan K. Wilhelm and Frank Meely assisted with the coding of data in chapter 6. Several SAU students and staff reviewed various chapters to help make them more readable and compelling: Jennifer Timm, Sarah Shirlen, Megan K. Wilhelm, and Rebecca Negron. Rebecca Negron also worked diligently on formatting all chapters into a single document and creating the Table of Contents. Our faculty colleagues at SAU reviewed various chapters for style and substance: Mary Darling, Paul Patton, Reed Sheard, Stephanie Davis, Mike Jindra, and Cindy Meredith.

Various colleagues within the Council of Christian Colleges and Universities (CCCU) and other non-CCCU institutions provided feedback as well: Diane Badzinski, Samuel Ebersole, Rebekah Woods, Carrie Steenwyk, and Ron Rienstra. Bert Polman and Lester Ruth spent time reviewing the conclusion. Our friend John Strodtbeck took time to review the introduction and offer insightful comments. Betty Walrath reviewed the manuscript for typographical and grammatical errors.

Marsha Daigle-Williamson's masterful copyediting work during the final stages reinforced the unity among the chapters and greatly increased the book's readability. Quentin Schultze's sage advice about organization, readability, and publishing in general was instrumental as we considered ways to serve our audiences with this work.

We thank Abingdon Press for their immediate interest in this project. We are grateful to Harriett Jane Olson, senior vice president for publishing, who championed the idea. Robert Ratcliff, senior editor of Academic and Ministry Leadership Resources, and Tim West patiently shepherded us through the process. John Kutsko and the rest of the academic team, including but not limited to Chris Czynszak, ensured that the process went smoothly. We thank them for their professionalism and dedication to a quality product.

Our wives, Rebekah Woods and Betty Walrath, provided daily nurture and perspective. They served as sounding boards and encouraged us to be patient and transparent. Their early input shaped the tone and tenor of the manuscript. They are constant sources of joy.

We dedicate this book to Robert Webber. Bob's contributions to the field of worship studies are significant, to say the least, and his generosity and collegiality continue to inspire generations of scholars. When we told Bob about the idea we had for this book before he passed away, his positive response and willingness to be involved in some way gave us the extra spark we needed to move forward. We are extremely grateful. We will miss you.

INTRODUCTION

Robert Woods and Brian Walrath

In 1999, the cover of *Christianity Today* boldly proclaimed the following: "The Triumph of the Praise Songs: How Guitars Beat out the Organ in the Worship Wars." Although the reality and scope of the worship "wars" has been challenged by some,[1] if we accept Don Hustad's suggestion that praise and worship music began officially in 1968 with the release of David and Dale Garratt's *Scripture in Song*,[2] then it took about a generation and a half (thirty-eight years) to bring about the victory Michael Hamilton describes in this cover story.[3]

For many, Hamilton's statement stirs strong feelings—both positive and negative—and at the very least demands serious consideration. Even six years after first seeing it in print, it is still a little shocking for us. The title made whatever had transpired between the guitar and organ sound—how shall we say—long and bloody. You may have wondered a few things after first seeing this statement in 1999 or just now in the paragraph above, such as who fired the first shot, who or what survived, and what does all this mean for us now? If you did, you are not alone.

This book is about taking a closer look at the so-called victors, that is, the contemporary worship music that triumphed in what is often referred to as the "worship wars." The authors we have assembled in this volume sidestep the wartime propaganda to take an in-depth look at 77 of the most frequently sung worship tunes in America. In the process, we have asked the authors to reflect on what this so-called triumph means for us as twenty-first-century worshipers and how future wars might be avoided.

Before we present you the ten chapters in this volume, we need to first trace the "triumph" of the praise song and consider why this music has evoked such strong reactions, both positive and negative, among worshipers. Why we focused our analysis on 77 contemporary worship songs among the hundreds of thousands available requires brief explanation as well. Before we conclude this introduction we will give a brief overview of each chapter and suggest ways for readers to make practical use of their contents.

Tracing the "Triumph" of the Praise Song

When the Jesus Movement swept America in the late 1960s and early 1970s, a new type of Christian music began to emerge. Using song forms and instrumentation of the popular culture from which these young musicians came, this new "Jesus Music" at first focused on testifying to personal salvation experience. The songs reflected the gratitude of the writers for being saved from their former lifestyles and circumstances. As these artists matured in their faith and moved into Christian concert ministries and recording contracts, the genre of Contemporary Christian Music (CCM) was born.[4]

Openness to ministry through pop/rock music, church culture shifts sparked by Vatican II, and the explosion of the worldwide charismatic movement combined to produce the first "praise and worship" choruses. Known initially as "scripture choruses," these short paraphrased scriptures set to pop-style music were composed by and found homes in the Sunday worship of Pentecostal and other "charismatic" churches by the mid 1970s.[5] The composers of many of the earliest of these songs are unknown since they did not file copyrights on them. Ultimately, others collected and published collections of this music.[6] The limitation of setting only scripture passages to music soon gave way to writing a broader range of praise songs expressing one's personal relationship with Jesus and intimate worship by the individual believer.[7]

By the 1980s youth from noncharismatic churches had also developed a taste for this style of worship music and were becoming increasingly influential in the planning and leading of Sunday worship in their own churches. At the same time a large modern church in suburban Chicago was pioneering what soon became known worldwide as the "seeker service." Using contemporary music, drama, and multimedia, Willow Creek Community Church sought to produce "church for the unchurched," a culturally comfortable introductory church experience for non-Christians. A component of the Willow Creek model was a "believers'" service, held on a different weekday, which continued to feature the use of similar music, drama, and multimedia in a worship setting. The stunning growth of this church and others like it sparked a flood of interest in imitating this model, which included "believers'" worship services based on this design.[8]

Praise and worship music, more broadly contemporary worship music (CWM),[9] has been steadily growing in popularity and use in American churches since the 1980s.[10] CWM began replacing traditional hymns in a small number of churches in the late 1980s and early 1990s. By the end of 1990 a significant minority of American Protestant churches (31%) were using CWM either in conjunction with other hymnody or as the exclusive musical style of the Sunday service.[11]

In 2003, CWM accounted for 11.1% of the 47.1 million albums sold in the Christian music industry. Four of the top ten best-selling albums of 2003 were praise and worship. The CWM song *I Can Only Imagine* rated high on mainstream pop charts that same year.[12] John Styll, president of the Gospel Music Association, commented, "Nearly half of the top albums are worship records, telling us that our consumers desire a real connection to God with their music and are actively seeking music that extends their church experience into daily life."[13] This surge reversed a downward trend in CCM sales of the previous year.[14]

Pastor Jack Hayford, author of the popular praise chorus *Majesty* and supporter of renewal worship, suggests that what is taking place is nothing less than a new reformation in worship music. Just as the reformation of the sixteenth century was a reformation of doctrine (words and message) to recover biblical truth, this generation's reformation in worship is just as historic and just as necessary.[15] CWM composer and author Barry Liesch gives further insight into the central issues of the "reformation" when he concludes, "No group or denomination can sidestep the hot debate over the benefits of hymns versus choruses, seeker services versus worship services, choirs versus worship teams, traditional versus contemporary styles, and flowing praise versus singing one song at a time."[16]

So, whether you consider what has transpired between the hymn and praise chorus to be a heated debate, war, or reformation, the church you attend has most likely responded to one or more of these issues.

Michael Hamilton offers good advice for twenty-first-century worshipers at the conclusion of his article—advice we find particularly encouraging as we are about to embark on the analytical journey in the ten chapters that follow. He reminds us that the Body of Christ is too diverse to ever settle on just one style of music as appropriate for worship. He also notes that the living church needs to welcome creative new ways of singing the gospel. "We need . . . to welcome any worship music that helps churches produce disciples of Jesus Christ" and "banish fears that grip us when familiar music passes away."[17] To this we might add that such welcoming must always be done wisely and without aversion to self-criticism.

The Good, Bad, and Ugly of CWM

Along with many of you, we have been active participants in and students of the "worship wars" for quite some time. As professors at an evangelical Christian university, we are immersed in CWM. One of the fastest-growing majors at Spring Arbor University (and other Christian colleges), and a major in which we both teach, is Worship Arts. In the first three years of its existence at our institution, its enrollment doubled every year. Many of our students on campus, whether worship majors or not, listen to CWM, perform it, analyze it, compose it, and record it. Our students engage us in lengthy discussions about what makes a quality worship song, how to blend contemporary and traditional music, what the difference between worship and performance is, and what their roles are as the next generation of contemporary worship leaders. Outside of the university, we are actively involved in the rehearsal and use of CWM as members of our church's worship team.

But what is it about this music that has generated such excitement and emotional response, both good and bad—and sometimes ugly?

As a guitarist (Robert) and drummer (Brian) for Sunday worship, we see people encounter God's presence in powerful ways through CWM. There are some CWM songs that we ourselves cannot sing without being brought to tears. We agree with Barry Liesch and others that praise and worship choruses have the potential to communicate the Christian faith in a fresh way to contemporary culture. They are often a means of intimate and enjoyable worship expression for the younger generation who values direct experience. They effectively educate children and are understood by the visiting nonbeliever. We have seen CWM help new believers become spiritually grounded and give expression to their faith. We have seen how praise choruses can have a cultural "broadening effect" by putting worshipers in contact with other ethnic groups and their musical styles.

At the same time, despite CWM's increasing use in American churches and the benefits highlighted above, it has received much criticism. Thus, while we wholeheartedly acknowledge CWM's value, we wrestle with its quality and usage on a near weekly basis.

Many traditional church musicians take exception to the style and quality of the music.[18] Others describe CWM as faddish "pop worship" that mimics the latest popular styles.[19] CWM has been charged with being merely entertainment, treating worshipers like consumers—giving them what they want musically rather than what they need spiritually, relying on manipulation of emotions rather than the movement of the Holy Spirit.[20]

But it is the texts, or lyrics, of the songs that have received most of the criticism, given their potential influence on worshipers and mainstream perceptions of Christianity. The songs' lyrics have been accused of reflecting values of popular culture, such as "instant gratification, impatience, ahistorical immediacy, and incessant novelty." In many cases the songs lack intellectual rigor and "shortchange the full reality of sin and human weakness."[21] We have heard pastor friends of ours suggest that CWM fails to adequately capture human suffering and the suffering of Christ on the cross. Others have noted that the songs' lyrics tend to "emphasize sin defeated, gloss over persistent sin in our lives, and provide little emphasis on corporate confession or repentance." In much of the CWM we have sung in recent years, the cost of discipleship and need for perseverance seem to get little attention. On top of this, the lyrics of most choruses are so short that "thoughts about God cannot be developed or expanded." All of these criticisms have led some to conclude that CWM's lyrics are too "me-centered," repetitive, and lacking in "mature exposition of the broad range of biblical doctrine."[22] Raymond Gawronski poignantly summarizes the concerns surrounding the typical modern religious song when he states:

> Written, no doubt, within the past 20 years, it is a piece of that resigned sentimentality that is characteristic of "easy listening music." Although pleasant enough, it

is spiritual Wonder Bread: It utterly lacks roots, depth, sustenance. It is all right as a starter, to open the heart to prayer. But unless fed by some solid food . . . serious seekers will turn elsewhere.[23]

Strong words, but certainly deserving of a response.

A Timely and Traditional Response

In light of the concerns mentioned earlier, there have been numerous calls for serious analysis of CWM by worship scholars, pastors, worship leaders, lay leaders, composers, and musicians. However, to date neither the lyrics nor the music of CWM has been subjected to much serious scholarly attention.

Indeed, scholars have long been interested in the content of church music. Hymns, for example, were subjected to formal content analysis techniques as early as the eighteenth century when church officials suspected that the *Songs of Zion*, a collection of ninety hymns published in 1743, were propagating the pietistic doctrine of the Moravian Brethren over against that approved by the State (Lutheran) Church.[24] Such reflection on the content of hymns has remained popular up to and including the twenty-first century.[25] More recently, there has been growing interest in the lyrical content of CCM given its popularity and mainstream success,[26] although CWM has been conspicuously overlooked. We consider this somewhat surprising since CWM is the fastest-growing form of CCM[27] and, like CCM, it is a popular genre similarly defined by its lyrical content.

The majority of available scholarship on CWM to date has centered on its development and current role in worship renewal.[28] Nearly all of the work we have encountered dealing with CWM involves essays, editorials, or commentaries related to a specific song's word choice or message, along with a few general raves or rants about the whole of CWM.[29] Such work more often than not is propagandistic in that it promotes the authors' personal theological or denominational biases. Furthermore, such work often fails to adequately represent the breadth of CWM and tends to confuse musical style with lyrical content.[30]

To address the lack of systematic inquiry related to CWM's lyrics and music and respond to widespread concerns regarding CWM's suitability for worship, we have assembled a group of scholars and musicians to review the Top 25 praise and worship song lists as reported by Christian Copyright Licensing International (CCLI) between 1989 and 2005. (As explained in greater detail below, the Top 25 lists during this time period provide 77 songs for analysis.) The thirteen authors assembled represent nearly a dozen Christian colleges in North America and half a dozen academic disciplines, from anthropology to liturgical studies. Following a common organizational scheme, the authors critically analyze the 77 CWM songs from their unique perspectives and frames of reference. Chapters 1–7 analyze CWM's lyrical content while chapters 8–10 analyze its musical content. Each chapter concludes with recommendations and practical advice for music ministers and other lay leaders involved in planning and performing corporate worship that includes CWM.

We believe that the scope of this book follows a rich Christian tradition as it relates to concern about appropriate communication and expression in worship. At the end of the fourth century, Jerome raised his voice against pagan literature and its embellishments, banishing their use among Christian preachers and writers.[31] Writing a few years later, Augustine (354–430) disagreed, arguing that Christian teaching and doctrine deserved the same decorations and rhetorical embellishment as did pagan literature and religious teachings.[32] By the seventh and eighth centuries, the iconoclastic controversy raged as Christians on both sides questioned whether images had any place in worship. The Reformation followed within 75 years of the invention of printing from movable type. As Christian churches adapted their communication to the printing press, they also returned to the earlier debates about the proper use of physical, rhetorical, and musical decoration in worship and in Christian life.[33]

Throughout this rich tradition, which continues in various new media forms today,[34] reflection has tended to follow practice. In other words, people make use of various popular means of worship communication first and only later come to a theoretical judgment about that practice. For the last four decades, with rare exception, CWM practice has outpaced theoretical and theological judgment. This book is thus both traditionally grounded and timely. Our authors seek to bring clarity to an area of popular worship practice that is ripe for reflection. We trust that their conclusions will open doors of conversation and spark interest in future study of CWM in the twenty-first century.

How We Selected the Top 77 CWM Songs for Analysis

Since CWM first appeared in the late 1960s, thousands of songs fitting this genre have been written. Currently, there are over 150,000 songs listed on the Christian Copyright Licensing International (CCLI) site. CCLI is the major clearinghouse for the handling of license fees paid in by churches and paid out as royalties for CWM. The number of churches holding licenses has expanded rapidly since CCLI first appeared on the scene. In 1989, 9,500 churches held licenses. Currently more than 176,000 churches hold licenses with over 136,000 of these in the United States.[35] More than 130 denominations are represented among CCLI's license holders.

In order to have a manageable, yet representative, number of songs to analyze, we acquired CCLI's Top 25 lists between 1989 and 2005. CCLI publishes a list of the Top 25 songs for each of its twice-a-year royalty payout periods. Thus, two Top 25 lists—the first published in October and the second in February of the following year—comprise a single year's list. Between 1989 and 2005, there were a total of thirty-three Top 25 lists. The first list appeared in April 1989. The lists beginning in 1990 were published twice per year.

The two Top 25 lists each year reflect the CWM songs most used by CCLI license-holding churches in the United States during a twelve-month period, factoring in frequency of use and size of worshiping congregations, as indicated on these churches' reports to CCLI. The reporting for any time period is a sampling of the churches holding licenses at that time. All 136,000+ license-holding U.S. churches do not report during each six-month period: churches in the U.S. report songs used in a six-month period once every two-and-a-half years.

Although the combination of Top 25 lists for each year between 1989 and 2005 yielded 825 potential songs to review, closer analysis of these thirty-three Top 25 lists comprising the time period revealed that only 77 different songs appeared between 1989 and 2005. Put another way, only 77 songs made up CCLI's Top 25 lists between 1989 and 2005. As mentioned above, this list of 77 songs constituted the repertoire for each author's chapter and appears at the end of this introductory chapter in alphabetical order (see table 1). Each chapter author was given the lyrics for each of the 77 songs to assist in his or her analysis. Authors for chapters 8–10, who analyzed the musical content of the 77 songs, shared the musical scores for each song. The 77 songs identified in the manner described above and listed in table 1 were then listed in a spreadsheet in alphabetical order along with their copyright date and the reporting periods in which they appeared.

There were several advantages and disadvantages of using CCLI to determine the top CWM songs for analysis. One advantage is that CCLI is the only major clearinghouse of CWM usage in the world. From 1989 to present day, CCLI has served as a central data collection agency for cross-denominational usage of CWM in churches across North America. Second, CCLI is updated regularly (every six months) and provides researchers with comprehensive and current data that allow comparisons over an extended period of time. CCLI also provides modest thematic categorizations that were a helpful starting place for some of our authors as they considered their analysis of the songs.

In addition, CCLI's Top 25 lists provide a snapshot of current CWM songs that receive the highest level of activity in a significant number of Protestant churches across North America. Songs with high levels of activity are important to study because they will likely influence Christians' ways of thinking about worship. Non-Christians and "seekers" too may draw conclusions about the church's values, beliefs, and priorities based on the lyrics and music of the songs performed during worship. Also, it is possible that songs on the Top 25 lists may be more frequently sung than others because they embody relevant personal experiences or struggles better than others, respond to larger cultural trends better than others, or permit authentic expression for worshipers in ways not permitted by other songs in CCLI's storehouse. So even though a systematic random sample may have allowed us to generalize to all 150,000+ songs licensed by CCLI, such a sample would not have told us which songs were having the greatest potential impact on worshipers.

As noted above, there were several disadvantages of using CCLI. First, every church that licenses music from CCLI does not report its CWM usage each six-month period. It is not clear from CCLI's website or personnel we contacted what processes CCLI employs to select reporting churches for each six-month period. According to their customer service representative, churches representing broad demographics of location, denomination, and church size are selected to report, with all license holders reporting once every two-and-a-half years.

Second, although a significant number of denominations across conservative and mainline Protestant churches are represented by CCLI (over 130 denominations),[36] the list of denominations is not exhaustive.

Third, although we believe the Top 25 lists between 1989 and 2005 provide a representative sample of the songs having the greatest possible impact on worshipers during any given Sunday, because we did not employ random sampling procedures to all the songs, the conclusions in each chapter cannot be generalized to all songs CCLI licenses.

Furthermore, we are limited in our generalizability since hymn usage is often not reported by churches to CCLI. Since hymns are a large part of blended worship, where contemporary and traditional music is performed, several hymns that might otherwise appear on the Top 25 lists may be excluded.

Finally, copyright dates listed on songs may not be accurate. For example, *Turn Your Eyes upon Jesus* is listed in some places with a 1989 copyright when it is actually the chorus of a hymn with three verses that was written in 1922 and is in the public domain. And *Joy to the World*, a Handel Christmas carol in the public domain, was included in the Top 25 lists.

How Can This Book Help You?

Music ministers and worship leaders could benefit from a more specific indexing of content that could result from this study, with an eye toward finding songs specific to an upcoming sermon theme or season of the church year. Most worship leaders have few guidelines to follow when it comes to making choices about worship music. These chapters may help you make selections wisely rather than on "felt needs" or musical style preferences of your worship team or congregation.

For senior or lead pastors, this book will provide you with a thematic and theological overview of the content of the most widely used CWM songs that influence both the wider culture and the worshipers in your pews. Since the ultimate responsibility for what happens in Sunday worship rests with you, the book could help you understand the breadth and depth of CWM topics in order to support and justify its use in a given service format. It may also be a way for you to open up discussion with worship leaders about the proper use of contemporary praise music in worship.

For the average worshiper in the pew, whether fully immersed in, doubtful of, or simply curious about the "worship wars," be prepared to discover something new about the songs you have been singing. A frightening, overarching impression among many Christians is that few worship leaders and churches care about the kinds of analyses presented in this book. An older friend of ours at church remarked, "They seem more interested in performing what is popular to keep the people entertained than singing what is good." We trust that your concerns that leaders "do not care" will be dismissed after reading the following chapters.

For students of worship, this book will provide you with examples of how to conduct your own critical analysis of CWM in ways that wed theory with practice. Writing from theological, sociological, psychological, communication, and musical perspectives, our authors have made significant contributions to the analysis of the quality and usefulness of this type of church music. This kind of perspective is foundational to your education in worship ministry.

We think everyone will benefit from the attempt our authors have made to lay to rest much rumor and innuendo about CWM while simultaneously raising levels of consciousness about more important theological and sociological issues. Moreover, the suggestions and correctives offered throughout will help guide the development and use of new worship music in the twenty-first century. The suggestions may also form the basis of a heuristic, or stimulant, for ongoing research on the technical and artistic components of the corporate worship service. We hope that our academic colleagues will be challenged to follow up this initial research with analyses of their own that will contribute to a truly comprehensive body of literature on this and similar subjects.

Organization of the Book

The traditional categorization of worship songs is divided between musical characteristics and textual characteristics.[37] Since most of the criticism facing CWM has revolved around its lyrics, part 1 (chapters 1–7) focuses on the lyrical content. Part 2 (chapters 8–10) focuses on the musical content and styles of the top 77 songs.

In chapter 1, Lester Ruth (Asbury Theological Seminary) analyzes the trinitarian content of the lyrics. More specifically, he asks, "To what extent do the songs facilitate praying and worshiping the Triune God?"

In chapter 2, Jenell Williams Paris (Messiah College) explores the extent to which CWM expresses the American romantic ideal versus authentic biblical love. Jenell responds to concerns that CWM is "Jesus-is-my-boyfriend" or "romantic-pop" music.

In chapter 3, Keith Drury (Indiana Wesleyan University) draws on Jenell's observations in chapter 2 regarding romantic and erotic language in worship. Keith is concerned that our worship uses phrases that some males too easily perceive as having subliminal sexual overtones and thus brings less than enthusiastic participation in worship from some of them.

In chapter 4, Jay Howard (Indiana University–Purdue University Columbus) investigates the degree to which CWM addresses the relationship between worship of God and God's concern for righteousness and justice in our interactions with others.

In chapter 5, Wendy J. Porter (McMaster Divinity College) looks at the role that the expression of pain and suffering plays in our worshiping communities. Wendy explores some of the biblical foundations for this notion, lays out some basic criteria for determining which songs contribute meaningfully to this category, and specifically looks at some songs from the current CCLI list that do.

In chapter 6, Robert Woods (Spring Arbor University), Brian Walrath (Spring Arbor University), and Diane Badzinski (Colorado Christian University) ask how the 77 songs as a whole adequately model the threefold purpose or mission of the church. The authors conduct a quantitative content analysis to categorize each song as *kerygma* (preaching), *koinonia* (fellowship), or *leitourgia* (service, ministry, worship). The authors ask which category appears most often between 1989 and 2005, and how the percentages of categories have changed over time.

In chapter 7, David Pass (PassWord International) picks up where chapter 6 leaves off and takes the analysis of the *leitourgic* mode one step further by categorizing the 77 songs as songs of thanksgiving, petition, praise, and adoration. In the process, Dave explores the provocative notion that there are certain attitudes and emotions that worshipers must bring to the songs in order for the songs to function to their fullest potential.

In chapter 8, Bert Polman (Calvin College) offers the first of three chapters that focus on the musical content of the 77 CWM songs selected for analysis. Bert focuses on the extent to which the 77 are congregational and which others are better suited to soloists or small ensembles.

In chapter 9, Guy Jansen (Director, Choir of St Johns-in-the-City, Wellington, New Zealand) asks, "What are some characteristics of high musical quality in CWM?" Guy then reviews important artistic criteria for defining quality worship music. He spends the rest of the chapter examining the 77 CWM songs to discover their harmonic and melodic traits. He asks important questions such as, "Are the melodies of the 77 songs within a comfortable range and vocal expectation for most singers? And is there a 'hook' or motif with inherent musical worth and originality?"

In chapter 10, Margaret Brady (North Park Theological Seminary) examines the songs in their historical context to determine their structure and form before categorizing them according to their style and genre. To help determine their style and genre, the songs are compared to genres in secular (mainstream) popular music. The chapter concludes by examining the musical analysis of each song to discover similarities, differences, and trends among the 77 CWM songs on our list.

In the conclusion, John D. Witvliet (Calvin College) masterfully unites the previous ten chapters, reviews an emerging body of literature in worship studies, sets forth a compelling research agenda, and sounds the clarion call for scholars, students, worship leaders, pastors, songwriters, and worshipers in the pews to contribute to the ongoing dialogue.

Getting Started

We believe this book represents a positive step forward in the objective study of the relatively new genre known as CWM. By no means do we suggest that the ten chapters presented here are the final word. We trust that the work as a whole will function as a catalyst for ongoing analytical study of music in the worship arts and related disciplines. John Witvliet's conclusion offers a compelling call to interdisciplinary study of CWM. He offers several ways for others to take the analyses presented in the ten chapters to the next level.

We welcome dialogue with you beyond these pages. As you use this book for personal study, classroom, and small group discussion, feel free to pass along materials that you think extend, challenge, or reinforce what you read. We have collected discussion questions, class assignments, and test/quiz questions for many of the chapters in the book. We're happy to make these available to you upon request (Robert: rwoods@arbor.edu; Brian: bwalrath@arbor.edu).

Now, let the conversation begin!

Table 1

Top 77 CWM songs as reported by CCLI (in alphabetical order): 1989–2005

Name of Song	Authors & Composers	Year	Copyright Holder
1. *Above All*	Lenny LeBlanc & Paul Baloche	1999	Integrity's Hosanna!/ LenSongs Publishing
2. *Ah, Lord God*	Kay Chance	1976	Kay Chance
3. *All Hail King Jesus*	Dave Moody	1981	Dayspring Music
4. *Arise and Sing*	Mel Ray, Jr.	1976	Integrity's Hosanna!
5. *As the Deer*	Martin Nystrom	1984	Maranatha! Praise
6. *Awesome God*	Rich Mullins	1988	BMG Songs
7. *Because He Lives*	Gloria Gaither & William J. Gaither	1971	William J. Gaither, Inc.
8. *Better Is One Day*	Matt Redman	1995	Thankyou Music
9. *Bind Us Together*	Bob Gillman	1977	Thankyou Music
10. *Bless His Holy Name*	Andraé Crouch	1973	Bud John Songs
11. *Blessed Be Your Name*	Beth Redman & Matt Redman	2002	Thankyou Music
12. *Breathe*	Marie Barnett	1995	Mercy/Vineyard Pub.
13. *Celebrate Jesus*	Gary Oliver	1988	Integrity's Hosanna!
14. *Change My Heart, Oh God*	Eddie Espinosa	1982	Mercy/Vineyard Pub.
15. *Come, Now Is the Time to Worship*	Brian Doerksen	1998	Vineyard Songs (UK/Eire)
16. *Draw Me Close*	Kelly Carpenter	1994	Mercy/ Vineyard Pub.
17. *Emmanuel*	Bob McGee	1976	C.A. Music
18. *Father, I Adore You*	Terrye Coelho	1972	Maranatha! Music/ CCCM Music
19. *Forever*	Chris Tomlin	2001	worshiptogether.com songs/sixsteps Music
20. *Give Thanks*	Henry Smith	1978	Integrity's Hosanna!
21. *Glorify Thy Name*	Donna Adkins	1976, 1981	Maranatha! Music/ CCCM Music

<!-- Handwritten margin notes:
2069 (by 3), 2025 (by 5), 2040 (by 6), 364 (by 7),
2226 (by 9), 2015 (by 10), 3002 (by 11), 3112 (by 12),
2152 (by 14), 317b (by 15), 204 (by 17), 2038 (by 18),
3023 (by 19), 2036 (by 20), 2016 (by 21) -->

Name of Song	Authors & Composers	Year	Copyright Holder
22. *God of Wonders*	Mark Byrd & Steve Hindalong	2000	New Spring Publishing, Inc./Storm Boy Music/ Meaux Mercy
23. *Great Is the Lord*	Deborah D. Smith & Michael W. Smith	1982	Meadowgreen Music Company
24. *Hallelujah (Your Love Is Amazing)*	Brenton Brown & Brian Doerksen	2000	Vineyard Songs (UK/Eire)
25. *He Has Made Me Glad*	Leona Von Brethorst	1976	Maranatha! Praise
26. *He Is Exalted*	Twila Paris	1985	Straightway Music/ Mountain Spring Music
27. *Here I Am to Worship*	Tim Hughes	2000	Thankyou Music
28. *His Name Is Wonderful*	Audrey Mieir	1959, 1987	Audrey Mieir/ Manna Music, Inc.
29. *Holy Ground*	Geron Davis	1983	Meadowgreen Music Company/Song-channel Music
30. *Holy Is the Lord*	Chris Tomlin & Louie Giglio	2003	worshiptogether.com songs/sixsteps Music
31. *How Can We Name a Love*	Brian Wren & Malcolm Williamson	1975, 1995	Hope Publishing Company for the USA
32. *How Great Is Our God*	Chris Tomlin, Ed Cash, & Jesse Reeves	2004	worshiptogether.com songs/sixsteps Music/ Alletrop Music
33. *How Majestic Is Your Name*	Michael W. Smith	1981	Meadowgreen Music Co.
34. *I Could Sing of Your Love Forever*	Martin Smith	1994	Curious? Music UK
35. *I Exalt Thee*	Pete Sanchez, Jr.	1977	Pete Sanchez, Jr.
36. *I Give You My Heart*	Reuben Morgan	1995	Hillsong Publishing
37. *I Love You, Lord*	Lauren Klein	1978, 1980	House of Mercy Music

Name of Song	Authors & Composers	Year	Copyright Holder
38. *I Stand in Awe*	Mark Altrogge	1987	Sovereign Grace Praise
39. *I Will Call upon the Lord*	Michael O'Shields	1981	Sound III, Inc./ Universal—MCA Music Publishing
40. *I Worship You, Almighty God*	Sondra Corbett	1983	Integrity's Hosanna!
41. *In Moments Like These*	David Graham	1980	C.A. Music
42. *Jesus, Name above All Names*	Naida Hearn	1974, 1978	Scripture in Song
43. *Joy to the World*	Isaac Watts & Lowell Alexander	1990	Public Domain; Meadowgreen Music Company
44. *Let There Be Glory and Honor and Praises*	Elizabeth Greenelsh & James Greenelsh	1978	Integrity's Hosanna!
45. *Lord, Be Glorified*	Bob Kilpatrick	1978	Bob Kilpatrick Ministries
46. *Lord, I Lift Your Name on High*	Rick Founds	1989	Maranatha! Praise
47. *Lord, Reign in Me*	Brenton Brown	1998	Vineyard Songs (UK/Eire)
48. *Majesty*	Jack Hayford	1981	Rocksmith Music
49. *More Precious Than Silver*	Lynn DeShazo	1982	Integrity's Hosanna!
50. *My Life Is in You*	Daniel Gardner	1986	Integrity's Hosanna!
51. *Oh How He Loves You and Me*	Kurt Kaiser	1975	Word Music
52. *Open Our Eyes*	Bob Cull	1976	Maranatha! Music/ CCCM Music
53. *Open the Eyes of My Heart*	Paul Baloche	1997	Integrity's Hosanna!
54. *Our God Reigns*	Leonard E. Smith, Jr.	1974, 1978	New Jerusalem Music

2002
2071
246
2150
2588
176
2065
2032
2108
2086
3608

Name of Song	Authors & Composers	Year	Copyright Holder
55. *Praise the Name of Jesus* **2066**	Roy Hicks, Jr.	1976	Latter Rain Music/ Roy Hicks, Jr.
56. *Sanctuary* **2164**	John W. Thompson & Randy Scruggs	1982	WholeArmor/ Full Armor Music
57. *Seek Ye First* **405**	Karen Lafferty	1972	Maranatha! Music/ CCCM Music
58. *Shine, Jesus, Shine* **2173** *(Lord, the Light of Your Love)*	Graham Kendrick	1987	Make Way Music
59. *Shout to the Lord* **3042**	Darlene Zschech	1993	Hillsong Publishing
60. *Surely the Presence of the Lord* **328**	Lanny Wolfe	1977	Lanny Wolfe Music
61. *The Heart of Worship*	Matt Redman	1997	Thankyou Music
62. *The Wonderful Cross*	Chris Tomlin, Isaac Watts, J. D. Walt, Jesse Reeves, & Lowell Mason	1707/ 1824, 2000	worshiptogether.com songs/sixsteps Music
63. *There's Something About That Name* **171**	Gloria Gaither & William J. Gaither	1970	William J. Gaither, Inc.
64. *This Is the Day* **657**	Les Garrett	1967, 1980	Scripture in Song
65. *Thou Art Worthy* **2041**	Pauline Michael Mills	1963, 1975	Fred Bock Music Company
66. *Thy Lovingkindness*	Hugh Mitchell	1956	Singspiration Music
67. *Trading My Sorrows* **3108**	Darrell Evans	1998	Integrity's Hosanna!
68. *Turn Your Eyes upon Jesus* **349**	Helen H. Lemmel	1922	Public Domain
69. *We Bring the Sacrifice of Praise* **2031**	Kirk Dearman	1984	John T. Benson Publishing Company
70. *We Fall Down* **3187**	Chris Tomlin	1998	worshiptogether.com songs
71. *We Have Come into His House*	Bruce T. Ballinger	1976	Sound III, Inc./ Universal—MCA Music Publishing

Name of Song	Authors & Composers	Year	Copyright Holder
72. *We Will Glorify*	Twila Paris	1982	Singspiration Music
73. *What a Mighty God We Serve*	David Allan Cosand	1989	David Allan Cosand
74. *When I Look into Your Holiness*	Cathy Perrin & Wayne Perrin	1981	Integrity's Hosanna!
75. *You Are My All in All*	Dennis Jernigan	1990	Shepherd's Heart Music, Inc.
76. *You Are My King (Amazing Love)*	Billy Foote	1997	worshiptogether.com songs
77. *You're Worthy of My Praise*	David Ruis	1986	Maranatha! Praise/ Shade Tree Music

2087
2021
3016
3040
3102

HOW GREAT IS OUR GOD: THE TRINITY IN CONTEMPORARY CHRISTIAN WORSHIP MUSIC

LESTER RUTH

Introduction

According to the Bible, every good and perfect gift is a heavenly one, coming from the Father of lights (James 1:17). Such gifts must include the fullness of the revelation of God unless we want to say that humans have their own power to conjure up a true vision of God. The witness of the apostles, recorded in their writings and crafted by subsequent Christians into a statement of faith, is that God exists and acts as three Persons (Father, Son, and Holy Spirit) in one Godhead. This is the classic Christian faith.

If this is scriptural Christianity, then why should Christians settle for anything less in the content of worship than the fullness of this revelation of God, particularly when the revelation itself is a gift from God? Why should churches be happy with worship that is less than true to God?

Perhaps churches are satisfied with worship that does not reach for a full vision because a consumerist culture leads us to believe that the most critical thing is that worship be true to us. Perhaps some are scared that our worship will become cold if it becomes "theological."

But could not a fuller, richer vision of God actually stimulate love, not quench it? Could not a more complete vision of God lead to a deeper love, rather than away from it? Theology can give us more motives to love God, not fewer. And there is every reason why such theology could take lyrical form in songs. Christian history is full of outstanding examples of songwriters who offered up such lyrics for the church to adore the Triune God. It is not just the latest generation who knows passion for the God revealed in Jesus Christ by the power of the Holy Spirit.

The Trinity is not just an abstract concept, some theological idea that Christians are supposed to take a test on or write a paper about. It is not some detached doctrine that we know we are supposed to agree with, checking it off a list of right beliefs like items on a packing list for vacation. "Okay, kids, let's make sure we have the first aid kit and the doctrine of the Trinity just in case something happens."

The doctrine of the Trinity is a vision not only of God but also of our greatest longings for salvation and our deepest hopes in worship. It liberates by affirming the blessed thought that salvation and worship do not depend upon me. Both are gifts of participating through the Holy Spirit in the incarnate Son's communion with God the Father. People as diverse as theologian James Torrance and songwriter Matt Redman delight in this truth.[1] Thus, Trinitarian belief reminds us that God is not some passive bystander in worship or salvation, desperately hoping that we will work ourselves up before being happy with us.[2]

And this doctrine is important to help us avoid pitfalls, perhaps even idolatry. As one person put it, "Believing right things about God is an essential component in honouring God appropriately."[3] Worshiping the Trinity is a large part of what makes worship orthodox. ("Orthodox" comes from Greek words that mean "right glory.") Because how we relate to God is shaped by our worship experience of God, Trinitarian content in worship is very important. Long after the music has faded, worship songs have created in us a sense of how all this God and salvation stuff fits together. If we lose the Trinity, if we have worship that is less than true to God, we end up with a very different faith, a very different hope of salvation, and, ultimately, a very different God than the one revealed in Scripture.

In light of the foregoing, this chapter focuses on Trinitarian theological content by asking five questions about how the most-used contemporary worship songs lead Christian congregations to pray to and worship the Triune God.[4] I conclude this chapter by discussing some possible reasons the core repertoire is minimally Trinitarian and whether future worship songs will become more adoring of the Trinity.

Throughout this chapter, I will argue that the theological content of the lyrics of the top 77 songs that constitute the heart of CWM between 1989 and 2005 reveals that this core repertoire has few explicit Trinitarian aspects. The Christians who write and use these songs expect them to express a relationship with God that must be rooted primarily in the heart, not in a common faith. This emphasis provides the focus of this chapter: *lex amandi, lex orandi,* that is, the rule of loving establishes the rule of praying. The classic maxim from the ancient church was *lex orandi, lex credendi,* that is, the rule of praying establishes the rule of believing.

Method of Analysis

There are five questions that govern the qualitative analysis presented in this chapter:

1. Do the songs name the Trinity or all three Persons of the Trinity?
2. Do the songs direct our worship toward the Trinity as a whole or toward one of the Persons of the Trinity?
3. Do the songs remember the activity of the Divine Persons among Themselves?

4. Do the songs see Christian worship as participation of believers in inter-Trinitarian dynamics or activity?

5. Do the songs use the character of inter-Trinitarian relationships to explore a desired character for relationship among Christians, for example, unity, love, sacrifice, or humility?

These questions build upon each other. What they get at is an upward spiral of understanding how our salvation is communion with the Triune God. They try to point at dimensions of what theologians might call a Trinitarian economy of salvation, that is, how God has been revealed and acted on our behalf to bring us into fellowship with the Trinity. It assumes that redemption is a cooperative venture by the Father, the Son, and the Holy Spirit and that salvation involves being brought into the fellowship these Three have with each other. In some real way, we can experience this communion within the church, particularly as it worships.

Results

Do the Songs Name the Trinity or All Three Persons of the Trinity?

None of the 77 songs explicitly uses the word "Trinity" or "Triune," and only four songs explicitly refer to or name all three Persons of the Trinity: (1) *Glorify Thy Name*; (2) *Father, I Adore You*; (3) *Shine, Jesus, Shine*; and (4) *How Great Is Our God*. The first two songs are praise songs with three verses structured on the Trinity. The description of the Trinity in *Shine, Jesus, Shine* comes as the standard feature of the recurring chorus: "Shine, Jesus, shine, fill this land with the Father's glory / Blaze, Spirit, blaze, set our hearts on fire." *How Great Is Our God* is the truly exceptional song, both in this list of four and in the entire corpus of 77 songs. It alone worships the Triune nature of God ("Godhead Three in One / Father, Spirit, Son"). Only one song in addition to these four (*How Can We Name a Love*) speaks of God as "Father." In the handful of songs that refer to the Holy Spirit, seven refer to the "Spirit" (but none explicitly uses the name "Holy Spirit").

Beyond an explicit reference to the Father in the five songs above, seven more of the 77 songs make clear reference to the First Person of the Trinity, using terms other than "Father." Some of these songs use other names like "Holy One" (*Give Thanks*) or "Most High" (*Our God Reigns*). Some speak of "God," but the composer clearly refers to the First Person as in "God sent His Son / They called Him Jesus" (*Because He Lives*).

Thirty-seven of the songs, however, make explicit reference to the Son, or Jesus Christ, the Second Person of the Trinity. Twenty-seven of these songs specifically speak of Jesus, Christ, or Jesus Christ. The other ten speak of Christ more generally as "Lord," "God," or "King," but Christ is clearly meant, for example, *Lord, I Lift Your Name on High* recalls Christ's coming, cross, and resurrection.

However, it is not always clear to which person of the Trinity the lyrics are referring. The most frequently used titles for the divine object of worship are "Lord" (47 occurrences), "God" (28 occurrences), and "King" (18 occurrences). In 29 of the 47 occurrences of "Lord," it is difficult to determine exactly who this "Lord" is, as seen in the most frequently appearing song among the 77, *I Love You, Lord*. In 14 of the 28 occurrences of the title "God," the lack of additional context or names likewise obscures the specific identity of "God." For the third most used title, "King," the level of clarity is much higher. Except in a few cases, the songs make clear that the "King" is Jesus Christ. But there is even less clarity in the five songs that do not explicitly use any common divine title or name: *I Could Sing of Your Love Forever*, *Breathe*, *Above All*, *Draw Me Close*, and *When I Look into Your Holiness*. *As the Deer* and *You're Worthy of My Praise* were not included because they speak of the recipient as King.

The same pattern of Christ-centeredness is seen in those songs whose purpose is to contemplate the divine name. Only one (*Glorify Thy Name*) shows an explicit intention to worship the entire Trinity, while six songs focus on Jesus Christ and three are generic contemplations of the divine name (*How Majestic Is Your Name*, *Bless His Holy Name*, and *Blessed Be Your Name*).

Do the Songs Direct Our Worship toward the Trinity as a Whole or Toward One of the Persons of the Trinity?

As noted above, only one song explicitly worships God for being Triune, and only two lead to direct worship of the Trinity. Directly addressing worship to the Trinity as a whole or to the Holy Spirit is the most minimal aspect of this body of 77 songs. Similarly, very few songs explicitly address the Holy Spirit in worship. Of the seven that name the Spirit, only four direct worship to the Spirit—the same four that name all three Persons of the Trinity (*Glorify Thy Name*; *Father, I Adore You*; *Shine, Jesus, Shine*; and *How Great Is Our God*). The other three songs that mention the Holy Spirit simply make reference to the worshiper's enjoyment of the Spirit.

Directly addressing worship to the First Person of the Trinity fares no better. Of the twelve songs that make clear reference to the First Person of the Trinity (God the Father), only four explicitly worship the Father in direct address: the two songs internally structured by Trinitarian naming (*Glorify Thy Name* and *Father, I Adore You*) and two others (*Give Thanks* and *How Great Is Our God*). One other song that distinguishes the First Person of the Trinity (*Bind Us Together*) possibly addresses God the Father in petition, depending upon whether its prayer to the "Lord" has God the Father in mind. (*Open Our Eyes, Lord* is another possibility.) Perhaps some of the composers had God the Father in mind in the songs that speak of the "Lord" or "God" generically, but the lack of context or content makes it difficult to tell. However, given the stronger tendency to name the Second Person of the Trinity throughout the entire body of 77 songs, it is more likely that most of these generic references are to Jesus Christ.

Directing worship toward Jesus Christ is a much stronger phenomenon. As noted above, 37 of the 77 songs make distinct reference to Jesus Christ. Thirty-two of these directly address Jesus Christ as the recipient of worship.

However, the basis for worshiping Christ varies in these 32 songs. Twelve acknowledge Jesus Christ's divine nature, either explicitly or implicitly. Several root worship of Christ in remembrance of His activity, usually referencing His death and resurrection. Others speak of Christ's exalted status, most clearly seen in those songs that are essentially strings of Christ's titles. Songs that speak of Christ's exalted status frequently connect it to His Kingship and occasionally to sheer contemplation of the name "Jesus" itself. Clearly, worship of Christ is more fully developed in the 77 songs than worship of God the Father or the Holy Spirit. Of course, this assessment omits whatever conclusions might be drawn from songs that speak of "Lord" or "God" in a generic manner.

Do the Songs Remember the Activity of the Divine Persons among Themselves?

It is not surprising that the answer is "no" or "very minimally." Without naming, and thus not distinguishing between, the Persons of the Trinity, it is difficult to discuss how these Persons have acted among themselves or in concert.

As a whole this body of 77 songs is what some might call "functionally unitarian."[5] In *Glorify Thy Name* and *Father, I Adore You* the composers symmetrically make each Person of the Trinity the object of worship but do not explore how they interact. The structure of the songs, with equal statements of adoration and petition, implies equality between the Father, Jesus, and the Spirit. The third, *Shine, Jesus, Shine*, has more nuance because the recurring chorus makes Jesus the mediator of the Father's glory and the Spirit the enabler of our participation in this glory. *Shine, Jesus, Shine* is exceptional in that it implies our reliance upon Jesus Christ or the Holy Spirit to experience God the Father. *How Great Is Our God* is exceptional, too, in being the only song that makes God's Triune nature the explicit basis for adoration.

Eleven songs among the 77 make clear reference to two distinct Persons of the Trinity: eight discuss the Father and the Son and two discuss the Son and the Spirit. Another song (*Better Is One Day*) distinguishes between the "living God" and the Spirit of this God, but it is unclear who is meant by "living God." If the Father is in view, then this is the only song that speaks of the Father and the Holy Spirit, without reference to the Son. (*Open Our Eyes, Lord* is also another two-Person song if the unspecified "Lord" is God the Father or the Holy Spirit.)

Of the eight songs that discuss the Father and the Son, six focus on the theme that the Father has given the Son to save us. Four of them have brief references: the "Holy One" has given Jesus Christ His Son (*Give Thanks*); God sent His Son for healing, forgiveness, and pardon (*Because He Lives*); we are "purchased" by God's Son (*Bind Us Together*); and Jesus is the Lamb of God (*You Are My All in All*). The two that explore this theme in greater depth are both derived from the "Suffering Servant" prophecy found in Isaiah 53. In *I Stand in Awe*, for example, God brings about the suffering of the Lamb of God for the singer's sin. The song *Our God Reigns* shares a similar perspective, although the emphasis on God bringing the suffering is muted.

The two remaining Father/Son songs have very undeveloped associations between the two Persons. In *Jesus, Name above All Names*, the composer speaks of Jesus as Son of God, Emmanuel, and God with us as part of stringing together names and titles for Christ without explanation. The connection between Father and Son in *How Can We Name a Love* is even more tenuous.

Similarly, the two songs that clearly speak of Jesus Christ and the Holy Spirit make only passing references to their relationship. In *You Are My King* the singer has the Spirit of Jesus as a result of Christ's crucifixion and resurrection. In *Surely the Presence of the Lord* the singer feels the "sweet Spirit" as a result of the Lord Jesus fulfilling the promise of His presence according to Matthew 18:20.

Apart from the lack of naming the Father and the Holy Spirit, three other factors contribute to the lack of emphasis on the activity of the Trinity.

The first is the tendency within many songs to emphasize character traits or the status of God/Jesus Christ/the Lord/the King singularly without contemplating the dynamics of the Trinity itself. The song *Forever* affirms that God is faithful, strong, and with us. *Shout to the Lord* proclaims that no one compares to Jesus as the singer's comfort, shelter, and tower of refuge and strength. *More Precious Than Silver* speaks of the Lord being of more worth than silver, gold, or diamonds. *He Is Exalted* rejoices that the King is forever exalted on high, while heaven and earth rejoice in His holy name. And *As the Deer*, a very popular song, speaks of the song's recipient being the singer's strength, shield, heart's desire, friend, brother, sole satisfaction, real joy giver, and apple of her/his eye without specifically naming the recipient as God. In these songs the nature of the Trinity and its activity are rarely put forth as the basis for the worship.

The second factor that contributes to the lack of emphasis on the activity of the Trinity is the relative de-emphasis on commemorating God's saving activity. The songs pay little attention to placing salvation within a broader meta-narrative—that is, any grand, all-encompassing master story—and thus providing opportunity to recite the specific activities or internal dynamics of the Father, Son, and Holy Spirit. Usually the saving work is attributed to a single entity, whether God, the Lord (unspecified), or the Lord Jesus Christ.

In the 19 songs that commemorate God's saving activity, almost all place the focus on the crucifixion and resurrection of Christ. For example, *Give Thanks* speaks of the Holy One having given Jesus Christ, His Son. Another, *Celebrate Jesus*, remembers only the resurrection. While it is acceptable for a single worship piece to remember only one redemptive act, one still wonders whether the overall effect in using these songs would be to create the impression that God's saving activities are isolated events—rather than part of a whole plan of salvation—and that these events are solely the work of one Divine Person—rather than being a cooperative work by God the Father through Jesus Christ in the power of the Spirit.

Only a few of the songs that recall the crucifixion place it in a wider context of saving activity: *Lord, I Lift Your Name on High* associates it with the *kenosis* (or the relinquishment of the form of God by Jesus in becoming man and suffering death), cross, burial, and exaltation; *Here I Am to Worship* associates creation, *kenosis*, crucifixion, and exaltation; and *Awesome God* makes the crucifixion the activity of the same God (Christ) who judged Adam and Eve in the Garden, brought judgment on Sodom, and is about to return. Two of the 19 songs remember creation.

Therefore, few of the songs, unlike the New Testament, explore the internal dynamics of the Father, Son, and Holy Spirit in this wider range of saving activity. Whereas the New Testament continually explores how the Father, Son, and Holy Spirit have acted in concert on our behalf (consider how God the Father promises the birth of His Son when the Holy Spirit overshadows Mary [Luke 1] or how the Father raises Jesus from the dead through the Spirit showing Him to be the Son of God [Romans 1]), these songs tend to see the great events of salvation as isolated works.[6] With respect to the Father and the Son, there is only occasional reference to Christ's saving activity being of the Father. The Holy Spirit as an active agent in our salvation is almost nowhere to be found. This leaves even the doctrine of the atonement underdeveloped in its Trinitarian aspects in this body of songs. The two possible exceptions are derived from Isaiah 53: *I Stand in Awe* and *Our God Reigns*.

Such omissions mean that possibilities for exploring the Trinitarian aspect of salvation are missed. For example, because this music's view of salvation emphasizes it as personal experience, the songs do not explore possible Trinitarian aspects in more cosmic or church-related understandings of salvation. There is also little emphasis on present aspects of God's work. There is no emphasis on ongoing mediation, whether it be on the heavenly ministry of Christ or the saving role of the Holy Spirit. God's saving activity seems to be something done in the past that is presently enjoyed. There is also little sense of God's ongoing mission in the world and little eschatology, or end-times thinking, in the songs.

The third factor that contributes to the lack of focus on the activity of the Trinity is a possible confusion of Persons, that is, "Lord" is often used in an ill-defined, generic way. Although the term is sometimes clearly used to refer to Jesus Christ, that is not always the case. *Open Our Eyes, Lord*, for instance, is a case where the Lord appears to be a very different Person than Jesus. *Awesome God* complicates the matter by tossing "God" into the mix: in this song "God" and "Lord" appear to be interchangeable names for whoever expelled Adam from Eden, experienced the crucifixion, and poured judgment on Sodom.

Do the Songs See Christian Worship as Participation of Believers in Inter-Trinitarian Dynamics or Activity?

There is little, if any, sense of worshipers being in Christ or Christ being in worshipers, particularly as a church-related reality during corporate worship. Because so few of the songs commemorate the internal dynamics or activity of the Trinity, little space exists for worship as participation in the Trinitarian activity.

On the whole these songs tend to objectify God as the recipient of worship to emphasize a distinction between the One worshiped and the worshiper. God/Christ/ the Lord/the King is Someone *out there* Who is to be worshiped and adored. The One worshiped is someone Whom we love and enjoy and Who is with us, but there is little sense of Christians being brought into the activity of this God, particularly if this God whom we worship is conceived of as a Triune community. Almost all the songs describe the dynamic between worshipers and the Divine recipient of worship, not the relationship and activity—past, present, and future—among the Persons of the Trinity. A more classic approach is to make God's activity on our behalf—from the Father through the Son in the Spirit—mirrored in the response of worship—in the Spirit through the Son to the Father. Thus the classic approach, in contrast to the tendency of these songs, puts the emphasis on God's graciousness from first to last. The classic approach keeps Jesus as the "lead worshiper" within the internal love of the Trinity.

Neither do these songs consider worship as participation in Christ's activity *through* us with reference to either the Father or the Holy Spirit. The 43 songs that are some sort of prayer (identified by the worshiper addressing a divine "You") have virtually no sense of being addressed to the Father through the Son in the power of the Holy Spirit. The songs mainly address Christ—and occasionally the Father—in prayer, but none speaks of us addressing the Father through Christ or the church's prayer being Christ praying through us. The songs also do not speak of Christ's intercessory ministry.

These omissions are partly a result of the absence of a strong emphasis on the Trinity's current activity and partly to the overwhelming character of the songs as expressing only our own human love to the divine Object of worship (in contrast to our sharing in the love which the Father, Son, and Spirit share among themselves). *I Love You, Lord* is perhaps the most representative song of the whole group. Not surprisingly, CCLI's database reveals over 400 songs with the phrase "I love you" in the title. Songs that would be truer to the Trinity would delight in how the Spirit brings us into the love the Father and Son share as described in the Gospel of John.

Do the Songs Use the Character of Inter-Trinitarian Relationships to Explore a Desired Character for Relationship among Christians, for Example, Unity, Love, Sacrifice, or Humility?

The answer is a strong "no."

These 77 songs have a very low explicit consciousness of the church. Only one (*Lord, Be Glorified*) uses the word "church," and only one (*We Have Come into His House*) has a church theme. There are a handful with an explicit sense of God's people as community, but only two are about fellowship: *We Have Come into His House* and *Bind Us Together*.

Moreover, only *Bind Us Together* derives a vision for the church from contemplating the nature and activity of the Triune God (although the song does not speak of the Holy Spirit). The song petitions the Lord for a greater measure of a unity of love, basing the request in the essential unity of God and in the activity of the Father and the Son.

Discussion

Acts of omission, not commission, cause the lack of a Trinitarian dimension in most CWM: Songwriters, marketers of the songs, and churches do not seem to value explicit Trinitarian content or even miss it if it is not included. Robin Parry's description of the British situation seems applicable to America: "If there is a problem with Christian worship songs, it is more a failure to bring out the Trinitarian dimensions of the God we worship than a problem of violating Trinitarian faith."[7]

To a significant degree the root for this omission is the lack of theological expectations for the songs. Even when theological review does come into play, the goals are often limited to either making sure the song avoids obvious error or making sure the song expresses a scriptural idea or sentiment. In general, few composers intentionally seek to include a wider breadth of theological contemplation of the Triune God and Trinitarian activity.

If explicit witness to the Trinity is not the high priority, then what is? The songs demonstrate a common concern: *the priority of a shared affective experience in the worship of God.* Worship is seen as the expression of our hearts and ministry to God's heart. It is this law of love, *lex amandi*, that determines the rule of praying, *lex orandi.*

This concern with affections is evident in writings from and about the composers of the 77 songs in this study.[8] One influential composer puts it this way: "As songwriters, our job is to hook people's hearts and emotions for the Lord. . . . So a worship song, more than almost any other type of song, needs to express a universal sentiment, something we can all agree on as our own expression of love to Him."[9] That "something" seems rarely derived from God's own Trinitarian nature and work.

This affective sentiment is frequent among the composers who describe worship as singing authentically from one's heart to express true affection to God. It is also reflected in how the composers describe the origins of their songs and contrasts with the composer's rejection of worship that is mainly singing about God. Occasionally, the composers speak of God's reception of these authentic worship songs in affective terms, too, as they speak of touching the heart of God. For these composers, then, worship is foremost about God's Presence affectively discerned and experienced. In this respect, they share a similar worship piety with many churches that use their music. Few of the composers seem to have a piety shaped by Trinitarian contemplation, so they are unaware of the omission of the Trinity.

The desire for the heart's authentic expression to God also shapes the nature of the language in the songs, which seldom leads to speaking of the Trinity. Following the lead of much recent popular music generally, CWM lyrics lean toward an oral, conversational style. Composers avoid complex sentences; attention to strict rhyming and metrical schemes is rare. Most seem to follow Paul Baloche's suggestion that "it's best to make your lyrics move straight ahead, as they would in conversation."[10] Consequently, the absence of Trinitarian content in many of the songs may be because it is not "conversational" to speak to and about the Trinity. Composer Graham Kendrick makes the same point in connecting CWM lyrics to their pop music counterparts: "It has to be said that the rock-pop genre, into which category many worship choruses fit, is not always ideal for carrying extensive, deep, or content-rich lyrics."[11]

The dynamics of composing also contribute to a lack of Trinitarian emphasis. Of the 44 songs for which I found background information, 29 were spontaneous creations. Some came about during private devotions, and a few were written while the composer was actually leading corporate worship. Four composers even wrote theirs while driving. This kind of composition allows no time for deeper theological reflection or revision.

In addition, some composers speak of their songs being God-given since many had no intention of writing a song when they "received" a song from God. *I Love You, Lord* is one example. The composer, a young, financially strapped housewife with no home church or friends, first prayed to God to give her a song that "He would be in the mood to hear." The resulting song, Laurie Klein reports, was "like an early Valentine" or what her editor called "a gift from God that emerged spontaneously from her lips."[12] So strong is this sense in a few composers that they speak of taking "dictation" from God, and, in such cases, there seems to be no need for further theological reflection or revision.

Another important compositional dynamic is that many of these songs were written at a low point in the composers' lives, expressing their encounter with God at that time. The economy of salvation in these songs is an intensely personal story of salvation, which would call for little theological reflection or revision.

A final compositional dynamic that tends to marginalize explicit Trinitarian content involves the sources for the songs. The most critical source for many of the songs is Scripture. The Psalms, in particular, are the scriptural material most mentioned in the accounts of composition. While the use of psalms is commendable and has an extensive historical pedigree in Christian worship, in the case of CWM it contributes to the lack of explicit Trinitarian content. Since the Trinity is not obvious in the Psalms, the composers are not likely to tease out their Trinitarian dimensions as have some past Christians who used the Psalms as Christ's prayer to the Father or the Father's address to the Son. The same is likely true for other biblical sources, even New Testament ones. The scriptural backdrop to the songs, then, precludes asking further theological questions about the songs. If a song is "scriptural," this biblical connection seems self-validating, and it does not occur to the composers to make Trinitarian concerns a factor.

Some potential sources that are not in play should likewise be noted. Few songs are shaped by formal theological reflection since few composers have theological training at the college or seminary level.[13] Few of the composers are from churches with written denominational liturgies, which are likely to have explicit Trinitarian content. Few speak of using written liturgical texts, either current or historical, as a source for inspiration. It is much more likely that over time extemporaneous praying shapes the composers' pieties from which they draw their songs, although this is far harder to document.

Although the 77 songs considered here generally lack a Trinitarian dimension, this is not the case for all CWM, even from the same composers. Thus, this omission is also a result of the system that produces and markets these songs to churches. The standard commercial sources through which CWM is made available to churches[14] seem to help marginalize Trinitarian concerns not only because they reinforce the piety that creates these songs but because they do not introduce more formal theological scrutiny of the music.

 Simply stated, Christians within this production and marketing system have not noticed the omission because they have valued the songs on other grounds. They also appear to use the same criteria and vocabulary in assessing the songs: Does it carry an "anointing" from God or usher people into the presence of God? Whether or not a song is explicitly Trinitarian is irrelevant because that dimension is not necessary for a positive worship experience. Many do not care about a song's theological content. As one CWM industry executive explains, "When listening to songs for the first time I try to turn off my brain and turn on my heart. A song can break all the normal rules of songwriting but bear such a touch of God that you can not ignore it."[15] For CWM distributors, too, *lex amandi* establishes *lex orandi*.

Because the sale of CWM is business as well as ministry, business concerns provide little motivation to address the omission of theological dimensions in these songs. Robb Redman, a former vice president at Maranatha! Music, acknowledges that decisions about repertoire and presentations often have been defined

> by the needs of the recording and marketing process (projected revenue and expenses, available musical talent, advertising, and so on) instead of the needs of the congregation for worship music people can sing with theological integrity. Most producers and executives would admit they have sometimes thought more about the bottom line of a CD than its potential impact on a congregation or the individual.[16]

As business, CWM promotion shapes a culture of trendiness among church musicians. As noted by another former publisher, the emphasis typically is on singing a *new* song to the Lord, meaning the system makes keeping up with the latest songs a high priority for church musicians.[17] CWM catalogs, magazines, and other promotional material often emphasize what is new or "hot," shifting their effective role from mere recording usage to promoting usage and thereby displacing more careful reflection on a song's lyrical content.

Finally, another reason these 77 songs have become the most-used CWM songs for the last 15 years resides with the churches. The range and number of churches represented in the CCLI data do not allow absolute statements, but it seems that the basis for choosing CWM for worship services is not tied to explicit Trinitarian content within the songs because it is not needed to accomplish the songs' liturgical purpose.

The Major Factor Causing Churches to Overlook the Missing Trinitarian Dimension

Several possible factors have caused churches to overlook a lack of Trinitarian dimension in the songs chosen for worship. For my analysis here I refer to the widespread worship performance practice of using an extensive musical "set" (to use a common term), which consists of multiple consecutive songs, with internal repetition of each song, for the beginning of the corporate worship service.

A major factor is the churches' expectation for an experience of God's presence in and through worship music. Oftentimes, particularly when the theology of the Vineyard movement has been influential, worshipers express this expectation in terms of intimacy. This musical worship allows a deep, affective connection between the worshiper and God. The criteria for discerning achievement of this goal are primarily affective, not doctrinal.

In these "sets," a strong emphasis is placed on the music and the worship leader(s) to create an experience of divine presence. According to the typology found in certain Pentecostal and Charismatic writings, the various areas of the temple in the Old Testament provide the framework for the musical journey to a deep experience of God's presence[18] through entrance into the "Holy of Holies." Using certain key biblical proof texts and supplemental types, proponents often use Psalm 100 to provide a biblical rationale for using this temple/tabernacle model as a way to sequence worship music. Second Chronicles provides a supplemental type to demonstrate God's honoring of this musical movement by manifesting His presence. Psalm 22:3 (God is enthroned on the praises of Israel) serves as a central text to establish the basic expectation that God inhabits sung praise.

Even if churches do not use this precise typology to explain the musical order, these churches often replicate a similar order for the set. The movement, generally, tends to be from "praise" or "high praise" to "worship," understood as intimate communion with God. There is also an increasing focus on the divine "You" directly addressed by the song lyric.

To achieve entering into God's presence, musical worship leaders often learn to structure the musical set by "flow"—which does not take into account broader theological concerns. They generally focus on key, tempo, and theme. Key allows easy and effective transitions between songs. Tempo allows the movement from faster to slower as the set develops. Theme allows songs to focus on a central topic, perhaps to anticipate the main idea of the sermon. This theme-based approach tends to emphasize nouns (names for God) and adjectives (attributes for God). What these songs lack is a corresponding emphasis on verbs, understood as the activity of God within the economy of salvation and inter-Trinitarian dynamics.

A good "flow" within the musical set, which allows worshipers to see themselves on a journey into the presence of God, has several characteristics, but none is necessarily related to the Trinity. One is the expressiveness of the songs and their authenticity, honesty, and passion. Another is the repetitiveness of the songs because, as C. Michael Hawn points out, such cyclical, repetitive worship music has the ability to strike the worshiper at a deeper, different level than more sequential, story-telling musical forms. It creates an experience beyond the words and "encourages a physical response, either toward the ecstatic or toward the meditative."[19] The music's percussive nature, too, as sociologist Tex Sample suggests, allows worshipers to hear the songs as "true."[20]

This emphasis on musical sets to facilitate an experience with God potentially erodes a classic understanding of Jesus Christ as the unique mediator between humans and God the Father. Perhaps displacing Christ as mediator goes hand-in-hand with the central focus on an exalted, divine Christ in CWM. If worship's primary end is communion with the Son, not necessarily with God the Father—a communion understood as personal intimacy—the need for Christ as mediator is itself lessened. Mediation is shifted to the music, it appears. Thus prayer in CWM is not primarily to the Father through the Son but to the Son through the music.

Conclusion

These conclusions about the 77 songs considered do not apply to all contemporary songs. Indeed, some songs from the same group of composers who wrote the 77 show a greater capacity for naming the Persons of the Godhead, which is the starting point for greater Trinitarian reflection in the lyrics. Some of these songs have great potential for Trinitarian worship.[21]

In addition to these songs from the same composers, there are other songs within the broader CWM corpus that are more explicitly Trinitarian. CCLI's song labels in its database, for example, point to 85 songs with the Trinity as a theme. (This number is actually low since not all songs with explicit Trinitarian connections have been so labeled.) Several traits connect these 85 songs. Just under 50 percent have a copyright date since about 2000, and almost 80 percent have copyright dates from about 1990—a promising sign. The songs much more clearly and consistently name the three Persons of the Trinity. Clear reference to the Holy Spirit is most numerous, perhaps because alternative names/titles for the Spirit are not as easily found as for the Father and the Son. These new songs are stronger in remembering God's activity, in having an ecclesial consciousness, and in having a tendency to be more dependent upon antecedent Trinitarian material. The well-known hymn *Holy, Holy, Holy* is the basis for many of the new songs.

What will the next 15 years of CCLI data indicate if this same kind of study is conducted? Several signs indicate a possible shift. One, noted above, is the increased number of recently written songs about the Trinity, including the exceptional *How Great Is Our God*. Another is the growing awareness by CWM composers of the power of songs to shape the faith of Christian peoples. Consequently, many new composers speak of the need for submitting songs to theological review. This increased dialogue with theologians is a sign of potential change, but whether or not it will result in a theological enrichment of CWM lyrics—and overcome the Trinitarian omission—will likely depend on composers. Greater theological breadth in CWM lyrics will occur as composers get beyond threshold questions like "Can the song's theme be found in the Bible?" or "Does it contradict good theology or the Bible?" Such questions set a minimal agenda rather than aspire to the full scriptural revelation of God.

Even now, a few composers address issues of theological fullness and breadth and include greater Trinitarian content as a goal for CWM. Notable examples include Graham Kendrick and Matt Redman.[22] Indeed, Redman now articulates an explicit Trinitarian understanding of worship:

> We praise Jesus the Son with everything within us—but we also join with Jesus in worship as He glorifies His Father. As the Holy Spirit reveals the Lordship of Jesus to the depths of our heart, He also takes us into the Son's relationships with the Father. . . . Worship is *to* Jesus, yes—absolutely. We glorify the Son and magnify His name. But worship is also *in* Jesus and *through* Jesus and *with* Jesus. . . . When our heavenly Father receives our worship, He receives it in the person of His Son and in the power of His Holy Spirit.[23]

A growing number of theologians and pastors within the CWM world—including Robert Webber, Brian McLaren, and Bert Waggoner, national director of the Vineyard Churches USA—supplement these composers' call for theologically enriched lyrics.[24] The emergence of Chris Tomlin's song *How Great Is Our God*, the only song among the 77 that intentionally worships because of God's Triune nature, is another promising sign of a Trinitarian piety.

While these signs indicate a potential shift for the next 15 years, widespread change will depend primarily upon developing a more Trinitarian piety. Christians will write and choose more Trinitarian songs only if love for the Trinity resides deeply in their hearts. The dynamics of *lex amandi, lex orandi* will not go away. As composer Brian Doerksen explains, the aim of a song is "to unlock the language of a people's hearts and for them to say, 'This is exactly what I wanted to say to God.' "[25] If Doerksen accurately assesses the way CWM is valued—and he does—then the implication is clear: A shift in the next 15 years will mean getting adoration of the Trinity to reside deeply within people's hearts. Songs will shift as Christians learn to love the Triune God for being Triune.

I COULD SING OF YOUR LOVE FOREVER: AMERICAN ROMANCE IN CONTEMPORARY WORSHIP MUSIC

JENELL WILLIAMS PARIS

Introduction

Contemporary praise and worship songs are often about love: how God loves humans, and how humans are to love God. First John 4:16 voices a theme found throughout Scripture, "And so we know and rely on the love God has for us. God is love. Whoever lives in love lives in God, and God in them" (TNIV). From the simple *Jesus Loves Me* to the classic *Jesus, Lover of My Soul*, Christians of all eras have sung about God's love in corporate worship.

When speaking of God's love, Christians, even when well-informed by Scripture, use the language and symbols of their culture. In American culture, that often means looking to romance when speaking of love. In academic conference conversations, Web logs, and books, many have argued that romance is overrepresented in praise and worship music. Some critically refer to this phenomenon as "Jesus-is-my-boyfriend" music or "romantic-pop" music, and argue that it has negative effects on congregations.[1] If romance is overemphasized in worship, it would not be surprising given the strongly sexualized understandings of love relationships in our culture. This chapter tests claims such as these by analyzing the romantic themes in popular praise and worship song lyrics.

Love from a Biblical Perspective

Biblical writers describe God in myriad ways, few of which are romantic in our sense of the word. In the Old Testament, the foremost name for God is "I AM," emphasizing God's everlastingness and sheer existence. God is also often described as a lord, king, or warrior, that is, a political or military leader who loves people by ruling them with justice and protecting them. God is described metaphorically as animals including a lion, a lamb, an eagle, and a hen, with associated characteristics of strength, tenderness, and protectiveness. Family terms are also used to describe God, including husband, brother, father, and mother. In Hosea, Jeremiah, and Isaiah, God is associated with maternal actions of gestating, giving birth, and nursing. These describe a God who goes to great lengths to call and create a people for Himself.[2]

Theologians have categorized biblical loves based upon Greek words used in the New Testament, including erotic love (*eros*), friendship (*philos*), family or maternal love (*storge*), and altruistic love (*agape*).[3] The Old Testament analogizes the love between God and Israel as marital, and the prophets Hosea and Jeremiah rely on this metaphor at length.

Similarly, the New Testament offers a few marital analogies for the relationship between God and humans or Christ and the church, such as Jesus as a bridegroom (Mark 2:20), but this does not mean the same as a "Hollywood leading man" groom. In biblical cultures, marriage relationships were formed for political or financial gain, for joining extended families, and for procreation. Intimacy could grow between a husband and wife over time, but passionate, intimate love would not be cultivated before marriage, nor developed in isolation from an extended family context.

Erotic love (*eros*) was certainly present in biblical times, but it was not the same as American ideals of romantic love. Though the Song of Solomon shows us that *eros* was present in biblical cultures, it was just one valued kind of human bond, not the be-all and end-all it often is in our culture. Even more important, however, romantic love was not ascribed to the relationship between God and His followers.

The American Romantic Ideal

Sociologist Ann Swidler interviewed white, middle-class Americans about their understandings and experiences of love.[4] She found that many Americans hold at least two competing frameworks for understanding love: the romantic ideal and prosaic realism. The *romantic ideal* comes from the medieval courtly tradition and is present still today in romance novels, Hollywood movies, and our imaginations. Lovers come together in sudden passion, each finding an idealized lover in the other. They persist through obstacles and find that love has magically transformed each lover into a more virtuous person. This romantic love separates individuals from society, because they need nothing but each other. Consequently, their union is often made in defiance of society or family expectations. In most of these romantic stories, the man is cast as strong, active, and initiative-taking, while the woman is in need of help, passive, and ultimately receiving of the man's initiative. Psychotherapist Stephen Mitchell sums it up well: "Romance is closer to 'falling' in love than to being in love."[5]

Even while they hold it as an ideal, the Americans in Swidler's study debunked the myth of romantic love, describing instead the *prosaic realist* view of love. In contrast to sudden, total, and permanent romantic passion, real love is often confused and ambivalent, and may grow or dissipate over time. Love that leads to marriage should not be defiant of society or family, but instead should be between lovers who are compatible in practical ways. Instead of automatically inferring virtue, love requires hard work, compromise, and sacrifice over time.

In the end, Swidler found that people use both models of love to shape expectations for and understandings of their own relationships. In particular, the romantic ideal is helpful when initially falling in love, while prosaic realism is a more helpful ideal for an ongoing, committed relationship. Indeed, both the romantic ideal and prosaic realism reflect aspects of biblical love, but each is only partial. Elements of romantic love may be seen in the Song of Solomon, and elements of prosaic realism may be found in marriage narratives such as those about Abraham and Sarah or Mary and Joseph since both couples faced significant obstacles in their relationships.

Both the romantic ideal and prosaic realism are, however, about the love shared between humans. Our culture offers few symbols or stories, if any, to image the love between God and humans. We may expect difficulties, then, when we create praise and worship music that, in an attempt to be relevant, inadvertently relies heavily on cultural understandings of love.

In analyzing popular praise and worship songs from 1989 through 2005, I pose the question, *In what ways do these songs use the American romantic ideal to describe the relationship between God and humans?*

I will argue that while romantic love serves to illuminate, in part, the divine-human relationship, an overreliance on the American romantic ideal in worship may have drawbacks. In conclusion, I offer applications designed to encourage worship leaders and worshipers toward greater faithfulness to Scripture and stronger discernment about how we contextualize the Word of God in American culture.

Method of Analysis

My method of analysis involved qualitative content analysis[6] of the lyrics of the Top 25 song lists of 1989–2005 as reported by CCLI and as described in the introductory chapter. First, I categorized each song as romantic or nonromantic based upon three criteria. A song was considered romantic if it fit any of these three criteria:

1. The first criterion was use of *American love colloquialisms*, such as "I'm desperate for You" (*Breathe*), or "You alone are my heart's desire" (*As the Deer*).
2. The second was use of *emotionally intimate language*, such as "for my soul longs and even faints for You" (*Better Is One Day*) or "Beauty that made this heart adore You / Hope of a life spent with You" (*Here I Am to Worship*).

3. The third was use of *physically intimate language*, such as "You are my desire / No one else will do / 'Cause nothing else could take Your place / To feel the warmth of Your embrace" (*Draw Me Close*) or "When I gaze into Your loveliness" (*When I Look into Your Holiness*).

My review of the 77 songs using these three criteria yielded a list of 27 romantic songs, which comprises 35 percent of the entire body of songs (see table 1 for a list of the romantic songs).

Table 1
Praise and worship songs identified as romantic

Above All	*I Love You, Lord*
As the Deer	*I Stand in Awe*
Better Is One Day	*In Moments Like These*
Breathe	*Lord, Reign in Me*
Change My Heart, Oh God	*More Precious Than Silver*
Come, Now Is the Time to Worship	*Open Our Eyes*
Draw Me Close	*Open the Eyes of My Heart*
Father, I Adore You	*Shout to the Lord*
Hallelujah (Your Love Is Amazing)	*Surely the Presence of the Lord*
The Heart of Worship	*There's Something about That Name*
Here I Am to Worship	*Thy Lovingkindness*
How Can We Name a Love	*When I Look into Your Holiness*
I Could Sing of Your Love Forever	*You Are My All in All*
I Give You My Heart	

The next step was to analyze the 27 romantic songs for ways in which they express the American romantic ideal. Based upon Ann Swidler's narrative description of romantic love described at the beginning of this chapter, I developed three questions to guide my in-depth analysis of the 27 songs identified as romantic:

1. First, *what is the role of God in the divine-human relationship?* If ascribed to the divine-human relationship, the American romantic ideal would have God taking the male role, being the stronger, more active, and more assertive partner. Here, I also looked for names of God, which emphasize certain actions and roles over others.

2. Second, *what is the role of humans in the divine-human relationship?* The American romantic ideal would cast humans in the feminine role, being passive, weak, dependent, and in need of rescue.

3. Third, *what difference does love make?* The American romantic ideal suggests that love is primarily for the self-fulfillment and pleasure of the lovers. This interpersonal fulfillment results in a separation from society, either because the lovers need nothing but each other, or because society presents obstacles to the pursuit of the romantic relationship.

Results and Discussion

God as the "Leading Man"

In her study, Ann Swidler found that Americans hold an idealized image of the masculine role in a romantic relationship. As in the movies, the "leading man" is assertive in pursuing the woman, persisting through obstacles to win the heart of his beloved. He takes risks to save the woman from some desperate situation. In romantic praise and worship songs, God takes this leading male role as well. We can see this in lyrics that describe God's actions, as well as in the names given to God.

Like the leading man in a movie, God saves, wins over, and enjoys His one true love. In the songs that describe divine actions, most refer to Jesus' salvific (salvation) acts. These songs are more likely to use referents such as "You" or "He," however, or avoid referents with the use of the passive voice. Jesus is praised for "taking my sin, my cross, my shame" (*You Are My All in All*), and honored for having "set me free" (*I Could Sing of Your Love Forever*). *I Stand in Awe* describes Jesus as a leading man, cast as hero against an antagonistic God: "Yet God crushed You for my sin." Similarly in *Here I Am to Worship*, Jesus "stepped down in darkness / Opened my eyes let me see."

Also in keeping with the "leading man" theme, in these songs God is an initiator of emotional intimacy. For example, in *Draw Me Close*, the worshiper longs for God to say "that I'm Your friend." *The Heart of Worship* describes God this way: "You search much deeper within / Through the way things appear / You're looking into my heart." *Above All* blends themes of God as rescuer and as lover. In *Above All*, Jesus (the name of Jesus is implied, not stated) is described as suffering for His beloved with a romantic sensibility: "Like a rose trampled on the ground / You took the fall and thought of me."

In many of these songs the climax of lyrics is the enjoyment of interpersonal intimacy between God and humans, mimicking the American romantic ideal of total fulfillment found between lovers. Songs present a static image of a believer resting in safety and intimacy with God, suggesting that God's primary purpose for acting in the world is to enter into romance-type relationships with individuals. *Draw Me Close*, for example, elevates intimacy in its final line, "You're all I want / Help me know You are near." *When*

I Look into Your Holiness ends with "When my will becomes enthralled in Your love . . . ." *Surely the Presence of the Lord* ends with "And my heart is overflowing / With the fullness of His joy / I know without a doubt / That I've been with the Lord." Other purposes of the divine-human relationship are minimized, such as spiritual growth, mission, acts of service, or even salvation.

God's role in the divine-human relationship is also apparent in the ways God is named. Though God's role mirrors the male part of the American romantic ideal, God is named in de-gendered ways, perhaps as a way of including both men and women in worship. In 81% of the romantic songs, God is referred to as "You," which avoids a gendered reference altogether. The next most common divine names are "Lord" (twelve songs, or 44%) and "God" (nine songs, or 33%). Though the acts of crucifixion and resurrection are mentioned in numerous songs, the name of Jesus is stated in only seven songs (26%). Fourth most common is "King," in just four songs (15%). Lord, God, and King are all male authority figures, yet the lyrics suggest a more intimate and equal relationship like boyfriend-girlfriend or husband-wife. Some lyrics could even be sung with a human companion in mind. In *Better Is One Day*, for example, the worshiper sings, "For my soul longs and even faints for You / For here my heart is satisfied within Your presence." Phrases like these would be better exchanged with a lover than with a political authority.

Limitations of God as "Leading Man"

In their pervasive portrayal of God as leading man, the 27 romantic praise and worship songs encourage people to view God primarily in terms of God's ability to deliver an experience of emotional fulfillment. In both God's role and God's name, worshipers are encouraged to imagine a divine partner who is the ultimate boyfriend—a strong, benevolent, wooing man. While this is not entirely inappropriate—indeed, it is important to encourage worshipers to develop a heartfelt relationship with God—it is also very limiting.

God's activities include more than personal salvation and interpersonal intimacy. To name just a few, God also created the world, formed a nation and then a church as His people, and continues to work through people to bring justice to the oppressed. These are all actions related to God's loving character that reach beyond an individual's experience of inner fulfillment or even individual salvation. As recorded in Scripture, God's intimate relationships with people, such as Jeremiah or Moses, were not primarily for the personal fulfillment of the individuals, but, rather, to empower the individuals to work for God's purposes in the world.

A second limitation related to the pervasive use of the American romantic ideal is that the simplification of naming—that is, using almost exclusively "You," "God," "Lord," and "Jesus"—may prevent worshipers from cultivating a rich scriptural imagination. Scripture offers many names for God and metaphors about what God is like, many of which could inspire worshipers to image and relate to God in ways faithful to

Scripture. Just a few examples include God as Jehovah, "I AM," a shade from the heat (Isaiah 25:4), the refuge of His people (Joel 3:12-16), or judge (Psalm 7:8). Jesus is referred to as the Word (John 1:1), the reflection of God's glory (Hebrews 1:3), the servant (Isaiah 42:1), the carpenter and son of Mary (Mark 6:3), and a man of sorrows (Isaiah 53:3). There are hundreds of metaphorical references, names, descriptions, and allusions to what God, Jesus, and the Holy Spirit are like. In addition to its romantic aspects, love includes care, justice, refuge, and service—all attributes of a loving God that could be included in worship.

Humans as the "Leading Lady"

In the romantic ideal—described by one of the participants in Ann Swidler's study as "movie love"—the leading lady complements the leading man by being weak, and passive, and in distress. In romantic worship songs, humans take this feminine role. A good example is found in *Draw Me Close*. In verse 1 the worshiper sings, "Draw me close to You / Never let me go," and in verse 2, "You are my desire / No one else will do / 'Cause nothing else could take your place / To feel the warmth of your embrace." Another, *Breathe*, has the worshiper singing, "And I / I'm desperate for You / And I'm lost without You."

In these songs, the human stance before God is one of longing and begging. Humans rarely initiate action or do anything good. Instead, humans ask for things to be done for them and speak of how wretched and pitiable they are. In *As the Deer*, the worshiper sings, "You alone are my heart's desire / And I long to worship Thee." In *I Give You My Heart*, the worshiper says what could easily be written in a love letter. After pledging her heart to the Lord, the worshiper adds, "Lord, have Your way in me." Humans and God are paired in a distress-and-rescue scenario, seen clearly in *You Are My All in All*: "You are my strength when I am weak," and later in the song where the worshipers comment on how Jesus picks them up when they are down.

Limitations of Humans as "Leading Lady"

While a stance of humility is essential in worship, these songs overemphasize the worthlessness of humans, which may limit worshipers from becoming agents of change in the world. *Thy Lovingkindness*, for example, leaves the worshiper "safe in thy shadow," and *Better Is One Day* has the worshiper "beneath the shadow of Your wings." In *I Stand in Awe*, the worshiper never moves, standing still in God's presence. There is a strength that comes through weakness, but the purpose of human weakness is not only to experience God's protection and rescue, but to become Holy Spirit–empowered agents of action in the world. As in our world, people in Scripture engage with God in a variety of ways. Moses argued with God, Jeremiah accepted his calling and acted boldly, David lamented, and Mary became an active partner in bringing Jesus into the world. For these followers of God, a love relationship with God offered strength and purpose for living, not emotional indulgence.

In these songs, when humans finally act it is in responsive and religious ways. In many songs, the most humans do is "give in" and let God take the lead. In *I Could Sing of Your Love Forever*, the worshiper says, "I will open up my heart and let the Healer set me free." Similarly, *I Give You My Heart* has the worshiper yielding in language that could be understood as erotic submission. After declaring that every waking moment and breath are to be spent for God alone, the worshiper concludes again with, "Lord, have Your way in me." The most active responses from humans are those individual religious acts that are mostly done in a church gathering, such as "I lift up my hands" (*Thy Lovingkindness*), or "I lift my voice" (*I Love You, Lord*).

While religious responses to God are necessary and valuable, most people spend only a few hours a week singing and worshiping at church. Worship songs might also speak of how a saved person might live in the workplace, family, or society. They also might include corporate acts of worship and service. God's love should prompt us both to praise Him in response and to change the way we live our daily lives.

Interestingly, there is much more elaboration upon themes of human frailty, humility, and need than on the character of God. As described earlier, descriptions of God are generally very simple, especially when compared to the elaborate lyrics describing humans. *The Heart of Worship* is an interesting example. The song's narrative is that the worshiper is apologizing for being self-centered and is coming back to the heart of worship: "And it's all about You / All about You, Jesus." Verse one focuses on the person coming back to God, and verse two focuses on the person being weak and poor. Much more briefly, God is described as looking into the worshiper's heart and being of "endless worth." Even here, God is described in terms of what He does for the worshiper.

Even more problematically, these songs suggest that personal fulfillment is the high point of being a Christian. *Better Is One Day* provides a good example: "For my soul longs and even faints for You / For here my heart is satisfied within your presence." *As the Deer* describes satisfaction and completion in romance with God: "You alone are my heart's desire," and "You're the apple of my eye." While it is true that human identity finds completion in God, the repetition of this theme to the exclusion of human service and community may promote an excessively personalized and pietistic vision of faith—as if feeling satisfied in life and experiencing romantic feelings of love toward God is the mark of Christian maturity. The love of God may sometimes bring intense emotional experience that may mimic human romantic love, but sometimes it does not, and the presence or absence of a particular experience should not be the mark of Christian maturity. Additionally, God's love does more than produce inner experience. It also helps free believers to express His love in the world by living rightly with others and with creation.

"Riding Off Together into the Sunset"

In Ann Swidler's study, Americans described the romantic ideal as "riding off together into the sunset." Lovers find completion and bliss in each other and distance themselves from society as they pursue their love. Connections to family or society become either unnecessary, because the lovers are fulfilled in each other, or harmful, when others present obstacles to the lovers pursuing their relationship. When people described their marriages in Swidler's study, however, they said love entangles people in commitments, families, and communities. Rather than exploring how God's love binds us to the church and to our communities, popular worship songs more often describe the divine-human relationship in romantic terms, with individuals becoming less and less connected to life on earth as they worship.

When I Look into Your Holiness describes a person losing touch with society as he or she becomes intimate with God. In the last line of verse 1, everything in the vicinity of the worshiper becomes darkness in God's light. *There's Something about That Name* compares Jesus' name to "the fragrance after the rain" and speaks of earthly things passing away. Evidence of worship, in fact, is sometimes considered the experience of detachment from earthly surroundings. In *Surely the Presence of the Lord*, the worshiper knows that he or she is worshiping because he or she "can feel his mighty power," "can hear the brush of angel's wings," and can "feel that same sweet spirit."

Limitations of "Riding Off Together into the Sunset"

Many romantic praise and worship songs conjure the sense of a person united with God, floating somewhere in open space. There seems to be no human or earthly context to the spiritual life, except for the general sinfulness of the world that needs to be blocked out of the mind. This overemphasis is problematic if for no other reason than that people worshiping at a church service will soon return to homes, neighborhoods, cities, workplaces—real world contexts in which their faith needs to make practical sense. Overemphasis on the romantic teaches that the spiritual life is one of disconnecting from the world, rather than engaging it. As Christians increasingly learn to engage social justice issues such as war, AIDS, poverty, and disaster relief, they should find a fullness of personal piety and social action in their worship music.

I Could Sing of Your Love Forever provides a helpful counterexample. It ends, "But when the world has seen the light / They will dance with joy / Like we're dancing now." Though the imagery of light is still otherworldly, the song suggests that God's love has influence in the here and now. Another counterexample is *How Can We Name a Love*. The lyrics encourage the worshiper to reflect on daily life: "Look at your life, your world / In each familiar face where joy is found, Love's echoes sound / Hid in the common place." In the final verse, life on earth is connected to the love of God: "Daily we all can meet / Signals of love unknown at work, at home or in the street / Yet on these terms alone, faith would be weak and dim / In Christ we see love's guarantee and fix our hopes on Him." Songs such as these encourage both intimacy with God and active service in the world.[7]

Conclusion

As metaphor and as art, music is a powerful instrument for helping people understand the scope and everlastingness of God's love. The near-exclusive use of the American romantic ideal in love-oriented worship songs uses only a fraction of what Scripture teaches about God's love, and it also may misinform worshipers' spiritual journeys, shaping expectations of an American romantic love story playing out in their spiritual lives. The widespread use in contemporary worship of romantic language that reinforces the American ideal to the exclusion of a fuller biblical perspective presents pastors, worship leaders, and worshipers with important challenges.

Romantic worship songs may be helpful in encouraging an intimate, heartfelt relationship with God, and such a purpose should be conserved. As participants in Ann Swidler's study said, however, romance is not the whole story when it comes to love. Love is also about commitment, hard work, change over time, and, at times, confusion and doubt. Below are several suggestions for addressing some of the challenges identified in this chapter:

1. *Increase reliance on Scripture in song lyrics.* As Scripture shows, God's love for humans is much more than just romantic. God's love cannot be pinned down to a simple definition, which is why the hundreds of scriptural metaphors for God help us envision its vastness and perfection. Images of and names for God could be broadened to include more than the most simple "God," "Lord," "King," and "You." Songs designed particularly to enhance the individual's heartfelt relationship with God could include the Savior (Acts 13:23), the good shepherd (John 10:11), or a sure foundation (Isaiah 28:16). In this way, worshipers will be more faithful to scriptural attributes of God and reduce the tendency to ascribe pop culture images and ideas to God. Additionally, worship songs can teach Scripture by using literal phrases and words.

2. *Broaden the language of love beyond the romantic.* Swidler's study would suggest including aspects of prosaic realism: the commitment, the hard work, the long-suffering, and the confusions of real love lived over time. The well-known appropriation of Greek words for love, including *eros* (erotic love), *storge* (family or maternal love), *agape* (altruistic love), and *pragma* (pragmatic love) would also provide a way of describing different facets of love.

3. *Expand the role of humans beyond passivity, weakness, and sinfulness.* Scriptural images of God often carry complementary images of humans—Creator and creation, father and child, friends, and teacher and student. In all of these, God is greater than humans, which is already reflected in romantic worship songs. But humans are also active participants in the divine-human relationship, doing important works of creativity, justice, and mercy. Additionally, humans make positive efforts toward their own

spiritual formation in realms including society and politics, the family, the workplace, and the church. The personal, private, and "other-worldly" part of the spiritual life is not the whole. Worship music should reflect more of what spiritual formation is, that is, the shaping of a person in relationship with God, living life in this world.

Finally, it is important to become aware of ways in which worship music may superficially "Christianize" elements of our culture. American music and popular culture are romanticized in ways that are easy to see and to critique. Worship music parallels this trend, however, in ways that may seem subtle to those who count on such music for meaningful worship experiences. Developing worship music that expresses the wonderfulness of God's love in ways that connect culturally, but do not capitulate, will be an ongoing adventure.

I'm Desperate for You: Male Perception of Romantic Lyrics in Contemporary Worship Music

KEITH DRURY

Introduction

As has been pointed out by Jenell Williams Paris (in chapter 2), many contemporary worship songs focus on the loving relationship between God and humans and feature phrases that are also used in a sexualized culture to express romantic or erotic love for another person. This chapter proposes that we have seen an increasing emphasis on the humanness—even maleness—of Jesus in our general perception and in worship songs. At the same time, romantic lyrics such as "I'm desperate for You" (*Breathe*) or "I sing out a love song to Jesus" (*In Moments Like These*) have become more dominant in CWM songs. When combined with an increasing emphasis on the humanness of Jesus, such lyrics produce a strong brew—for young adult males especially—of what can seem like "singing love songs to Jesus, the hunk." Romanticizing our relationship with Jesus may not be wise for female worshipers, but it could be a special problem for males if the relationship is sexualized—at least for some young adult males.

Research is at the early stages of development on gender and worship, although the quality of the work is better for females and worship than for males and worship.[1] A virtual avalanche of books has been published recently on maleness and "male spirituality," but these works are weak at two points. First, they tend to describe "what is obvious to everyone" such as the repugnance men have for "Jesus-is-my-boyfriend" songs in worship, though there is little testing of this claim. The second weakness in the literature on male spirituality is its tendency to give greater attention to a more solitary style of "lone wolf spirituality" and overlook the corporate role of the entire body of Christ that is theologically imperative.

This chapter reports the results of interviews with 45 young adult males in an attempt to discover the extent to which they may be aware of romantic lyrics in the 77 songs and their response to them in a worship context.

The Increasingly Human Jesus

Jesus is both divine and human, fully 100% God and 100% man at the same time. While these two natures of Jesus have widely been accepted through Christian history, there is often a disproportionate emphasis on one or the other: either the humanity or the divinity of Jesus.[2] Sometimes the emphasis is to correct error, for example, when a heresy arises and teaches that Jesus was not really human but only appeared to be so. In response, the church may heavily emphasize the humanity of Jesus to correct the imbalance. Likewise, when Jesus has been humanized to the extent that He has been stripped of His divinity, the church tends to respond with an emphasis on the divinity of Jesus. But even without heresy, the Christian church is constantly calibrating its understanding of Jesus to stay balanced and complete.

This emphasis on Jesus' humanity is readily apparent in the shifting arena of worship arts over the last half-century in representing the face of Jesus. When Warner Sallman drew his *Head of Christ* in 1941, it rapidly dominated the market.[3] Over the succeeding years more than 500 million reproductions were made. Sallman pictured a dark and sturdy man with just a hint of an aura. In the 1940s nobody would have mistaken the artwork for someone they might actually meet—it was clearly of a man from another era, even complete with a hint of an aura, though less than a halo. While Sallman's art of Jesus continued to dominate the market in the 1960s, Richard and Frances Hook's art portrayed a more inviting Jesus. Their *Head of Christ* appeared more modern, realistic, likable, and heroic.[4] I recall a college student in the 1960s remarking upon seeing my copy of the Hooks' picture, "Cool—great picture of Davy Crocket." He was serious. This was a "manly Christ" who appeared very human and recent—like someone you might meet on a hike in the woods.

This humanizing trend continued on after the 1960s. The Hooks then produced their popular *Smiling Christ*[5] and *Laughing Jesus*, which humanized and modernized the image even more, thereby making Jesus someone we would want to invite to our party or go fishing with us.[6] The more recent *Undefeated* by Steve Sawyer depicts Jesus as a powerful and buff boxer more akin to a male pin-up picture than a distant first-century prophet.[7]

What does all this talk about education and liturgical art have to do with romanticized lyrics in worship songs? Because "singing love songs to Jesus" when we are picturing a very manly person instead of a distant Godlike painting has greater sensual overtones. The 1941 painting by Sallman may have made Jesus too distant and unlike humans. We cannot say for sure. But we might say that the trend in representing Jesus artistically seems to be moving toward a more human, accessible, and very manly Jesus, and this gives romanticized lyrics focusing on the manly Jesus somewhat of a different meaning.

Christians today seem to picture Jesus as more human (and more male) than in the past. The human mind works visually. When we sing a song to Jesus, what visual symbol pops up in the mind, if any at all? Could it be that a song directed to Jesus in 1941 prompted a different imagination than one sung today? Is it possible the Jesus we sing to today is a very human person, that is, a man like me? A "real" man? Maybe even a buff, powerful man—and one who is clearly male?

If Jesus has been increasingly seen as human and male during the last 50 years, much of our music has continued to be (perhaps increasing so?) subjective and relational, even romantic in nature. Romantic-leaning lyrics are not new, of course. Almost 300 years ago Charles Wesley penned "Jesus, lover of my soul / let me to thy bosom fly." Such phrases may be difficult for some to sing today in an oversexualized culture. Yet there is a preponderance of similar though less explicit phrases in today's popular worship music. Love seems to be a primary binding agent in the relationship between Jesus and His followers in today's worship. Indeed, in these 77 songs, the terms "love," "loving," or "lover" are used more than 50 times. Even some of the songs that did not feature love used words like "adore" or "desire," which are generally considered romantic terms in today's pop culture. All this leaves us sometimes singing love songs to a very human and very male Jesus—which has the potential to sexualize the relationship between worshiper and Jesus for both women and men.

Being sensitized to the potential response of males to romanticized music by the alert writing of Jenell Williams Paris (chapter 2) and others, I started noticing how many lyrics of contemporary (and some traditional) songs do indeed have lyrics that are romantic-leaning or could even be taken with double meaning. For example, "I'm desperate for You" (*Breathe*, Michael W. Smith) has a totally different meaning in a worship service than those identical lyrics have in *Drop Dead, Gorgeous*.[8] I have often wondered if young men were troubled at all by these double-meaning lyrics or overtly romanticized lyrics in worship songs.

In chapter 2, Jenell Williams Paris addressed the use of the American romance lyrics in the 77 CWM songs. Jenell's study suggested that CWM heavily relies on the American romantic ideal with God as the "leading man" and humans as the "leading lady," consummated in "riding off together into the sunset."

If this model is continually used today, I wondered how it would strike young males, especially when combined with an increasing view of Jesus as very human, and male—even a "hunk." While an overemphasis on the American romantic motif in the divine-human relationship is problematic for both genders, I focused on how it might strike males—especially single young adult males. A late adolescent male might burst out, "I'm desperate for you" to his girlfriend to denote one sort of feeling. I wondered how that young man might feel about singing these same words to divinity, especially to Jesus. It seemed to me that young adult single males are especially sensitive to a sexualized culture and might be most sensitive to the romantic or erotic overtones of these lyrics. I decided to ask them directly.

Method of Analysis

I conducted unstructured interviews with 45 male young adults 18 to 26 years old. The population comprised students at Indiana Wesleyan University (IWU), a private, liberal arts, Christian institution in Marion, Indiana. IWU has a predominantly residential student population of which 39% are male; there are approximately 2,600 traditional-age students total. The students represent 60 different denominations with Wesleyan, nondenominational, Baptist, United Methodist, and Nazarene being the five most common denominations. The students come from Indiana (54%), Ohio (14%), and Michigan (10%). The students in the traditional-age programs are 98% Caucasian. Religion or ministry majors make up 12% of the university's majors.[9]

Those surveyed did not fully represent the overall makeup of the student body. Of those surveyed, slightly more than half (28) were from one of the various religion majors. Less than 10% were freshmen (3), 20% were seniors (9), and the largest portion were sophomores or juniors (33). None of the students interviewed was from the worship major at our university.

Before conducting the interviews, I examined Jenell Williams Paris's analysis of the 77 songs in chapter 2 and determined to test the extent to which her examples might be taken romantically by young adult males. I prepared a slip of paper with the example lyrics that she had cited in her chapter as examples of romantic lyrics. I did not mention other lyrics that could be interpreted romantically or with double meaning. I did not mention the many lyrics where God can be seen as a "leading man" providing shelter, protection, or strength, or those where God whisks the worshiper off into the sunset to live happily ever after. These are actually by far the most common references in the list. The lyrics I consider to have potential romantic or sexual double entendre in the 77 songs are listed in table 1 below, though in my interviews I only mentioned those cited in chapter 2.

Table 1	
Lyrics with potential sexual double entendre or romantic overtones	**Song Title**
And hush to praise our Lover and our Friend	*How Can We Name a Love*
And the warmth of Your embrace	*We Bring the Sacrifice of Praise*
Beauty that made this heart adore You	*Here I Am to Worship*
Bring me back to You	*Draw Me Close*
Come once again to me / I will draw near to You	*Better Is One Day*
Draw me close to You / Never let me go	*Draw Me Close*
Enthralled in Your love	*When I Look into Your Holiness*

Ev'ry breath that I take / . . .	
Lord, have Your way in me	*I Give You My Heart*
Father, I adore You	*Father, I Adore You*
For my soul longs and even faints for You	*Better Is One Day*
Hope of a life spent with You	*Here I Am to Worship*
I could sing of Your love forever	*I Could Sing of Your Love Forever*
I love You more than any other	*As the Deer*
I sing out a love song to Jesus	*In Moments Like These*
My heart and flesh cry out for You	*Better Is One Day*
No one else will do	*Draw Me Close*
Nothing I desire compares with You	*More Precious Than Silver*
Oh, I feel like dancing	*I Could Sing of Your Love Forever*
One thing I ask and I would seek / To see Your beauty	*Better Is One Day*
Only You can satisfy	*As the Deer*
To feel the warmth of Your embrace	*Draw Me Close*
When I gaze into Your loveliness	*When I Look into Your Holiness*
Yes, Lord, yes, Lord, yes, yes, Lord	*Trading My Sorrows*
You alone are my heart's desire	*As the Deer*
You are beautiful beyond description	*I Stand in Awe*
You are my desire	*Draw Me Close*
You're all I've ever needed	*Draw Me Close*
You're altogether lovely	*Here I Am to Worship*

I interviewed students in a neutral setting, either following a non-worship-related class or at the campus coffee shop. I asked the interviewees how they felt when singing songs to Jesus (identified in the table above) that included lyrics such as "When I gaze into your loveliness" (*When I Look into Your Holiness*); "Draw me close" (*Draw Me Close*); "You're all I want" (*Draw Me Close*); "My soul longs and even faints for You" (*Better Is One Day*); "Feel the warmth of Your embrace" (*Draw Me Close*); "I'm desperate for You" (*Breathe*); and "You alone are my heart's desire" (*As the Deer*). I gave no follow-up explanations verbally or in print other than the phrases printed on a slip of paper for them to ponder before answering. Each interview lasted approximately three minutes. I asked the student to read the phrases, and then write his immediate response to the question. I gave no other comments and did not introduce the subject of the research. If a young man asked a follow-up question for clarification, I responded, "Just respond to the question on the slip without my comments, ok?" Following their initial responses to the primary question outlined above, I asked follow-up or probing questions designed to get at deeper levels of meaning and took careful notes of the phrases they used. I never raised gender issues in any of these discussions except to ask follow-up questions when they raised the subject first. After all the interviews were completed, I performed qualitative content analysis on the responses in an attempt to group responses into broad categories for discussion.

By selecting what I considered to be the most explicitly romantic phrases from Jenell Williams Paris's work (chapter 2), I assumed a large number of these younger males might say something about the romantic overtones of the phrases. The majority did not. However, those who did make remarks on the romantic aspects of lyrics registered strong negative feelings about that aspect. The following is a summary of how the 45 young male adults I interviewed responded to the interview questions.

Results and Discussion

Positive Response

The most common response to the romantic lyrics among the 45 interviewees was positive toward the lyrics. Even when presented with explicitly romantic lyrics identified in table 1 above, the most common response (about a third of the males interviewed) gave wholly positive remarks on the lyrics and said nothing at all about romantic overtones.

Many interviewees saw the lyrics I identified as "romantic" as representing a relationship with Jesus of comfort and closeness. One interviewee said, "I feel like Jesus is my comforter and friend and the one I seek when I'm going through a rough time." Another remarked, "I feel like I'm speaking straight to Him when I sing songs like this, and I feel closer to Him." Several described how they wanted to respond while singing with comments like, "I feel a longing and desire to close my eyes and be alone . . . and to let the words sink in and help me to be calm and relaxed." Several mentioned the usefulness of such songs to "get me in the mood to worship" or "to help me forget the outside world and just to focus on Jesus." Some cited sensory experiences such as "I feel especially close to God when singing like this. It is as if God's hand is resting on me and encouraging me to continue."

What was notable among these interviewees was that more than half the young adult males switched Persons of the Trinity in their responses. Recall that the question specifically asked about "singing such phrases to Jesus." More than half of the males who favorably responded to the lyrics switched from "Jesus" to "God" in their responses. I wondered, were they coping with the romantic phrases this way or was there some other factor that influenced this change of Persons in the Trinity from the question posed? Is it possible that males feel more comfortable using romantic language when applied to their relationship with God the Father than Jesus Christ?

That so many young men did not react negatively to the romantic overtones of the lyrics was somewhat surprising to me. How could they not be bothered by explicit phrases so widely considered romantic/erotic in our culture? Were these worship lyrics cemented into their thinking during their prepubescent years and thus had never taken on romantic overtones? Or, had these worship phrases taken on significance in their church context so that what would be explicitly romantic in another context was absolutely appropriate for worship? It is also possible that there may be a sense of shame associated in admitting that they recognized any romantic/erotic overtones in the phrases, so they simply opted to embrace the musical lyrics. We do not know. What I did discover is that most of the males responded positively to the lyrics, giving no negative response to the lyrics that I thought had romantic overtones.

Negative Response Unrelated to Romantic Overtones

The second most common response was negative, but not about the romantic aspect; they condemned the shallowness and subjectivity of the phrases. One young man said in response to the list of romantic lyrics, "My first thought is that these are the typical worship songs we sing that do not go deep in thought." Another said, "Honestly, it seems very emotional and lacking in content." Several remarked that such phrases are "too me-focused" or "all about I, me, and my." One young man considered the romantic phrases I presented as representative of "subjective" music: "I would rather sing [objectively] of God's greatness than my subjective feelings for Him. These songs may have a place, but . . . [they are too] subjective and response-oriented."

None of this second category of responses mentioned the romantic flavor of the phrases directly. It is possible that this group's rejection of the lyrics based on subjectivity and shallowness could have been a "coded answer" related to the romantic flavor. While not all subjective lyrics are romantic-leaning, all romantic lyrics are subjective. Therefore, one could argue that the second most common response may have implied a negative response to romantic lyrics while using nonromantic language of "subjectivity" or "shallowness."

It is also possible that this response was second most common because the young men have been sensitized to notice subjectivity and shallowness by the current church culture that has derided the "Jesus-is-my-boyfriend" songs. There are probably more articles and speakers who have addressed the shallowness and subjectivity of contemporary songs than those who have even mentioned any erotic or romantic overtones of some lyrics. Though some worship experts have addressed this matter in private, few have published their concerns. With more attention given to the romantic allusions in our songs than I have outlined above, we might expect more males to notice in the future. But, in these interviews, the second most prominent response was not about romantic overtones in the lyrics but about what has been a charge for several decades against "the new praise choruses": their shallowness and subjectivity.

Negative Response Related to Romantic Overtones

Concern for romantic overtones was the third most frequent response. About one-fourth (11/45) of the male students interviewed mentioned this concern immediately. Yet even though this response was not the most frequent response, the feelings were especially strong with this group. Respondents sometimes used words like "sickening" or even "revolting" in their answer.

One young man saw the parallel to popular love songs by saying, "I don't feel totally right [singing these lyrics]. . . . They sound too much like secular love songs." A college sophomore said, "Some of these songs make me sound like I want to make out with Jesus and that thought is revolting to me." In another case a young man said, "It's almost more of a conversation between two lovers than between a sinner and their savior. . . . I feel awkward singing these kinds of things though I usually go along when we do." One young man said the lyrics caused him to feel uncomfortable: "I would rather emphasize my relationship with Christ as my Lord or my shelter than my lover—the lover thing makes my skin crawl." One young man admitted the songs had no romantic overtones until he had heard of it: "I started singing these songs before I knew of the 'Jesus-is-my-boyfriend' thing, so I never thought of it—but now that I am aware of that aspect it has gotten much harder to worship with them than it used to be." One male student brought up the subject of switching tracks while singing romantic lyrics: "Sometimes when we sing those songs my mind wanders to thinking about my girlfriend and I start applying the words to our relationship instead of a spiritual one with God." This was the only response indicating this switchover among males, but it brought to light another factor I had missed. My own concern about romantic or sexualized lyrics has been primarily focused on the impropriety of a romantic or erotic flavor of a relationship with Jesus—for either females or males. However, this last response raised an additional area that had not occurred to me: *To what extent do romantic-erotic lyrics in worship trigger interpersonal human feelings that are romantic or erotic?* Perhaps this is a single response of a particularly honest young man, or it could be a hint of a more extensive issue that is just as problematic as romanticizing the human-divine relationship. This is certainly an area inviting further research.

While most of the males did not indicate that the romantic overtones presented a problem, the depth of feelings and breadth of distraction for those who did complain (11/45) should make us sit up and take notice. It is not just a tiny minority of oversexualized males who notice these romantic overtones, but perhaps as many as one out of four males sitting (more likely *standing*) in worship. It is enough of a response to consider the matter more carefully.

Authenticity

The final category of response revolved around the lack of authenticity and honesty in worship. A surprising number of men started off their comments with "I feel awkward" or "I have difficulty with these songs" as if they were going to cite romantic aspects, but then went on to describe that their problem singing the phrases was that these phrases were not totally true—they felt like hypocrites singing these lyrics. One said, "I have difficulty singing such phrases because I wonder if I really mean it." Another said, "God is not my whole heart's desire—I have many competing desires, and when I sing phrases like these I feel like I'm being a hypocrite and not telling the truth." Another said, "Singing words such as these makes me ask if I am really being authentic when I am singing them—to sing them without authenticity would be useless." One young man simply said he sometimes did not sing at all: "Sometimes I feel like I'm being dishonest and singing somebody else's song and that is not really what I feel, and then I am lying when I sing those kinds of words, so sometimes I am just silent and let others sing."

The concern for authenticity and honesty among young adults is often reported,[10] but apparently for some it is a factor in singing romantic song lyrics of the kind identified in this study. About one out of ten young adults I interviewed (five) mentioned the authenticity or honesty matter. That is worthy to note and invites further study.

Conclusion

My findings showed that only some males considered romantic lyrics a problem. Observing this barrier for some males is easier than offering solutions to the problem. Considering the low reporting of such a problem, perhaps the recommendations could be to ignore the issue altogether—considering it to be "a problem some males have." But, if we wish to address the matter for this minority, there are several actions we might take in local church worship and in the Christian worship movement at large. These actions might address the more serious stumbling blocks we could be placing in the path of young men and young women as it relates to romantically suggestive lyrics. Here are several follow-up observations and suggestions to consider in light of the results presented above.

Perhaps There Is No Problem at All

Most males I interviewed did not mention romantic lyrics as a problem, though it does not follow that romantic motifs are indeed not a problem. Through history Christians have often found refuge and solace in mistaken, imbalanced, or even heretical ideas. Yet using romantic motifs as expressions of our relationship with God is legitimate and biblical (Matthew 22:1-14; Ephesians 5:1-2, 22-33; John 14:1-3; Revelation 19:7-9). Our question may be one of balance when it is the *dominant* means of expression.

In a related shorter process, I interviewed 12 young women using the same procedure. Not a single young woman mentioned having problems with the romantic aspects of the phrases. Yet that does not mean that seeing their relationship with Jesus in this light is not imbalanced or even unhealthy for women, as well as for men. Using phrases in songs that are usually construed as romantic or erotic in our culture *is* a problem for some, perhaps for more than will admit it. It would be a mistake to conclude from my interviews that only a few young men even notice these things. More than a few young men did notice it, and it is likely a problem for older men as well as women too, even if they do not recognize it as such.

Select Songs That Include the Father

At least some males seem to respond more positively to devotional-romantic phrases when they are applied to the Father as divinity. While emphasis on all three Persons of the Trinity is ideal and correct, loading our romantic phrases into our songs to Jesus may hamper the worship of at least some young males. Lester Ruth's chapter on Trinitarian references (chapter 1) in the 77 songs highlights this point. His conclusion is that very few songs actually facilitate praying to and worshiping the Triune God. As new songs are written and find their way into common use, a correction in this imbalance can surely take place.

Develop More Corporate Love Lyrics

The romantic motif is not a secular idea that has "crept into religious songs" lately. It is a sound biblical idea in the following way: the church *is* the bride of Christ, our lover, and we are all headed for a marriage supper of the lamb. But it is the *group* that is betrothed to Jesus, not each of us as individuals. One of the strengths of recent songs has been the personalizing and privatizing of lyrics so that we sing them directly and personally to Jesus, thereby making worship more personal and individual. However, the danger of this approach arises with the use of romantic lyrics where the individual is improperly placed in the spot where the corporate body should be. None of us alone can be the bride of Christ; only together collectively are we His bride. Thus, the church could use more lyrics expressing the love relationship between Jesus and the collective church, replacing "I, my, and mine" with "we, our, and ours." In this group context, the romantic aspect—even the marriage metaphor—can be wholesome, biblical, and proper.

De-emphasize Songs with Explicitly Erotic Nuances

Some phrases have such strong double meanings that even if only one out of ten young males notices the suggestiveness of the lyrics, the sexual meaning could be so repugnant to a few that a wise worship leader would deselect them altogether—or at least use them rarely. We might let pass a single romantic phrase in a song by considering those who respond negatively as outliers who are overreacting (e.g., *We Bring the Sacrifice of Praise*). However, when a song repeatedly uses romantic or erotic double-meaning phrases (*Better Is One Day; Draw Me Close*), we should use greater caution—even if the song has great meaning to the majority. After all, many contemporary worship leaders have discarded traditional songs that have great meaning to a majority of older people because they are "a problem" for younger people.

It is not a helpful solution to dismiss those who notice these double meanings (e.g., "Yes, Lord, yes, Lord, yes, yes, Lord" in *Trading My Sorrows*) as young men with dirty minds or people with some sort of Freudian obsession with sex. Our culture is so sexualized, with much of our media humor riding on sexual double entendre, that we cannot ignore lyrics loaded with these meanings. Worshipers come to church predisposed by the culture to recognize double-entendre references to sex. Thus, even the most innocent worship leader who has never imagined such thoughts must become more aware of what these double meanings might be conveying to a significant number of young males.

Considerable additional study is called for in the arena of gender and worship. Do today's worshipers see Jesus skewed too much to the human and excluding the divine? How do women experience romantic or erotic references in songs differently than men? Do young men see these songs differently than older men? In what ways do non-Christian secularists see such lyrics differently than Christians? How might the Jesus-as-the-ideal-man affect women in their human relationships with other men?

My initial investigation concluded that some young adult males are sensitive to romantic or erotic allusions in worship lyrics, and it hinders their worship. Perhaps the concern registered by Jenell Williams Paris (chapter 2) can be dismissed. The majority of males did not immediately register responses expressing any concerns. Indeed, they spoke of other matters addressed in this book, including the shallowness of the lyrics.

Yet romanticized lyrics did bother some males. The question for worship leaders is how much weight to give to a minority population in the church who might "have a problem" with songs or lyrics. We always have people who are bothered by some of our music or lyrics. The question for us is how many it takes to make a problem. If my findings above are any indication of the general male population, would this be enough to worry about? How many people does it take to make a problem? That is a longtime question for veteran worship leaders.

Let the Weak Say I Am Strong: Contemporary Worship Music and God's Concern for Righteousness and Social Justice

Jay Howard

Introduction

In the book of Amos, God condemns the lifestyle and, in particular, the worship of Israel for the people's lack of concern with justice and righteousness:

> Away with the noise of your songs!
> I will not listen to the music of your harps.
> But let justice roll on like a river,
> righteousness like a never-failing stream!
>
> Amos 5:23-24 (NIV)

Howard Snyder argues that worship is always closely linked with God's kingdom and justice and, therefore, with repentance.[1] The first chapter of Isaiah calls offerings "meaningless" and assemblies "evil" while admonishing believers to seek justice, defend the fatherless, and plead for the widow. In Isaiah 58, the prophet describes God's chosen type of fasting as loosening the chains of injustice, setting the oppressed free, and sharing food with the hungry. The first chapter of James indicates that religion is "pure and faultless" when it concerns itself with looking after widows and orphans. In the chapter on worship in Richard Foster's classic book, *Celebration of Discipline*, Foster concludes:

> We worship the Lord not only because of who he is, but also because of what he has done. Above all, the God of the Bible is the God who acts. His goodness, faithfulness, justice, mercy all can be seen in his dealings with his people.[2]

In his book *The Politics of Jesus*, John Howard Yoder suggests that New Testament studies can and should be connected with contemporary social ethics. Yoder points out that in the passage known as the "Magnificat" in Luke 1, Mary praises God for putting down the mighty from their thrones and exalting those of low degree as well as for filling the hungry with good things and sending the rich away empty. In Luke 4, Jesus "states the messianic expectation in the most expressly social terms" when He describes the platform that comprises His messianic mission: preach good news to the poor and proclaim release for the captives, recovery of sight for the blind, liberty for the oppressed, and the year of Jubilee.[3] Yoder concludes that Jesus was the bearer of new possibilities for human, social, and political relationships. It was this call to a new kind of life that threatened the established social order and ultimately led to the cross.

Thus, in both the writings of the Old Testament prophets and in the Gospels, we find a direct connection between Christian worship and biblical justice and righteousness. Does contemporary worship music (CWM) envision a different type of social order based on a vision of Jesus' present and coming kingdom of righteousness and justice? Does CWM focus on what God indicates is at the heart of what it means to know Him? In addition to recognizing the holiness and majesty of God, are the themes of God's demands for justice and righteousness in social relationships also emphasized in CWM? Or does CWM imply that it is possible to love the Lord your God with all your heart, soul, and mind *without* loving your neighbor as yourself (Matthew 22:37-40)?

In this chapter, I will analyze the extent to which the top 77 contemporary worship music songs address issues of biblical righteousness and justice. First, I will explore the biblical notions of justice and righteousness. Then, I will identify the songs that address these topics before concluding with a few suggestions for worship leaders and worshipers alike.

Justice and Righteousness in a Biblical Perspective

What exactly is meant by biblical justice and righteousness? Andy Crouch notes that the words *mishpat* and *tsedaqah*, which most English Bibles translate as *justice* and *righteousness*, occur together more than 30 times in the Hebrew Bible.[4] In separate analyses, both Ruth Ann Foster and Brian Edgar also conclude that justice and righteousness are consistently linked in scripture.[5] In scripture, justice is not merely providing equal treatment under the law as we tend to define it in contemporary terms today. Instead, biblical justice is tied to "putting power at the service of the powerless and wealth at the service of the poor."[6] God's justice involves relationships within the life of the community and is inevitably intertwined with God's love, mercy, compassion, grace, and truth. Without God's love, mercy, compassion, grace, and truth, justice would require that everyone be condemned.

And because we have been justified by God's grace, we are called to show justice to others, especially the poor and the marginalized. Jeremiah 22:15-16 reveals that doing what is right and just, defending the poor and the needy, is at the heart of what it means to know God and thus at the heart of God's justice. The prophet Ezekiel (16:49) describes the sin of Sodom as being their failure to help the poor and needy. Christians' work for and concern with justice is a sign of God's work re-creating our hearts in His image and is an anticipation of God's forthcoming restoration of the world to what He intends for it to be. We can say that acts of justice are what a righteous person does. Righteousness involves aligning one's life with God's original good intentions for creation.[7] So a righteous person is one who is concerned with and actively seeks the well-being of the poor and the oppressed, widows and orphans, the helpless and the weak, the alien in the land and the prisoner—all of society's marginalized.

Have Christians sung about justice in the past? In his analysis of hymnody through history, Paul Westermeyer concludes that "Christians have always sung about justice."[8] However, he notes that the attention paid to justice in Christian hymnody has fluctuated over time. Whenever the Christian message has been "domesticated," when we remove the Christian obligation to do acts of compassion for our neighbor out of the context of a concern for the dispossessed and oppressed, and whenever Christians have tried to "shut out the world and its needs" in worship, justice gets omitted from worship and worship music, according to Westermeyer.[9] Although the subject of justice could not be avoided in the singing of biblical psalms and canticles, in the German and English hymnody of the sixteenth century onward, justice, while not entirely absent, is a much less highlighted theme of Christian worship music today.[10] Nevertheless, Westermeyer and others note that a concern for justice is implicit in corporate songs of praise to God. Howard Snyder also recognizes the connection between justice and corporate worship. He suggests that in worship we praise God not only for what He has done (including offering salvation by grace through faith) and is doing, but also for what He will do (including the restoration of all of creation to His original intention, including establishing justice for the marginalized).[11]

From a biblical perspective the historical debates about whether modern music styles are appropriate for worship or whether such styles inherently result in entertainment rather than worship may be causing us to ask the wrong questions about CWM.[12] Critics, in their focus on "high culture" versus "low culture," express a social-class elitism. By focusing on their general dislike of popular music styles, these critics miss entirely the standards of acceptable worship that Amos 5 articulates.[13] In Amos 5, the worship of Israel is condemned not for mimicking the popular musical styles of surrounding culture or confusing entertainment with worship, but for the lack of focus on justice and righteousness. Put another way, God condemned their lifestyle, which included among other things a lack of focus on justice and righteousness, and their worship was not accepted.

Given the Bible's frequent attention to these categories of people, one might expect to find them frequently referenced in the lyrics of CWM. Ronald Sider states,

"The sheer volume of biblical material that pertains to questions of hunger, justice, and the poor is astonishing."[14] Jim Wallis puts the number of Bible verses on the poor and God's response to injustice at "several thousand."[15] Are the themes of God's expectation for justice and righteousness present or are they conspicuously lacking in the 77 CWM songs analyzed in this volume? Are CWM and the worship services of which it is a part guilty of the same shortcomings for which the Old Testament prophets condemned ancient Israel? Based on a careful reading of the prophets and the Gospels, one can conclude that we should be asking, "Does CWM lead worshipers to a focus on God's concern for justice?" In particular, we should ask, "Does CWM lead to a form of worship that is consistent with the biblical demand for justice and righteousness in relationships among humans?"

Method of Analysis

In the following analysis I identify which of the 77 top contemporary worship songs from 1989–2005 include reference to God's concern for justice and righteousness.

First, I searched all of the song lyrics for the words "just"/"justice" and "righteous"/ "righteousness." Before submitting these songs to closer analysis, I examined how each occurrence was used in the context of the song. For example, "just" may be used as a conjunction or as a synonym of "only." This approach yielded a total of seven songs for analysis. (Only four of these seven songs were eventually used for analysis; see Results.)

Second, I searched all of the song lyrics for words that identify people and groups who, as described above, are of special concern to God in regards to receiving just and righteous treatment. Twelve terms (e.g., "poor") or groups of synonymous or similar terms (e.g., "fatherless"/"orphan") were selected based upon a review of the scriptures cited above, which emphasize justice and righteousness. The selected terms were "fatherless"/"orphan" (Isaiah 1, James 1), "widow" (Isaiah 1, James 1), "the hungry" (Isaiah 58, Matthew 25, Luke 1), "the rich" (in the sense of being "sent away empty" as in Luke 1), "the poor" (Ezekiel 16, Luke 4), "the captive"/"prisoner" (Matthew 25, Luke 4), "the blind" (Luke 4), "the oppressed" (Isaiah 58, Luke 4), (Year of) Jubilee (Luke 4), "alien"/"stranger"/"sojourner" (Leviticus 23, Deuteronomy 10, Psalm 146, Matthew 25), "the weak" (Psalms 12 and 41), and "compassion" (Zechariah 7, Matthew 22, Ephesians 4, Colossians 3). This approach yielded a total of six songs for analysis (see Results).

The two approaches described above yielded ten total songs for analysis. I followed with a close reading of the ten songs to determine the ways in which justice and righteousness are characterized. The ten songs are listed in table 2 at the end of the results section. As part of this in-depth analysis, I sought to determine whether righteousness and justice were viewed as characteristics of God, as traits that should characterize worshipers, or both. I also sought to determine whether concern for others who are marginalized was reflected in the lyrics (e.g., "Let the weak say I am strong"), and whether the worshipers themselves were identified as being among the marginal (e.g., "When I am weak").

Results

Depictions of Justice in CWM

There were seven songs that used "just." However, six of the seven songs used the word "just" in a sense other than a concern with righteousness. *Awesome God* includes the word as a synonym of "merely" as do *Surely the Presence of the Lord* ("It can be just two or three") and *The Heart of Worship* ("Longing just to bring"). *Because He Lives* uses "just" to mean "only" ("Just because He lives"). *There's Something about That Name* includes the word "just" to imply "simply" or "certainly" ("There's just something about that name"). "Just" is used to mean "exactly" or "precisely" in *Come, Now Is the Time to Worship* ("Come just as you are to worship").

Only a single song includes "just" in reference to a characteristic of God. *Great Is the Lord* includes "just" as one of several of God's attributes—along with holy, powerful, faithful, true, merciful—that make Him great and worthy of praise and glory. So while "just" is included as one of the characteristics of God, it is not the predominant theme of the song.

None of the other 76 CWM songs included in this analysis make note of God as "just," nor do they refer to God as demanding or bringing "justice." Likewise, there is no direct mention of "just" behavior or "justice" as something that is expected of one who is devoted to God. The word "justice" itself is not found in the lyrics of any of the 77 CWM songs analyzed.

Depictions of Righteousness in CWM

The word "righteousness" fares a little better in the 77 songs. While none of the songs includes the word "righteous," three songs include the word "righteousness." *I Worship You, Almighty God* includes the line "For you are my righteousness," thus acknowledging that it is God who through His grace and mercy (and not through our own efforts) makes us "righteous." It is possible that this view of righteousness is a passive one requiring no action on the part of the believer. Still, it does communicate the expectation that "righteousness" should be characteristic of Christians.

The second CWM song to include "righteousness," *We Will Glorify*, emphasizes a more active role for the worshiper. "We will worship Him in righteousness" implies that the worshiper is one who is righteous just as God is righteous. The rest of the song lyrics offer no insight as to how a righteous person ought to behave other than to worship God alone. There is no reference to establishing right relationships with other believers, no listing of acts of justice that ought to characterize a righteous person's behavior, nor is there any mention of specific groups (poor, widows, orphans, aliens, etc.) for whom God has expressed special concern.

The final song to include the word "righteousness" is *Seek Ye First*, which includes the lines "Seek ye first the kingdom of God / And His righteousness." These lyrics, taken from Matthew 6, reflect an even more active orientation on the part of the worshiper. In the context of advice about the futility of trying to serve two masters (God and money) and worry about life, eating and drinking, and clothing, Jesus tells His followers to instead seek God's kingdom and righteousness. As I noted in the section above titled "Justice and Righteousness in a Biblical Perspective," God's righteousness includes a special concern that society's weak, oppressed, and marginalized are well treated. So while the song lyrics make no direct reference to orphans, widows, the hungry, the poor, prisoners, or aliens in the land, in light of the broader scriptures—especially the prophets and the Gospels—one could argue that the worshiper is at least implicitly directed to reflect God's concern with these categories of people.

God's Concern for the Marginalized in CWM

The results in this section were produced by examining the 77 CWM songs for twelve themes: fatherless/orphan, widow, hungry, rich (in the sense of being "sent away empty" as in Luke 1), poor, captive/prisoner, blind, oppressed, (Year of) Jubilee (e.g., Leviticus 25, where the weak and poor are objects of God's special attention and concern), alien/stranger/sojourner, weak, and compassion.

Despite the Bible's emphasis on justice in these categories, nine of the twelve terms identified above were absent from the lyrics of the 77 CWM songs analyzed. There was no mention of orphans/fatherless, widows, the hungry, the rich, captives/prisoners, the blind, the oppressed, the Year of Jubilee, or aliens/strangers/sojourners. Thus, to a significant extent, the worship of God expressed in the 77 songs is divorced from worshipers' relationships with society's outcasts.

Three themes (the poor, the weak, and those needing compassion), which identify those for whom God expresses special concern regarding just treatment, were found in six songs. Those songs were *Give Thanks*, *Here I Am to Worship*, *How Can We Name a Love*, *Stand in Awe*, *The Heart of Worship*, and *You Are My All in All*.

The word "compassion" was found only in a single song, *I Stand in Awe*. The line "Who can grasp such tender compassion" is used to describe Christ's sacrificial atonement for sinners. In none of the 77 CWM songs is "compassion" used in reference to empathy for or action on behalf of society's marginalized.

Three songs include the word "poor" and four include the word "weak." See table 1 below.

Table 1
Songs including the words "poor" and "weak"

"Poor"	"Weak"
1) *Give Thanks*	1) *Give Thanks*
2) *Here I Am to Worship*	2) *How Can We Name a Love*
3) *The Heart of Worship*	3) *The Heart of Worship*
	4) *You Are My All in All*

With the exception of a single song, these terms are not used to identify those upon whom God's concern for justice and righteousness is centered. Instead, they depict characteristics of a worshiper in a spiritual, rather than physical sense, or they describe a state that Christ willingly chose for the sake of His creation. In *The Heart of Worship*, the worshiper describes himself/herself as both weak and poor, but surrenders everything to God, saying, "Though I'm weak and poor / All I have is Yours." *How Can We Name a Love* enumerates various loving relationships among humans (parent/child, husband/wife, co-workers) but suggests that "Faith would be weak and dim" apart from hope fixed on Christ.

Here I Am to Worship uses "poor" to describe Christ as the king of glory in heaven who humbly "All for love's sake became poor." Christ is described as the strength of a weak worshiper in *You Are My All in All* ("You are my strength when I am weak"). In each of these cases it is believers who are being described. The terms "poor" and "weak" are not being used in reference to a group for whom God has special concern with regard to just treatment.

Only one song among the 77 CWM songs included in this analysis addressed the "poor" and "weak" as the object of God's concern for justice and righteousness. In lyrics reminiscent of the Year of Jubilee (Leviticus 25), Mary's song (Luke 1:46-55), and Jesus' own self-proclaimed mission (Luke 4:18-20), *Give Thanks* makes reference to the "weak" and the "poor" as objects of God's special attention and concern. The lyrics anticipate God's restoration of the world to what was intended at creation. The "poor" and "weak" are encouraged to see themselves as "strong" and "rich" because of the Lord's action. Of the ten songs identified in this analysis, only *Give Thanks* makes the connection between worship and justice and righteousness in relationships among humans.

Table 2	
CWM including justice and righteousness concerns	
Song	**Emphasis**
1) *Great Is the Lord*	Just/Justice
2) *I Worship You, Almighty God*	Righteousness
3) *Seek Ye First*	Righteousness
4) *We Will Glorify*	Righteousness
5) *Give Thanks*	Poor, Weak
6) *Here I Am to Worship*	Poor
7) *The Heart of Worship*	Poor, Weak
8) *How Can We Name a Love*	Weak
9) *You Are My All in All*	Weak
10) *I Stand in Awe*	Compassion

Discussion

In his book *Whatever Happened to Worship*, A. W. Tozer warned that we always risk the "heresy of Samaritanism" in choosing what we like to worship and rejecting what we do not like.[16] This analysis of the lyrical content of 77 contemporary worship music songs suggests that much of CWM ignores an aspect of worship that the prophet Amos viewed as essential—a concern for justice and righteousness. Throughout scripture, both God's righteousness and His demands for righteousness on the part of His people and His concern that the marginalized receive justice and right treatment are empha-sized. Yet in the 77 CWM songs analyzed in this book, this theme is largely absent. This absence is particularly striking in light of Micah 6:8 where acting "justly" is the first thing required of humans who want to do what is good:

> He has showed you, O man, what is good.
> And what does the LORD require of you?
> To act justly and to love mercy
> and to walk humbly with your God. (NIV)

Christians worship God not only for who He is and what He has done but also for what He will do. Howard Snyder concludes that "in worship believers come to see the world from God's perspective and come to share the divine impulse for doing the works of Christ."[17] Worship, therefore, should be closely tied with God's establishment of jus-tice in human relationships. However, in only one of the 77 songs analyzed do we find this anticipation of God's kingdom of righteousness as both present and future. Richard Foster in his analysis of Amos 5 concludes that "because social righteousness is a divine mandate, liturgical life can never be divorced from it."[18] Brian Edgar calls the "alien-ation of the two great Christian activities of *worship* and *biblical justice*" disturbing. He suggests that there is a need to reconnect worship and biblical justice in a manner that will "enhance our understanding of God and His action in the world and lead to greater praise and worship."[19]

Themes of God's concern for the poor are present in some of the broader contours of contemporary Christian music. Songwriters such as Terry Scott Taylor, whose musi-cal incarnations include the bands *Daniel Amos, The Lost Dogs,* and *The Swirling Eddies* as well as solo work, has sprinkled such themes throughout his thirty-year career in CCM. *Faces to the Window*, his 1981 song with the band *Daniel Amos*, tells of a Christian who goes to church and tries to be a witness but who also tries to avoid the hungry people who press their faces to the window. Twelve years later, Taylor and *Daniel Amos* released a song called *Banquet at the World's End* that depicts all of soci-ety's marginal people (e.g., the poor, lame, blind) running to the banquet at the world's end while the rich and beautiful "send their excuses." However, the rock and new wave performance style of these songs probably eliminates them from consideration as wor-ship music in most churches. Taylor writes more Americana and country-influenced music for his band *The Lost Dogs. That's Where Jesus Is* (2006) describes finding Jesus in the midst of society's neglected—alcoholics, the elderly, prisoners, AIDS victims. Likewise, Mark Heard in the title song from his 1990 CD *Dry Bones Dance* dreams of a world where the mute speak, the deaf sing, the blind see, and "dry bones dance." Yet these are not true CWM songs. But if CCM artists more generally can write songs that reflect God's concern for justice and righteousness, why not CWM songwriters?

It is not impossible to find CWM that addresses such topics. For example, the CWM CD *City on a Hill: The Gathering* (2003) includes a song called *Table of the Lord*, which describes little children leading worshipers into the sanctuary and in the name of Christ admonishes: "Let the strong carry the sick / Let the rich embrace the poor."

But why is the theme of God's righteousness and justice, and His expectation of righteousness and justice from His followers, so rare in CWM, especially those songs in the Top 25 lists? Lack of participation in contemporary worship music by historic Anabaptist and peace churches (Church of the Brethren, Mennonite, Society of Friends [Quaker], etc.) may account, in part, for lack of voice given to righteousness and justice in CWM. One exception is the late Rich Mullins, author of *Awesome God* and *Sing Your Praise to the Lord*, who was raised a Quaker. That theological tradition perhaps encouraged Mullins's compassion for the poor and his decision to lead a simple lifestyle. This was reflected in Mullins's work as a spokesman for Compassion International, a Christian children's development organization. Compassion International has partnered with contemporary Christian musicians for decades to raise awareness of Christians' responsibility to care for poor children around the world. Working on behalf of the poor through organizations like Compassion International and World Vision is one way in which contemporary Christian music in general has raised awareness of God's calls for righteousness and social justice even if these concerns are largely absent from contemporary worship music.

A second possible explanation is that CWM with themes of God's demand for righteousness and social justice is being written and produced but is being largely ignored in the evangelical churches that utilize CWM. Christian Copyright Licensing International (CCLI), which provides copyright services to Christian songwriters,[20] maintains a list of 215 "themes" for thousands of songs included in their contemporary worship music database. A close examination of the CCLI's list of 215 CWM themes reveals three related themes: (1) jubilee, (2) righteousness, and (3) God's attributes/righteousness. A search for songs with the CCLI theme "jubilee" using the CCLI website database located 28 songs (none of which were in the 77 CWM songs analyzed herein), several of which appear to have references to the Year of Jubilee. A search for songs with the theme "God's attributes/righteousness" produced 162 songs including *I Worship You, Almighty God* and *We Will Glorify*, which were among the 77 analyzed in this chapter. Additionally, a list of 585 songs resulted from a search of the theme "righteousness." Again, from among the 77 CWM songs analyzed herein only the same two songs appeared in the search results.

Perhaps one might respond that while the larger number of songs does reflect God's concern with justice and righteousness, they are not as well written or user-friendly as those that are in popular use. Yet some of the songs that turn up in the CCLI search include songs written by popular CWM songwriters such as Michael W. Smith, Rick Founds, Michael Card, and Twila Paris. This suggests, perhaps, that the problem is not the quantity or quality of music being written which addresses issues of God's demands for righteousness and social justice, but rather a general lack of interest in the topics in the evangelical church. Future research is necessary to test this hypothesis. Clearly, a survey of worship leaders would be helpful here. Maybe an investigation of sermon themes or themes of best-selling Christian nonfiction books could provide insight as well. How frequently are the topics of justice and righteousness addressed in evangelical churches as compared to evangelism and individual devotion to God?

Mark Noll noted that beginning in the 1930s with the rise of Fundamentalism, Christian political involvement was replaced with an almost exclusive focus on personal evangelism and personal piety.[21] This, coupled with what Noll calls a "docetic tendency" among Evangelicals to see the world as hopelessly polluted and on a downward spiral, may contribute to a viewpoint that because "this world is not my home," the structures of society that contribute to injustice are unworthy of Christians' attention.[22] Often, worship leaders select their music to reflect the theme of the pastor's sermon. It is likely that God's concern for the poor and for justice and righteousness for society's marginalized are not frequent sermon topics despite thousands of Bible verses that address the topics. It may be that because justice and righteousness in social relationships are perceived primarily as matters of politics rather than personal piety, they are neglected as themes for worship music and worship services.

Another possible explanation for the relative lack of interest in God's demands for righteousness and justice in CWM is that these issues are associated with the social gospel tradition, which came to ignore other equally important Christian concerns such as evangelism and sanctification by grace. Given the Republican political leanings of many evangelical Christians, including pastors and worship leaders, it may be that our American political and cultural biases toward individual achievement and responsibility blind us to difficulties inherent in social structures—difficulties which both the Old and New Testament clearly recognize.[23] This focus on individual responsibility certainly has merit when balanced with the recognition that the structures of society can also create injustice and a lack of righteousness. However, when we view righteousness and justice as purely individual, not collective, matters, we might conclude that they are inappropriate topics for worship music.

Conclusion

The CWM in this study is sorely lacking in its attention to the very issues raised by the prophets who condemned the worshipers of ancient Israel. Evangelical Christians have largely limited their concern with righteousness and justice to their opposition to abortion and gay marriage. According to George Barna, while only 46% of adult Americans see homosexuality as "not an acceptable lifestyle," 95% of Evangelicals find it unacceptable. In the same survey, 61% of Evangelicals indicated abortion should be illegal in all cases compared to 23% of all adults. Barna also reports that while a majority of believers say "serving the needy" is important to do, only 34% gave any time or money to serve the poor in the past year. This led Barna to conclude that while "compassion" is a term most believers endorse, surprisingly few practice acts of compassion.[24] Despite overwhelming biblical emphasis on Christians' responsibility to widows, orphans, and aliens in the land, these themes are rarely emphasized in evangelical churches and in the contemporary worship music produced for and sung in those churches. This is not an issue that can be solely laid at the feet of songwriters and worship leaders. Pastors and teachers in the American evangelical church have also largely overlooked the call of the prophets and the Gospels for attention to matters of righteousness and social justice, in favor of an almost exclusive emphasis on an individual relationship with God. Perhaps we are guilty, as Tozer charges, of choosing to worship what we like (and what fits with our social and political preconceptions) and neglecting what we do not like (and what challenges our social and political preconceptions). In the end, it is difficult to avoid the conclusion that the prophet Amos would respond to the lack of attention to righteousness and social justice in modern worship and worship music by saying, "Away with the noise of your songs!"

To improve the situation will require intentional and concerted effort on the part of songwriters, worship leaders, and ministers. Those who write contemporary worship music need to carefully consider the call of the Old Testament prophets who intrinsically link righteousness and justice in social relationships to worship and incorporate this perspective into their songwriting. Taking a careful look at the songs included under the theme of righteousness in the CCLI database, worship leaders need to seek out the songs with an emphasis on righteousness and justice that are available and cry out for more from songwriters. Finally, ministers need to link righteousness and justice to their teaching in worship services. After all, while the first and greatest commandment is to love the Lord your God with all your heart, soul, and mind, the second is to "love your neighbor as yourself" (Matthew 22:39).

Trading My Sorrows: Worshiping God in the Darkness—The Expression of Pain and Suffering in Contemporary Worship Music

Wendy J. Porter

Introduction

In his treatment of pain, C. S. Lewis implies that what we normally think of as pain or suffering is not, in fact, the greatest problem we face; the deeper problem is trying to understand why God does not *do* something about it![1] Does not He *want* His creatures to be happy? Worse yet, what if God *cannot* do anything about it? What if He does not have the power? And if I mention these thoughts out loud, will God punish me and make my life even more miserable?

Songwriter and author Michael Card draws attention to the missing role of lament in our worship today and what role it played in the lives of major biblical characters.[2] In Psalm 13, for instance, the psalmist cries out, "How long, O LORD? Will you forget me forever? / How long will you hide your face from me? / How long must I wrestle with my thoughts and every day have sorrow in my heart? / How long will my enemy triumph over me?" Many of the psalms interweave joyful praise with cries of utter despair, anguish, and even anger at God's willful silence and apparent impotence; some of them include an almost shockingly honest expression of pain and suffering.[3] The book of Job lays out the "unfair deal" that Job receives.[4] His immense pain and suffering begin with the physical devastation of his possessions and livelihood and family, and continue on to even greater depths with the dubious assistance of his friends, further aided by his own mental torment and physical ailments.

The New Testament also contains a surprising and astonishing range of expressions of pain and suffering. Jesus teaches His disciples that, just as He must suffer, they must suffer too: "Whoever wants to be my disciple must deny themselves and take up their cross and follow me. For whoever wants to save their life will lose it, but whoever loses their life for me and for the gospel will save it" (Mark 8:31-36 TNIV). Jesus lets them know that there *will* be pain and suffering for His true followers. His words in John 16:20 are clear: "Very truly I tell you, you will weep and mourn while the world rejoices. You will grieve, but your grief will turn to joy" (TNIV). It is Paul, however, who teaches us most directly about the importance of pain and suffering within the worshiping community, and about the need to *share* it with the community. He writes to the Philippians that it is their duty to "suffer for him [Christ]," and that he is going through the same struggles that they are (Philippians 1:29-30 TNIV). He is not ashamed to share His suffering with His fellow believers.

Together, Old and New Testament observations suggest that vibrant worshiping communities must have a place for genuine expressions of pain and suffering. More important, perhaps, our musical worship is one place where such expressions should take place.

In light of the foregoing, in this chapter I focus on whether or not there is a place within the current canon of 77 worship songs to voice our questions, our pain, our sorrow, and our suffering. In other words, do we have CWM that assists us to worship God in the darkness—something more substantial than just a "whistling in the dark" that superficially props up our courage? I wanted to know which of the top 77 songs actually say something about pain and suffering, and then which ones might contribute meaningfully to worship.

Method of Analysis

With these observations about the presence of pain and suffering in worship in mind, in order to determine if the 77 worship songs express pain and suffering, I start with a definition and then specify three levels of analysis.

Definition of Pain and Suffering

To begin, how can "pain and suffering" be defined? Definitions of "pain" include the word "suffering" or distress, while definitions of "suffering" refer to it as the bearing of "pain" or distress, so it is reasonable to group pain and suffering here as a single category.[5] Although "pain and suffering" may refer simply to physical distress, I also use the term with regard to the kind of mental, emotional, or spiritual distress that Christians may endure. This distress may be brought about by an event, such as the physical disability or death of a loved one through a car accident, disease, or war. It may be brought about through broken or troubled relationships, through internal stresses that are difficult to identify, or through the person's own actions.

Levels of Analysis

As noted above, I was interested in how many songs in the top 77 not only express pain and suffering, but how many do so in meaningful and focused ways. On this basis,

I gathered songs among the 77 that do more than simply use words or phrases that refer to pain and suffering, although such words and phrases were a necessary first step in selecting songs for analysis. My method of analysis thus included three levels: (1) the lyrics, (2) the lyrical-musical interchange, and (3) the context in which the song focused on pain and suffering is performed.

The first level of analysis focused on (1) *the lyrics*. At this level I looked for lyrics that made some reference to pain and suffering in each song before examining the meaningfulness of such expression. Some of the words I considered were "affliction," "agony," "bewilderment," "condemned," "crucified," "crushed," "crying," "cut off," "darkness," "desert," "despair," "despised," "forsaken," "hurting," "pain," "persecuted," "pressed," "shame," "shedding his blood," "sorrow," "suffering," "the cross," "the crown of thorns," "troubled," "weeping," "wilderness," and "wound."

As for meaningfulness of lyrical expression, this becomes somewhat subjective. However, as a worship leader I must make this decision since a simple word or phrase that refers to pain or suffering may not be enough to establish a song as meaningfully expressing pain and suffering. To help consider how meaningful the lyrics related to pain and suffering are, I looked primarily at (a) whether pain and suffering is the overt focus (central theme) of the song; (b) if the expression is not overt, whether there is a strong underlying or implicit expression of pain and suffering that calls out to God; and (c) whether the lyrics are theologically appropriate when it comes to expressing pain and suffering.

The second level of analysis looked at (2) *the lyrical-musical interchange*, which assesses the sound of the music in combination with the lyrics. This level helped explore further the meaningfulness of the songs identified at the first level. After my first level of analysis of the lyrics helped me formulate a list of worship songs that could potentially allow for meaningful expression of pain and suffering, the second level focused on (a) the music itself and (b) how the music fits with the lyrics. In terms of the "music itself," I asked, does the music *sound* musical and could a congregation sing it? When it comes to how the music fits with the lyrics, I observed whether the music supports the *meaning* of the words and aids in their *expression*.

Finally, the most important practical question (or level) for any worship leader follows from the first two levels and focuses upon (3) *the context*, that is, "Is this song meaningful in my context?" I need to determine if the worship song (or songs) of pain and suffering fits with my congregation. Without this final step, the overall discussion of lyrics or lyrical-musical interchange is not particularly useful. It is in making this third decision that I would say many worship leaders fall short.

Results and Discussion

In this section, I present the results of my method of analysis described above and discuss the results in the context of my central research question.

The Lyrics

a. Which songs include lyrics that express pain and suffering?

The first level of analysis looked at the lyrics in two stages. Applying the list of words and phrases dealing with pain and suffering described above in the method of analysis section, I identified 22 songs that make some reference to pain and suffering. See table 1 below for this list of songs and relevant words or phrases I considered.

Table 1		
Song title	Relevant words or phrases	Comments
1. *Above All*	"like a rose trampled on the ground / You took the fall . . ."	Pain and suffering [=P/S] of Jesus
	*additional language and imagery of the crucifixion are used	
2. *Awesome God*	"it wasn't for no reason that He shed his blood"	P/S of Jesus Christ: shed his blood, at the cross; possibly P/S of God in relation to Adam and Eve in Garden of Eden, and in relation to Sodom
	"mercy and grace He gave us at the cross"	
3. *Because He Lives*	"face tomorrow / fear is gone, because I know He holds the future"	implied personal emotional/physical/ psychological P/S
	"life is worth the living just because He lives"	implied personal spiritual P/S requiring healing, forgiveness, pardon
	"Son . . . came to love, heal and forgive / he bled and died to buy my pardon"	personal P/S of parent
	"child can face uncertain days"	personal physical P/S
	"fight life's final war with pain"	
	"death gives way to victory"	

Song title	Relevant words or phrases	Comments
4. *Better Is One Day*	"for my soul longs and even faints for You"	personal spiritual P/S
	"my heart and flesh cry out for You, the living God / Your Spirit's water for my soul"	
5. *Blessed Be Your Name*	"when the darkness closes in Lord still I will say / blessed be the name of the Lord"	personal P/S
	"when I'm found in the desert place / though I walk through the wilderness"	personal P/S
	"on the road marked with suffering / though there's pain in the offering"	personal P/S
	"You give and take away / You give and take away / my heart will choose to say, Lord, blessed be Your name"	personal P/S and cost of choosing to bless the name of the Lord
6. *Breathe*	"I'm desperate for You, and I'm lost without You"	personal spiritual P/S
7. *God of Wonders*	"and as I stumble in the darkness, I will call Your name by night"	implied personal P/S
8. *Here I Am to Worship*	"Light of the world, You stepped down into darkness"	implied P/S of Christ
	"and I'll never know how much it cost to see my sin upon that cross"	a quality of personal spiritual P/S in recognition of P/S of Christ
9. *I Could Sing of Your Love Forever*	"and let the Healer set me free"	personal physical or spiritual P/S

Song title	Relevant words or phrases	Comments
10. *I Stand in Awe*	"yet God crushed You for my sin" . . . You are beautiful beyond words for your compassionate and merciful act of dying for me on the cross	a quality of personal spiritual P/S corresponding to seeing P/S of Christ
11. *Lord, I Lift Your Name on High*	"from the earth to the cross my debt to pay, from the cross to the grave"	a quality of personal spiritual P/S corresponding to seeing P/S of Christ
12. *Lord, Reign in Me*	"Lord, reign in me, reign in Your power / over all my dreams in my darkest hour"	personal P/S
13. *Oh How He Loves You and Me*	"what He did there brought hope from despair"	personal P/S
14. *Our God Reigns*	"He was despised / and we took no account of Him"; "our sin and guilt that bruised and wounded Him"; "on His shoulders bore our shame"; "Meek as a lamb that's led out to the slaughterhouse . . . His life ran down upon the ground like pouring rain"	mostly identifying the P/S of Christ; corresponding corporate P/S
	"Waste places of Jerusalem break forth with joy . . . the Lord has saved and comforted His people"	P/S in these places, people needing to be saved and comforted
15. *Praise the Name of Jesus*	"He's my Rock, He's my Fortress, He's my Deliverer, in Him will I trust"	implication of personal P/S: needing a rock, fortress, deliverer

Song title	Relevant words or phrases	Comments
16. *Shine, Jesus, Shine*	"consume all my darkness"	personal P/S
17. *The Heart of Worship*	"I'm sorry, Lord, for the thing I've made it / when it's all about You, all about You, Jesus"	personal spiritual P/S
18. *The Wonderful Cross*	"cross, bids me come and die"	a call to personal and spiritual P/S
	"When I survey the wondrous cross / on which the Prince of Glory died / my richest gain I count but loss / and pour contempt on all my pride"	P/S of Jesus on the cross; corresponding personal P/S as response
	"See from His head, His hands, His feet / sorrow and love flow mingled down / Did e'er such love and sorrow meet / or thorns compose so rich a crown?"	P/S of Jesus on the cross
	"Were the whole realm of nature mine / that were an offering far too small / love so amazing so divine / demands my soul, my life, my all"	corresponding recognition of personal P/S as response
19. *Trading My Sorrows*	" . . . my shame"	personal P/S
	*the worshiper describes being in different types of pain—both physical and emotional	
20. *Turn Your Eyes upon Jesus*	"O soul, are you weary and troubled / no light in the darkness you see?"	question about P/S spiritual/physical
	"then go to a world that is dying"	P/S of world at large

Song title	Relevant words or phrases	Comments
21. *You Are My All in All*	"taking my sin, my cross, my shame"	implied spiritual P/S?
22. *You Are My King (Amazing Love)*	"You, my King, would die for me"	P/S of Jesus on our behalf
	"You were forsaken / You were condemned"	

b. *Do the lyrics meaningfully express pain and suffering?*

Of these 22 songs, I then asked the important qualitative question, *Do the lyrics meaningfully express pain and suffering?* To answer this, I used the additional criteria presented above—that is, overt focus, strong implicit expression, and theological appropriateness.

As for the main focus or central theme, nine of the 22 listed in table 1 above have words or phrases that refer briefly to Jesus' pain and suffering, or to one's own, but do not make pain and suffering their focus. These nine songs include *Awesome God; God of Wonders; I Could Sing of Your Love Forever; Lord, I Lift Your Name on High; Lord, Reign in Me; O How He Loves You and Me; Praise the Name of Jesus; Shine, Jesus, Shine;* and *You Are My All in All*. For instance, Rich Mullins's *Awesome God* uses the phrase "he shed his blood" and mentions "the cross," but these are used as points of reference to outline a narrative of biblical events. *I Could Sing of Your Love Forever* refers to letting the Healer set us free, but this phrase is not its focus. *God of Wonders* mentions stumbling in the darkness and calling out God's name by night, but does not focus on this aspect.

After I eliminated the nine songs identified, 13 songs remained: *Above All; Because He Lives; Better Is One Day; Blessed Be Your Name; Breathe; Here I Am to Worship; I Stand in Awe; Our God Reigns; The Heart of Worship; The Wonderful Cross; Trading My Sorrows; Turn Your Eyes upon Jesus; You Are My King (Amazing Love)*.

Several of these remaining 13 songs are more overtly about *our* pain and suffering, two of which I will mention here. One focuses on the pain and suffering of life experiences: *Because He Lives*. Although the lyrics imply a sense of victory, they actually name some of the very issues that can cause the most pain and suffering. The chorus acknowledges that there has been fear, but "because he lives, all fear is gone," and alludes to a contemplation of not going on with life, but that "life is worth the living just because he lives."

The second song focuses more on a spiritual form of pain and suffering: *The Heart of Worship*. It deals almost exclusively with a personal and spiritual pain and suffering, recognizing a person's own sinfulness and self-preoccupation. This is seen especially in the lines, "I'm sorry, Lord, for the thing I've made it / when it's all about You, all about You, Jesus."

One of the 13 songs that deals almost exclusively with the pain and suffering of Jesus Christ is *The Wonderful Cross*, although much of this is within the traditional hymn, *When I Survey the Wondrous Cross*. Notice, however, that the much-more-recently written chorus makes use of the New Testament model of intentionally suffering for the sake of Christ: "O the wonderful cross bids me come and die and find that I might truly live." This alone sets this song in a unique category of worship songs that express pain and suffering.

Overall, I found these 13 songs to have some meaningful expression of pain and suffering, although some have a subtle underlying expression that is not immediately evident just through vocabulary. For instance, *Better Is One Day* speaks of a person's soul longing and even fainting for God, and of one's heart and flesh crying out for Him, the living God. The words themselves do not use direct language of pain and suffering, but the underlying sense concerns a suffering that can only be alleviated by God's Spirit.

Finally, regarding the theological appropriateness of the lyrics, there will never be one answer to this question, but it must be considered. One very important reason for this consideration is that for many churchgoers, especially those without previous theological foundation and spiritual formation, the songs that they leave church singing may well be the main foundation of their theology, that is, their understanding of the Bible and of God and their relationship to God. If the theology of a song is not biblically supportable, it is questionable whether it should be included in congregational worship.[6] This concern is an essential part of being a responsible worship leader.

There are two of the 13 songs identified above that express some level of pain and suffering, but should be removed from the list for theological reasons. One is very popular and beautiful in almost every way: *Above All*. It offers a window into the suffering of Jesus, especially with the chorus. But the imagery and analogy get confused once we get to the "rose" and talk about "taking the fall," and the latter phrase also seems to trivialize the imagery here. More troubling is the theological concern about the concluding statement—that Jesus thought of *me* above everything. It is not, after all, *all* about me, no matter how much I may want it to be.

The second song among the 13 that I would remove for theological reasons is *Breathe*. Even though the words "I'm desperate for you and I'm lost without you" do have an underlying sense of personal and spiritual pain and suffering, the nebulousness of the lyrics (that is, God is not mentioned) and the inescapable sense of girlish lovesickness are not what I consider theologically appropriate for corporate worship today.

After subtracting two for theological reasons, that leaves 11 songs on my list: *Because He Lives; Better Is One Day; Blessed Be Your Name; I Stand in Awe; Our God Reigns; The Heart of Worship; The Wonderful Cross; Trading My Sorrows; Turn Your Eyes upon Jesus; You Are My King (Amazing Love)*.

The Musical-Lyrical Interchange

I admit that it is difficult to reduce musical evaluation to a step-by-step linear procedure. There is always a song that has such poor music that it is eliminated from any potential list on the very first hearing—even if the words *might* be excellent. However, I assume that the words must primarily express pain and suffering in the context of worship, because it is the lyrics that are at the heart of this worshipful expression.

a. *The Music Itself*

My initial question here is simply, Does the music *sound* musical? In practical terms, that means if I play the song without focusing on any lyrics, does it have a melody that I and others want to sing? Do the chords of the song carry it along in a creative yet logical way, with harmonies that are potentially expressive of pain and suffering? This by no means suggests that the chords must be minor chords, but the harmonies combined with the melody will have an inherent expressiveness. A good example is the chorus of *Draw Me Close* ("You're all I want / You're all I've ever needed / You're all I want / help me know You are near"). The song—though not about pain and suffering—has a particular sound and feel to it that would make it excellent for this purpose.

There is no set formula to determine whether the music sounds musical, however. The study of why the sounds of a musical composition are perceived by their listeners the way they are is at least as old as the Greek philosophers. Musical background and worship experience work together to determine which worship songs have music that may help express pain and suffering to the listeners in a specific subculture. In some cases the "fit" of text and music is so obviously mismatched that the average layman can sense it immediately. In other cases, evaluating whether a given musical setting is helpful or harmful to communicating a message of pain and suffering may require significant musical training on the part of the evaluator.[7] If the music seems ill-fitting, then as a worship planner I will usually eliminate it from my prospective worship song list.

In the final analysis, I did not eliminate any of the 11 remaining songs strictly on the basis of the music, although there are two that have musical problems: *Blessed Be Your Name* and *You Are My King (Amazing Love)*.

The more problematic of the two is *Blessed Be Your Name*. In my experience, this song is not easy for a congregation to sing. Apart from some tricky syncopation and a couple of instances where there are too many word-syllables for the musical phrase, the main problem is that the melody begins very low and ends quite high. If one adjusts the key up to accommodate the low notes at the beginning, one ends up with a song that is uncomfortably, even piercingly high in the chorus; conversely, if one gears the song to accommodate an average vocal range for the chorus, the verse is too low for most to sing. One common solution is to have the opening lines of the verses sung by a soloist or small group, with the congregation joining later. The irony that I have observed and experienced with this song, however, is that although the musical difficulty is rarely totally overcome, congregations still want to sing the song, and they want to *sing it all*! (See Bert Polman's analysis of this song in chapter 8.)

Another song that has been difficult for the average congregation to sing is *You Are My King (Amazing Love)*. The syncopation of this song makes it very tricky for a large group to sing well, and most congregational singers do not succeed in articulating many of the notes. Interestingly again, it is a song that congregations have warmed to, no matter how many of the tricky notes they do or do not sing.

b. *How the Music Fits with the Lyrics*

There used to be some choice about what music went with what hymn text. The poetry of the hymn texts was frequently written independently and without reference to a particular tune. As long as the meter of the poem matched that of a given tune (that is, the number of syllables of the lyrics matched the notes of the melody line), tunes and poems could be mixed and matched by the worship leader.[8] This allowed for flexibility and often provided performance options. If one tune did not seem to match the sense of the words, you could choose another tune that did! Contemporary worship music, however, locks music and text together, and they are not easily interchangeable. The music and texts of contemporary worship songs usually are written together from the beginning and incorporate short or unique sections that do not conform to the exact shape of another song.[9] The way that worship leaders often learn a song first is by hearing it from a recording, possibly performed by the very person who wrote both the words and music.

Therefore, it becomes increasingly important to determine whether the music supports the *meaning* of the words and aids in the *expressiveness* of those words. Professional musicians and experienced worship leaders instinctively make these assessments; even if these kinds of questions are rarely explicitly formulated, they are underlying questions nonetheless. Examples of problematic music with lyrics might include a melody that sounds mournful with words that seem to be cheerful and uplifting. Or there is the song that sounds joyful while we are singing of despair. Part of my role as worship leader is providing music that allows and encourages the congregation to sing the words. I am not leading a congregation of professional musicians; I am giving laypeople in the church an opportunity to contribute their own voice in corporate worship that can express pain and suffering. If I have chosen a song to aid a community of worshipers in expressing pain and suffering, then I want it to be simple (though not simplistic) enough that people can sing the music and get to the heart of that pain and suffering, without the music becoming a hindrance.

Of the remaining 11 songs on my list, I would remove one on the basis of what I consider to be a mismatch of text and music, and that is *Our God Reigns*. The music hinders it from effectively contributing to worship that is expressive of pain and suffering. Three of the verses clearly speak of the pain and suffering of Christ (see the lyrics in table 1). The words themselves are from Isaiah, but the music does not adequately support the sense of the words. The song *should* allow us to focus on the immensity of Jesus' pain and suffering on our account, but the rhythm and shape of the musical line does not fit with the nuances in the text and the normal accenting of the syllables, which results in making the words sound superficial and unimportant.

After I removed *Our God Reigns* from the list, all of the remaining 10 songs are excellent examples of good lyrical and musical "fit." The 10 songs that remain are *Because He Lives; Better Is One Day; Blessed Be Your Name; Here I Am to Worship; I Stand in Awe; The Heart of Worship; The Wonderful Cross; Trading My Sorrows; Turn Your Eyes upon Jesus; You Are My King (Amazing Love)*.

Of these 10, some that stand out musically and lyrically focus on the pain and suffering of Jesus: *Here I Am to Worship* ("glorious in heaven above / humbly You came to the earth You created / all for love's sake became poor"; "and I'll never know how much it cost to see my sin upon that cross"); *I Stand in Awe* ("yet God crushed You for my sin . . ."); and *You Are My King (Amazing Love)* ("How can it be that You, my King, would die for me? / I'm forgiven because You were forsaken / I'm accepted, You were condemned").[10]

One song that I already mentioned above has an especially apt musical and lyrical interchange. It focuses almost exclusively on the suffering of Jesus and forces our attention to the cross. It is the combination of hymn and "chorus" (an appropriate use of this term), *The Wonderful Cross*. The most eloquent words are those of Isaac Watts, in the hymn *When I Survey the Wondrous Cross*, but the marriage of the music with this hymn text is exquisite. Not only beautiful, it is extremely user-friendly because almost anyone can sing its melodic range of only five notes. The chorus, now woven with this hymn, takes us back to the New Testament imagery of the suffering of dying to self in order to follow Christ: "O the wonderful cross, bids me come and die and find that I may truly live," which also corresponds with the third verse of Watts's classic hymn. This song stands alone as one that focuses our attention on the suffering of Jesus on the cross and the appropriate response to that suffering in our own commitment to Him.

Two other songs in my final list of 10 have a wonderful interchange of music and text, and although pain and suffering is not their overt subject, it is the strong underlying thread. The first is *The Heart of Worship*, which voices a spiritual pain and suffering resulting from a broken or half-hearted relationship with God, but it is not only the lyrics that contribute to the song's expressiveness, it is the combination of the music with those words. The second is *Turn Your Eyes upon Jesus*, whose opening lines speak directly to the sufferer: "O soul, are you weary and troubled, no light in the darkness you see?" It clearly reminds us what we are to do in the darkness: "turn your eyes upon Jesus." When we cannot hear or see God, when we cannot find answers to our "whys," when we cannot find relief from the pain—we must turn our eyes upon Jesus, the Light of the world. I have been interested to see this refrain used in numerous live worship settings and on recent worship recordings.

The Context

The final level of analysis is determining the context, or determining how the worship song (or songs) of pain and suffering fits with *my* or *your* congregation. I could argue that we have already determined which songs are *about* and meaningfully *express* pain and suffering, and that is enough, but I would find it troubling to leave things there.

It is in this final level of analysis where the decision is made about whether the song is incorporated into *my* (or *your*) worshiping community. If the song is in the CCLI list, but it does not belong in the list of songs for *my* own church, then the previous categories are of little value to me, except as an academic exercise. One of the most important questions that the discerning worship leader must answer—and I believe that discernment is absolutely crucial for a serious worship leader—is this: *Does the song give voice to the people in my own congregation, or are the words and/or musical style mismatched with my own worshiping community?* Just because the church down the street uses a song or I find it on a list of top songs does not mean that it is the right choice for my church.

The one song that stands out for its unique role in helping my worshipers voice their own pain and suffering is Beth and Matt Redman's *Blessed Be Your Name*.[11] I mentioned earlier that I initially had reservations about the music, but I also noted my experience with this song—that people want to sing it!

The opening words of the song give both sides of the life story. At first we sing, "Blessed be your name in the land that is plentiful where Your streams of abundance flow / blessed be Your name." This sounds archaic, and it would be easy to dismiss this song as disconnected from contemporary life. The second line has a surprising twist: "Blessed be Your name when I'm found in the desert place, though I walk through the wilderness / blessed be Your name." Who in their right mind is going to take desert/ wilderness experiences as the occasion to bless the name of the Lord? But the song does not say that I will *feel* like blessing the Lord; it does give me the words to say—perhaps with increasing faith—when things seem very dark around me.

The title, *Blessed Be Your Name*, comes from Job's incredible words in the first chapter of Job. We look in on a conversation between the Lord and Satan about Job: the Lord says, "There is no one on earth like him; he is blameless and upright, a man who fears God and shuns evil." Then, Satan negotiates the right to take away Job's great blessings, and we see a series of events that deprives Job of almost everything. The result of this devastation is amazing. Job gets up, tears his robe, shaves his head, falls to the ground and says this: "Naked I came from my mother's womb, / and naked I will depart. / The LORD gave and the LORD has taken away; / may the name of the LORD be praised" (Job 1:20-21 TNIV). Wow—what an amazing response!

The chorus of *Blessed Be Your Name* begins positively, "Every blessing You pour out I'll turn back to praise," but then ventures into uncomfortable territory: "When the darkness closes in, Lord, still I will say, 'Blessed be the name of the Lord.'" Repetition in the chorus plays a vital role in reminding us of our need to continually repeat these words, even when we do not know *where* God is in the midst of our pain and suffering. We may not understand God's ways; we simply affirm that we will continue to worship Him even in our darkness.

The second verse is similar to the first. We bless His name when the "sun's shining down on me, when the world's all as it should be," and we bless His name "on the road marked with suffering, though there's pain in the offering." We are reminded that the "road marked with suffering" is normal. We also can admit that there is genuine pain in offering up our trust to God when we do not understand what is happening or why; when we are clearly so crippled by pain and suffering that we can hardly even croak out the words, let alone say them with confidence and joy.

The bridge of this song brings us back to the unfathomable ways of God and the fact that we are called to trust Him anyway: "You give and take away, You give and take away / my heart will choose to say, Lord, blessed be Your name." This song is a profound gift to the church: It feels real, rings true, and strongly lays out for us the mandate of blessing and worshiping God, regardless of circumstances. It provides an excellent aid to genuine worship. Warm feelings may or may not come as a result of singing this song, but the affirmations of this song are a legitimate tool for Christians to use to learn how to worship God in the genuinely bad times of life.

Many people are aware of the personal heartache in the Redmans' lives that led to composing this song, that of losing a baby. Their story can make this song even more meaningful, but it alone cannot account for why the song has become so well-used and loved. The song captures the essence of the struggle between good and bad things happening to us as God's children, and the unanswered questions about why God does not seem to intervene. The lyrics, with the full support of the music, bring us back to the determined, even passionate response that we will *choose* to trust and bless God in every situation, regardless of those missing explanations. Even those who struggle with singing the music of the verses or articulating all the syllables in the opening lines can join in with fervor as the music of the chorus lifts us to join together as a congregation to sing, "Blessed be the name of the Lord."

But I come back to the need of determining whether a song fits my congregation. This is difficult. For instance, my own musical experience is fairly wide, so I cannot use it as the criterion for making decisions for my congregation or chapel. I come from an evangelical tradition, and I like some things about contemporary worship music; I write it for my church and chapel and I lead it with my worship teams. I love working with worship bands. My studies, however, focused on early Anglican musical traditions of sixteenth-century England, and I attended Westminster Abbey in London for a number of years. I have worked on ancient Greek musical papyri fragments and have studied early musical notation in lectionaries. I occasionally sing in a "Gregorian" chant choir at vespers in a local Anglican church and enjoy singing in a Bach cantata. I was invited to sing in a black gospel choir as backup for a leading pop musician and consider that a huge privilege as a non-black. I lead worship at casual family camps and have been the guest soloist for an audience of 10,000 people. I read and play classical music at my piano or improvise on any melodic theme that comes into my head. I love to creatively integrate the best (in my opinion) of contemporary worship songs with classic hymns. *But* my musical experience does not represent the worshiping communities that I lead. Many of the members of my church congregation and semi-nary chapel have little exposure to a wide range of musical styles, either historical or contemporary. One of my goals for these two communities is to develop a musical lan-guage and biblical grounding for our music that expresses the cries of our hearts and voices our meaningful worship back to God. I draw on the musical literature of the ear-liest hymns to the most recent of worship songs, combined with new settings of scrip-tural texts and other songs that allow these worshipers to sing meaningful words and prayers.

So how do I, as a discerning worship leader, choose music for my congregation that would help *us* meaningfully express pain and suffering in *our* worship?

It is the "us" and "our" here that are important. I need to be able to enter into this kind of worship myself, and, as I lead my congregation personally into this kind of wor-ship, I must enter the very space that I am asking them to enter. There is always a risk in this kind of leading. I am not just pointing down a path and saying, "Go down there." No, I am walking there myself and asking them to follow. This is true whether I am simply choosing music and leading it in a service, or whether I have written some-thing and present it as a vehicle for this unknown journey. But this discussion is one that would require more time and space and probably some personal interaction. It will have to be saved for another day.

Conclusion

The bottom line is that, of the 77 CCLI songs on our original list, only a few songs— 10 at most—lyrically and musically contribute at some level to the meaningful expres-sion of pain and suffering. Many of the songs that might initially be selected are inadequate for a variety of reasons, and of the remaining few, only a couple (*Blessed Be Your Name*, which focuses on personal pain and suffering, and *The Wonderful Cross*, which focuses on the pain and suffering of Jesus on the cross) rise to the surface as out-standing. So if meaningful expression of pain and suffering is a vital part of corporate worship, where do we go from here?

I think there are a number of things that we still need to learn about this kind of honest worship, and several ways that we could contribute to it. The Redmans' song provides some guidance. It is honest, and it does not avoid the fact that our under-standing of God is not laid out in black and white. At the same time it turns us back to praising God in the midst of very dark times. We could benefit from these points. We do need to be honest about our suffering. We do not need to make complex things simplistic. We do need to find a way of continuing to worship God even when we are feeble. And we do need to be willing to admit that there is no guarantee that the pain and suffering will be removed just because we have great faith in God. But honest wor-ship will teach us how to worship God *through* our pain, in the *middle* of our suffering, in those lonely places of isolation and in the ambiguity of all the questions that begin with "why."

We know that everybody experiences physical, mental, or spiritual pain and suffering to some degree at some time. Often this is what first brings people into our worshiping communities. What we cannot rely on is a list of popular worship songs to be our sole guide to finding music that gives expression to that pain and suffering in our own worshiping community.

The ongoing life of contemporary worshiping communities demands that worship leaders and songwriters contribute intentionally to the meaningful worship life of those communities. I need to have the pulse of my own church, so that I have some idea of the experiences represented by this gathered group of God's people, and those still journeying toward God. It is this kind of knowledge, coming out of my own congregation's experience, that prompted me to write a particular song for them, and us, to sing. This simple song has expressed pain and suffering for a wide range of people—even, in one case, for a woman who had suffered so deeply that she had not cried for 20 years until she began to sing it. No one knows if a song that he or she writes will be a vehicle for others to also worship, but let me explain some of the things that go through my mind when I am trying to contribute to this particular aspect of worship services that I lead.

First, I need lyrics that are accessible to others and meaningful to me. The words can be simple, but they need to speak to the deepest parts of my own heart in order for them to potentially speak to others; I can never be sure that they will speak to anyone else, but they must be meaningful to me.

Second, they need to be words that come out of a life deeply in touch with God's Spirit and immersed in His Word, whether anyone else knows that or not.

Third, the melody needs to be easily sung, so that it does not become the obstacle that prevents a congregation from participating.

Fourth, if possible, the harmonies need to be relatively straightforward, so that those who do sing by ear can find them.

I think part of the way forward is to begin writing our own songs for our own worshiping communities. Pastors, youth leaders, teachers, musicians, and laypeople who work with each of the four elements just described can all contribute to the content of these songs. We need to bring the sound of our own voices together to sing about our deepest needs. We need to understand that God knows all about those darkest moments, and that this is why Jesus came to earth in the first place. The reason we can worship God in the darkness is because Christ went there first, on our behalf: "'By his wounds you have been healed'" (1 Peter 2:24 TNIV).

WE HAVE COME INTO HIS HOUSE: KERYGMA, KOINONIA, LEITOURGIA— CWM THAT MODELS THE PURPOSE OF THE CHURCH

ROBERT WOODS
BRIAN WALRATH
DIANE BADZINSKI

Introduction

As Harold Best, Dean Emeritus of the Wheaton College Conservatory of Music and President Emeritus of the National Association of Schools of Music, remarked, "Excellent church music . . . must be embedded, not primarily in the nature of music and musical types, standards of practices, and scholarly excellence, but in a bed-rock theological perspective."[1]

Best's concern, which he formally stated at a church music conference in 1982, has been echoed resoundingly by others in both Protestant and Catholic church music circles ever since: church musicians, worship leaders, songwriters, not to mention average worshipers, do not know philosophically and theologically what they are all about when it comes to worship.

As we experience a revolution in church and contemporary Christian music all over the world, the concern is that we do not have an intellectually and theologically defensible rationale to answer such questions as *How should worship music function within the church? What purposes should it address?* and *What could it, or should it, look like today?* Without a biblically informed model we run the risk of producing and performing worship music that is inarticulate and driven by cultural trends, the latest musical fads, or some popular artists.

As a way to answer the questions above about how worship music should function, worship scholar David Pass argues that we should begin with the nature of the church: "The nature of church music is determined by the nature of the church, and the nature of the church is determined by its mission."[2] We understand the appropriate use of worship music when we understand ecclesiology, or what the church "is." Put another way, as we understand the nature of the church, we understand how worship, and worship music, should function within the church.

To develop models of the church, theologians often use certain terms from the Greek New Testament. According to New Testament scholars there is strong evidence based on Acts 2:42 that the nature of the church revolves around three basic purposes or functions: *kerygma* (proclamation), *koinonia* (fellowship), and *leitourgia* (service, ministry, worship). These three "address-modes," or modes of communication, as David Pass describes them, are interconnected and necessary for the church to fulfill its mission of mediating the message and fact of forgiveness to an alienated world.[3] More important, perhaps, the church's mission is to incarnate all three modes "regularly, creatively, systematically, and carefully."[4] Thus, if the mission of the church dictates its nature, and by implication the nature of church music, then balanced worship music should reflect these three modes "regularly, creatively, systematically, and carefully."

In light of the foregoing, as a way to evaluate the content of CCLI's top 77 contemporary worship songs, we suggest beginning with this threefold model of the church. To what extent do the top 77 praise and worship songs reported by CCLI between 1989 and 2005 demonstrate a balance of purposes? Which category—*kerygma*, *koinonia*, or *leitourgia*—appears most often during this time period, and how have the percentages of categories changed over time? Do the top 77 songs as a whole adequately model the purpose or mission of the church?

Kerygma, Koinonia, Leitourgia

The main source of the threefold church model is found in Acts 2:42. In verse 42, Luke gives us the first picture of the early church: "They devoted themselves to the apostles' *teaching* and to the *fellowship*, to the *breaking of bread and to prayer*" (NIV, emphasis ours). The church has always felt that the description in Acts 2:42 is a model for how the church should function in the world.[5]

In *The Cost of Discipleship* Dietrich Bonhoeffer provides further explanation of the threefold model described in Acts 2:42. As Bonhoeffer explains, "Every word in this sentence is significant"[6] since it is this verse that lists the basic elements of the church's life: the Word (the apostles' teaching), fellowship, and the Sacrament (breaking of bread and prayers). The church is made visible to the world as Word-Fellowship-Sacrament.[7] Word–Fellowship–Sacrament may also be understood as *kerygma*, *koinonia*, and *leitourgia*, respectively.

Kerygma

Kerygma, referred to as the apostles' teaching in Acts 2:42, is translated "proclamation" in the New Testament and is said to originate with God.[8] The church is committed to proclaiming the message of Jesus Christ, calling people to repentance, faith, and discipleship. The proclamation of the church is "more than historical instruction concerning the words and acts of Jesus"[9]; it also proclaims the significance of that event, in that complete forgiveness is now offered by God in Christ for those who will repent and be baptized. The ultimate goal of *kerygma* is conviction and change. Evangelism is thus a definite by-product of a worship service that includes *kerygma* (1 Corinthians 14:24-25).

Communication during worship in the *kerygmatic* mode tends to be one-way (monologic), or hierarchical, that is, one person or a few address the many (from speaker to audience). Someone preaches or sings while others receive or listen to the message. In Acts 2:14, *kerygma* was demonstrated when Peter "raised his voice and addressed the crowd." Paul encourages *kerygmatic* contributions during worship gatherings, for example, sharing a psalm, teaching, or revelation (Colossians 3:16). *Kerygmatic* communication during worship can also occur when the congregation proclaims the attributes and work of God by means of song, for example, when they sing, "He Is Risen and He lives forevermore" in *Celebrate Jesus*, or "With a mighty hand and an outstretched arm His love endures forever" in *Forever*. At times proclamation may involve comparing God to others (e.g., *He Is Lord*) or calling individuals to repentance and faith (e.g., *Come, Ye Sinners, Poor and Needy*).

Koinonia

The second purpose of the church described in Acts 2:42, hinted at by "fellowship" and "breaking of the bread," is *koinonia*. *Koinonia* is translated as "participation," "fellowship," and "partnership" (Philippians 1:4-5). This "coming together" or "uniting" function of the church involves establishing and enhancing relationships, maximizing participation, and maintaining unity in the Body of Christ.[10]

The *koinoniac* mode of worship is a concept unique to the Apostle Paul. It is "body-life worship in action."[11] In a worship service characterized by *koinonia*, no one person tends to dominate. Whereas *kerygma* is hierarchical or monologic in expression, *koinonia* communication in worship is more horizontal and omnidirectional or dialogical. *Koinonia* worship recognizes a plurality of leadership and exercises the gifts of the Spirit for the common good, for strengthening the church (1 Corinthians 14:26). A *koinoniac* mode resembles a family get-together and is a hands-on service that fosters encouragement, nurture, comfort, and affirmation (Philippians 2:1-4). The ultimate purpose of this spontaneous, informal expression is edification of the church.[12]

Koinoniac worship music tends to be congregational and cohesive. It comforts and promotes unity. Songs such as *Bind Us Together* and *We Have Come into His House* or lyrics such as "Come, now is the time to worship" and "We are one in the Spirit, we are one in the Lord" fulfill this purpose.

Leitourgia

Leitourgia, translated "service, ministry, or worship," is alluded to by the word "prayers" in Acts 2:42 and describes a group of individuals addressing God in vertical praise and prayer. It is the "summit toward which the activity of the Church is directed."[13] In both Old and New Testament contexts, *leitourgia* is used in reference to formal priestly service, ministry or liturgy carried out by Moses (Hebrews 9:19-21), Zacharias (Luke 1:5-23), and Christ (Hebrews 7–10).

Whereas *kerygmatic* communication is hierarchical or one-to-many (done to the people) and *koinonia* is horizontal or one-to-another sharing (done for one another), *leitourgia* is primarily vertical and is the response by the people to God. God is addressed directly as communication flows from the "many," or congregation, to God with the purpose of thanking, praising, and adoring Him. Whereas the choir in *kerygma* functions separately from the congregation, in *leitourgia* they join the congregation in praise. In this mode of communication, there may also be prayers of confession and guided prayers. Hands may be lifted, eyes may look upward to God, and knees may bow. There may be multiple corporate scriptural readings and Communion.

In light of the vertical focus of the mode just described, *leitourgic* music tends to be Godwardly directed and personally oriented. It is common to see in this mode God addressed directly as "You" or personally as "my God" or "my Savior." Expressions of adoration and praise (e.g., "Praise be to You, Father"), and thanks (e.g., "Thank You, Lord, for saving my soul") are included along with urgent requests for help (e.g., "Change my heart, oh God") and confession (e.g., "Create in me a clean heart"). Additionally, as a response to God's grace, singers may tell God who He is or what He has done (e.g., "You have been good"), or what the singer himself or herself is doing in response to who God is and what He has done or will do (e.g., "I could sing of your love forever"). In the final analysis, *leitourgic* music is music "not necessarily new and surprising in its language, not necessarily too difficult to perform, but so suited to what it is celebrating that it would be an inexhaustive source of prayer, meaning and feeling."[14]

How the Three Modes Relate: Finding a Balance in Worship

As hinted throughout, the three modes of communication in the church that serve as a model for worship are interconnected and interdependent. As David Pass explains, there is a "sequential dependence" among the modes.[15]

The *kerygmatic* mode is the foundation of the other two modes. *Koinonia* comes only through the gospel preached, the forgiveness of sins, baptism in Jesus' name, and the gift of the Holy Spirit (Acts 2:38). Evangelism (or proclamation) is also a part of *koinonia*. Unbelievers who see body-life interaction and proclamation may be convicted by the Spirit (1 Corinthians 14:24-25). Unbelievers experience God's presence as they encounter a community of believers demonstrating *koinonia*.

As Bonhoeffer explains in *The Cost of Discipleship*, fellowship fits neatly between the Word and the Sacrament, which is "no accident, for fellowship always springs from the Word (*kerygma*) and finds its goal and completion in the Lord's Supper."[16] The believing response to the *kerygma*, on which basis the *koinonia* is formed, is taken up in *leitourgia*.

Problems occur when there is a lack of balance in worship among the three modes. Because the modes are inextricably intertwined, changes or deficiencies in one will affect the others. If there is too much *koinonia*, for example, worship may lose its moorings in the *kerygma* since the community depends on the gracious acts of God in Christ (1 Corinthians 1:18–2:5). If *koinonia* loses touch with its *kerygmatic* basis, then it has no option but to depend more on its own resources whether those be cultural, political, aesthetic, or social, rather than biblical.

Furthermore, the interdependence among the modes described above means that worship representing the mission and communication of the church will have a balance of *kerygmatic*, *koinoniac*, and *leitourgic* expression. As mentioned earlier, the church's mission is to manifest all three modes regularly, creatively, systematically, and carefully. In light of these assumptions, our central research question revolves around the extent to which the top 77 worship songs identified between 1989 and 2005 reflect just such a balance of expression.

More specifically, first, we wanted to know what percentages of songs in the top 77 emphasize *kerygma*, *koinonia*, and *leitourgia*. As the church, some suggest that we define ourselves primarily as evangelists (*kerygma*) and only secondarily as worshipers (*leitourgia*).[17] Will such an emphasis appear in the top 77? Second, others suggest a trend over the last two decades toward songs that emphasize "Jesus and me" to the exclusion of *kerygma* and *koinonia*.[18] Will such a trend be detected in CWM songs between 1989 and 2005? Finally, not only will a systematic trend analysis provide a snapshot of balance in worship over time as it relates to the three modes, but it will also help to identify the most popular songs performed throughout this same time period.

Method of Analysis

To determine which of the 77 songs were *kerygmatic*, *koinoniac*, or *leitourgic*, we followed a three-step process. First, two independent coders were trained to divide the lyrics of each song into discrete thought-units. A single, discrete thought-unit was defined as a complete idea or thought that appeared in a single line or required more than one line to express. A thought-unit was further defined as something that (1) may be repeated several times in the exact or nearly exact same form (e.g., "Yes, Lord, yes, Lord, yes, yes, Lord"); (2) may be repeated in a parallel form (e.g., "Better is one day in Your house; better is one day in Your courts"); (3) may use parallel words or synonyms to reinforce a single idea (e.g., "Taking my sin, my cross, my shame"); (4) may appear as antithesis (e.g., "I am weak, but Thou art strong"); or

(5) may appear as a completion or progression (e.g., "From the cross to the grave, from the grave to the sky").

Once individual thought-units in each song were identified, the second step involved categorizing each thought-unit as *kerygmatic*, *koinoniac*, or *leitourgic*. To help coders categorize each thought-unit, we provided operational definitions, or a check-list of criteria, for each communication mode as defined in the previous section. There were several key words and phrases that helped coders to identify which mode a thought-unit fit best:

1. *Kerygma*: "God is . . . (has, does)"; "Our God is . . . "; "Jesus is . . . (has, does)"; "Christ is . . . (has, does)"; "the Holy Spirit is . . . (has, does)." A kerygmatic phrase might *proclaim God's attributes and work* (e.g., "Great is the Lord"; "The Steadfast Love of the Lord"; "Jehovah-Jireh"; "God is so good"), *proclaim God's attributes and work in comparison to others* (e.g., "There's no one God like Jehovah"; "Jesus, Name above all Names"), or *call someone to repentance, faith, and discipleship* ("Softly and tenderly Jesus is calling"; "His return is very close and so you better be believin'").

2. *Koinonia*: "We," "Our," "Us," "Let us," "one another," "family," "body," "fellow-ship," "join," "friendship." *Koinoniac* music might include statements of *interdependence and commonality* (e.g., "Blest be the tie that binds"; "One in the bond of love"), *asking or urging something of others* (e.g., "Come, now is the time to worship"; "Let's just praise the Lord"), or *admonishment* (e.g., "Beloved, let us love one another"; "Let us break bread together on our knees").

3. *Leitourgia*: "my" God (Savior, King, Lord, Master, [other names of God]), "You," "Your," "Yours," "Thee," "Thou," "Thy," "Thine." *Leitourgic* music might include statements of *confession* (e.g., "Create in me a clean heart"; "Purify my heart"), *adoration* (e.g., "Father, I adore You"; "Abba, Father"), *praise* (e.g., "Thou art worthy"; "Praise be to You, Father"), or *thanks* (e.g., "Thank you, Lord, for saving my soul"). Additionally, singers may *ask or request something* of God ("Change my heart, oh God"); *tell God who He is, what He has done, what He is doing, and what He will do* (e.g., "You are good / have been good"; "Almighty God, my redeemer"; "You are the air I breathe"); or *tell God what the singer has done, will do, could do, can do, or is doing in response to what God has done or is doing* (e.g., "I'm coming back to the heart of worship"; "As the deer panteth for the water, so my soul longeth after Thee").

Finally, in step three, we labeled each song as a whole as *kerygma*, *koinonia*, or *leitourgia* based on the most frequently appearing thought-unit categorized in steps one and two above. So, if coders in step one identified 10 thought-units in a particular worship song and in step two determined that 6 of the 10 thought-units were *leitourgic*, 3 were *kerygmatic*, and 1 was *koinoniac*, then in step three we labeled the whole song as *leitourgia*. After following this procedure for each song, we counted the total number of songs in each category. We then created a spreadsheet that included each of CCLI's Top 25 lists between 1989 and 2005 along with each song's designation as *kerygma*, *koinonia*, or *leitourgia*.

To help ensure that the songs were classified correctly, the level of agreement between the two coders in terms of identifying the thought-units and then classifying each thought-unit as *kerygma*, *koinonia*, or *leitourgia* was assessed on a randomly selected 10% of the songs. The two independent coders achieved high levels of agreement in both identifying (85% agreement) and classifying (93% agreement) the thought-units. Disagreements in identification and classification in the random selection were resolved through discussion. The remaining songs were classified by one of the two trained coders.[19] A statistical software package called SPSS was used to perform data analysis and answer the research questions stated above.

Results

Which Communication Mode—Kerygma, Koinonia, or Leitourgia—Appeared Most Frequently in the Top 77 CWM Songs between 1989 and 2005?

Of the 77 songs, the majority of songs were classified as *leitourgic* (36/77, or 47%) with the least number of songs classified as *koinonia* (11/77, 14%). Thirty of the 77 songs were *kerygmatic* (39%). Put another way, in terms of balance of worship, for every 10 of the 77 songs sung in worship, 5 fulfill the purpose of *leitourgia*, 4 *kerygma*, and 1 *koinonia*.

We then performed a statistical test to determine if the differences between the number of songs in each category identified above were significant, that is, whether the results were not likely to be the result of mere accident or chance. An overall chi-square test was significant (X^2 (2) = 13.27, $p \leqslant$ = .001), indicating that differences were not likely to have occurred by chance in terms of the number of songs classified in each category.

Thus, we are able to conclude that about half of the worship songs fulfill the purpose of *leitourgia*—songs which are directed to God with the aim of thanking, praising, and adoring Him. Likewise, songs that fulfilled the purpose of *kerygma* were well-represented: over 1/3 of the songs were devoted to proclaiming the message of Jesus Christ, calling people to repentance, faith, and discipleship. In contrast, few of the 77 songs centered on fulfilling the purpose of *koinonia*, that is, few focused primarily on worship that fosters encouragement, nurture, comfort, and affirmation among the Body of believers (Philippians 2:1-2).

What Is the Trend in Communication Mode— Kerygma, Koinonia, or Leitourgia—in the Top 77 Worship Songs between 1989 and 2005?

As shown in figure 1 below, the number of songs classified as *kerygma* decreased over the years, while the number of songs classified as *leitourgia* increased between 1989 and

2005. For example, approximately 48% of the songs were classified as *kerygma* in 1990, while only 29% of the songs were classified as *kerygma* in 2005. In contrast, 37% of the songs were classified as *leitourgia* in 1990, while 61% of the songs were classified as *leitourgia* in 2005. The change from *kerygma* to *leitourgia* as the most popular song type occurred in 1999, and by the year 2004 songs identified as *leitourgia* (n = 19) were over three times more likely to appear than songs identified as *kerygma* (n = 6). It should be noted that between 1989 and 2005 only 11 songs classified as *koinonia* made it to the Top 25 song list.

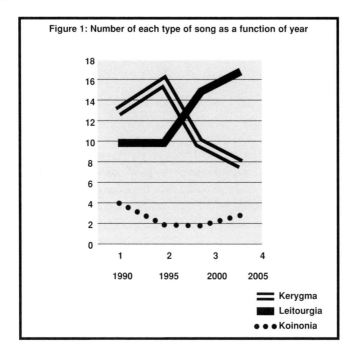

Figure 1: Number of each type of song as a function of year

Which Were the Most Popular Songs (Based on Frequency of Appearance on the Top 25 Lists between 1989 and 2005) and Which Category Did Each Represent?

To answer this question, we examined the 33 Top 25 lists between 1989 and 2005. The top 10 most frequently appearing songs are identified below in table 1. They appeared on the Top 25 lists 24-30 times out of a maximum of 33 times.

Note that this top 10 list in table 1 represents nearly the exact same percentages of songs identified among the 77 in our first research question. In other words, five of the top 10 songs were *leitourgic* (50%) (compared to 47% of all 77 songs), four (40%) were *kerygmatic* (compared to 39% of all 77), and only one of the songs in this top 10 list of most frequently occurring songs was *koinoniac* (10%) (compared to 14% of all 77).

Song	Table 1 Number of Top 25 lists on which the song appeared	Category
As the Deer	30	*Leitourgia*
Give Thanks	30	*Koinonia*
I Love You, Lord	30	*Leitourgia*
Majesty	27	*Kerygma*
Awesome God	26	*Kerygma*
He Has Made Me Glad	26	*Kerygma*
We Bring the Sacrifice of Praise	26	*Leitourgia*
He Is Exalted	25	*Kerygma*
I Exalt Thee	25	*Leitourgia*
Glorify Thy Name	24	*Leitourgia*

However, other popular songs among the 77 may not have been placed on our list in table 1 above because the song was simply not available during the entire period. For example, the song *I Could Sing of Your Love Forever* has been on every Top 25 list since it appeared in 2000, and the song *Shout to the Lord* has been on every list since it first appeared in 1998, yet prior to 2000 and 1998, respectively, neither of these songs was on the list. In contrast, *Praise the Name of Jesus* was on the Top 25 lists from 1990–1997 but has not been on a single list since that time. *All Hail King Jesus* has not been popular since 2000.

So, to address these concerns, we performed an additional analysis that took into account the date when the song was first published. A weighted percentage was applied to each of the songs in the top 77 based on the year the song was copyrighted and the number of times it appeared since that date. Thus, if a song was copyrighted in 2000, such as *I Could Sing of Your Love Forever*, it would be possible for that song to appear on ten of the Top 25 lists between 2001 and 2005, keeping in mind that two Top 25 lists are compiled each year. If the song appeared on each of the ten Top 25 lists between 2001 and 2005, it was given a ranking of 10/10, or 100%. But if a song copyrighted in 2001 appeared on only seven out of the ten lists between 2001 and 2005, it received a 7/10 ranking (70%). This analysis, however, produced the same top 10 list as that presented in table 1.

But using copyright date may be problematic since songs typically hit the charts several years, and in some cases much longer, after copyright date. Given this concern, a final analysis was performed examining the length of time remaining on the chart since the song's first appearance on the Top 25 lists. Thus, if a song first appeared in 2001 and remained on the list continuously through 2005, recalling that two Top 25 lists are generated each year, it was given a ranking of 10/10, or 100%. If, on the other hand, the song first appeared in 2001 and remained on the list only through 2003, it was given a ranking of 6/10 or 60%. Using such criteria, 22 of the 77 songs achieved a

100% ranking. An inspection of table 2 shows that the song *Lord, I Lift Your Name on High* has remained on Top 25 lists since its debut in 1994. It remains to be seen how long the songs that hit the chart in 2005, such as *Holy Is the Lord* and *How Great Is Our God*, will remain on the list.

	Table 2	
	The most popular CWM on the list of 77	
Song	**Year first appeared**	**Song Type**
Lord, I Lift Your Name on High	1994	*Leitourgia*
Shout to the Lord	1998	*Leitourgia*
You Are My All in All	1999	*Leitourgia*
I Could Sing of Your Love Forever	2000	*Leitourgia*
Open the Eyes of My Heart	2000	*Leitourgia*
Come, Now Is the Time to Worship	2001	*Koinonia*
Breathe	2002	*Leitourgia*
The Heart of Worship	2002	*Leitourgia*
We Fall Down	2002	*Koinonia*
You Are My King (Amazing Love)	2002	*Leitourgia*
Above All	2002	*Koinonia*
Better Is One Day	2002	*Leitourgia*
Draw Me Close	2002	*Leitourgia*
Trading My Sorrows	2002	*Kerygma*
Forever	2003	*Kerygma*
God of Wonders	2003	*Kerygma*
Here I Am to Worship	2003	*Leitourgia*
Lord, Reign in Me	2003	*Leitourgia*
I Give You My Heart	2004	*Leitourgia*
Blessed Be Your Name	2004	*Leitourgia*
Holy Is the Lord	2005	*Kerygma*
How Great Is Our God	2005	*Kerygma*

Of the 22 songs, 64% were classified as *leitourgic*, 27% *kerygmatic*, and 9% *koinoniac*. A comparison of these contemporary worship songs (table 2) with the overall top 10 lists (table 1) shows a 14% increase in the percentage of songs classified as *leitourgic* (50% compared to 64%) and a 12% decrease in the percentage of songs classified as *kerygmatic* (39% compared to 27%), with the percentage of songs classified as *koinonia* about the same (10% compared to 9%). It is important to keep in mind, however, that such conclusions are based on the comparison examining the percentage of songs classified as *leitourgic*, *kerygmatic*, and *koinoniac* of contemporary worship songs with those percentages of the overall top 10 songs between 1989 and 2005.

Discussion

Our results presented above indicate a significant imbalance in the type of CWM that we are using in corporate worship. *Leitourgia* now dominates, *kerygma* is decreasing, and *koinonia* is consistently a distant third. In the remainder of our chapter we consider possible explanations for the imbalance and what implications, if any, such imbalance may have on our worship today. Before concluding, we will consider what the imbalance says about the nature of the church and the nature of public worship.

From Kerygma to Leitourgia

In the first decade of CCLI reporting (1989–1999), we observed that *kerygmatic* songs were the dominant choice. This finding reinforces the long-standing perception that evangelical Christians are sermon-oriented in worship, defining themselves primarily as evangelists (*kerygma*) and only secondarily as worshipers (*leitourgia*).[20] This trend in North American worship services began with the Enlightenment preaching of Jonathan Edwards in the mid-eighteenth century and was later fueled by the evangelistic camp meeting movement of the 1800s. Evangelical Protestant denominations today, in pursuit of growth by conversion, have largely modeled their Sunday morning worship along the lines of the camp meeting or the evangelistic/revival meeting.[21]

The data suggest that 1999 was a pivotal year for CWM. In the five years following 1999, *leitourgic* music usage progressively outpaced *kerygmatic* music usage in CCLI reporting churches, with *koinoniac* remaining a distant third. There are several possible explanations for this shift from *kerygmatic* to *leitourgic* music.

First, over the same decade (1995–2005) in which we see the precipitous drop of *kerygmatic* music and the rise of *leitourgic* music, we also see a corresponding drop in the number of traditional worship services offered in America and a rise in the number of contemporary services. Surveys taken about every three years from 1993 to 2004 showed a steady rise in contemporary services over the same period during which traditional services declined. By 2004, the number of contemporary services surpassed those of traditional style.[22] The emphasis on participatory praise singing and active congregational worship within the contemporary service format may very well explain this trend.

Second, between the two denominational reporting periods of October 1996 and October 2003,[23] a period roughly paralleling the increase in *leitourgic* music and the increase in contemporary services, there was approximately a 35% increase in the number of charismatic churches reporting (e.g., Assemblies of God, Full Gospel, Pentecostal), while the number of noncharismatic and mainline churches (e.g., Southern Baptist, United Methodist, Nazarene) remained virtually unchanged.[24] By 2003, there were more charismatic churches than noncharismatic churches using CCLI-licensed music. Since charismatic churches are typically *leitourgic*-focused while Baptist and mainline churches are typically *kerygmatic*-focused,[25] the increased number of charismatic churches alone could be a significant factor in the overall CCLI-recorded growth of *leitourgic* music usage.

Finally, as Margaret Brady's analysis of CWM musical styles in chapter 10 will suggest, worship music performance practice historically has lagged between 10 and 20 years behind contemporary secular popular music composition until the 1990s. It is therefore possible that the type of music chosen by the mid-1990s finally caught up to the thematic *focus* of worship service planning. In other words, the church may have been moving the theme of its worship services toward *leitourgia* from *kerygma*, and worship leaders were finally starting to select music that fit.

Implications of the Imbalance for Worship

It is perhaps easiest to comment on the position of *koinoniac* music since it has maintained its status as the least-represented of the three forms over the course of the entire period of the study. If we agree with Dietrich Bonhoeffer's assertion that *koinonia* derives from *kerygma* and is worked out in *leitourgia*, then it follows that it would function in more of a transitional role between the other two larger components. This possibility does not diminish its importance, but it does assign it to a lesser position by comparison. Our data would support that conclusion.

Earlier in the chapter we described our concern for balance among the three components by suggesting that *koinonia* without *kerygma* would create an unhealthy situation similar to reducing the church to a social club. A worshiping community where *koinonia* trumps *kerygma* or *leitourgia* is one that celebrates itself more than it celebrates God.[26] Father Joseph Gelineau, composer of the first psalms for use in the reformed liturgy in France, illustrated this inevitability when he questioned whether many of the people in a given service have the kind of human relationships among one another that enable them "to hear the word in common in a fruitful manner, ready to share their prayers, and brotherly communion."[27]

As for the current imbalance between *leitourgia* and *kerygma*, the tendency to select and use predominantly *leitourgic* CWM to the neglect of *kerygmatic* CWM will be problematic only if the trend lines continue unchecked in the future. A worship service where *leitourgia* trumps *kerygma* and *koinonia* may produce a corporate worship setting in which the strong subjectivity and emotion of personal relationship to Christ is not adequately balanced by the objectivity of solid biblical exposition and evangelistic preaching. Worship becomes about "Jesus and Me" to the exclusion of the worshiping community, personal growth over public accountability, self-service over service and external outreach to others.[28] More important, perhaps, churches unable to feed, or fulfill, such individualistic needs for whatever reason may suffer in the "marketplace of consumerism," where the "product" may become a "stimulating Christian life."[29]

The issue of subjectivity over objectivity, *leitourgia* over *kerygma*, reflects the perennial concern of worship planners to achieve a balance in emphasis between immanence and transcendence. Through Immanuel—"God with us"—we experience God's closeness and approachability in and through Christ.[30] In worship we use the language of personal relationship to celebrate and convey this truth. However, we are not pantheists; God is not everything and everything is not God. So we must also remember that He is "high and lifted up,"[31] and His ways are higher than our ways. In worship we use the language of lordship, royalty, and majesty to celebrate His sovereignty and otherness. When worship errs on the side of immanence it can become self-centered and personal gratification–centered. When it errs on the side of transcendence, God becomes unapproachable to the point of being unknowable. Maintaining a balance in worship music selection plays an important role in helping the congregation walk a middle path between these extremes.

Conclusion

An ancient saying of the church was *lex orandi, lex credendi*—loosely translated as "the way we pray is the way we believe" or "the Law of prayer is the Law of belief." It also can be translated "the way we worship determines the way we believe." The music we select for corporate worship has great influence on the future of the church. If the way we worship/pray/sing actually does determine the beliefs of the people of God, then we must pay close attention to what we are singing.

In terms of addressing the imbalance identified in this study, worship pastors can use this study to focus and hone their awareness of the theological message of the songs they are selecting. In other words, they can be more intentional in choosing music that will be appropriate for the *kerygmatic, koinoiniac,* and *leitourgic* functions of their worship services. They can also apply our analytical method to evaluate other music as it appears on the CWM scene.

Worship planners—both lead pastors and worship/music pastors—would do well to note our discussion on the dangers of imbalance in worship and be intentional in maintaining an appropriate interplay among these three aspects of corporate worship. Songwriters and composers might respond to the relatively low usage of *koinoniac* music by producing new songs that reflect and celebrate life in the Body of Christ in the twenty-first century. Worshipers should appreciate this threefold model of worship communication and understand the importance of each element to a holistic corporate worship experience. They might respond by being supportive of pastoral leadership in their quest to bring such balance to the weekly Sunday worship service.

It may not be that a single service "out of balance" has a negative impact, but over the longterm our corporate worship should reflect a healthy mix of *leitourgia, kerygma,* and *koinonia*. Over a cycle of months and years our worship should rehearse the story of God in Christ. Sometimes we will be declaring who God is and what He desires of us. At other times we will be celebrating His presence with and within us and drawing near to Him as He draws near to us. And occasionally we will be speaking and singing to one another of His goodness and faithfulness and calling each other into accountability. These characteristics of holistic worship demonstrate the health of the church.

There are positive signs that a mitigating trend is on the horizon. According to figure 1 above, the ascending curve of the *leitourgic* line is not as steep for the last five years as it was for the prior five-year period. Similarly, the descending curve in the *kerygmatic* line has also become less pronounced. One would hope that this very preliminary data indicate a moderating trend in the imbalance between these two components (perhaps even including *koinonia*, since there is an upward trend there too). It will be interesting to see in ten years time whether or not this moderating trend actually continues and demonstrates a true change toward harmony among these three aspects of corporate worship.

Finally, we note that what our study *can not* tell us is whether the trends identified in the results section represent a change in the way worship music has been used in the American evangelical Protestant church in the past hundred or two hundred years. It may be that the proportion of *koinoniac* music to *kerygmatic* and *leitourgic* has always been lower, and may or may not be the proper balance of music types in public Christian worship. The answers to these questions are beyond the scope of this study but should be considered in future work.

Following Harold Best's advice, we have applied a theological model of the church's mission to our list of 77 songs. Our analysis has produced a snapshot of the state of the lyrical content of CWM at the end of the twentieth century, as viewed through the lenses of *kerygma*, *koinonia*, and *leitourgia*. The challenge before us in the coming century is to be wiser and more intentional in our worship planning so that we are truly "singing what we believe."

THE HEART OF WORSHIP: THE LEITOURGIC MODE AND CHRISTIAN SANCTIFICATION IN CONTEMPORARY WORSHIP MUSIC

DAVID PASS

Introduction

As our editors' introductory chapter explains, we are living in a time of rapid and substantive change in Christian worship, especially in the musical aspects of worship. There has, indeed, been a great explosion of new songs of praise, of which our sample is a tiny but, I hope, somewhat representative fraction. Yet what spearheaded these changes was a multifaceted revival movement that began in 1906 in Los Angeles and at the last count (A.D. 2000) included 523 million people worldwide: the Pentecostal/charismatic movement.[1] Many scholars see praise and worship songs as originating within this context of revival.[2] It is this context that is responsible for most of the songs in our 77-song sample.

The charismatic movement has been characterized by historian Peter Hocken as manifesting nine essential elements: (1) focus on Jesus; (2) praise; (3) love of the Bible; (4) God speaking today; (5) evangelism; (6) awareness of evil; (7) spiritual gifts; (8) eschatological expectation; and (9) spiritual power.[3] In elaborating on the second element, *praise*, Hocken has this to say:

> Being filled with the Holy Spirit always issues in the praise of God and of his Son Jesus Christ. The first result of the coming of the Holy Spirit is a flow of praise from within the believer, a verification of John 7:38. The believer has a new capacity to give glory to God, evident in the spontaneity of the charismatic praise and symbolized in the gift of tongues. Together with this flow of praise has come a great explosion of new songs of praise, possibly unparalleled in Christian history.[4]

There are two aspects in Hocken's concluding comments that are very significant, and they form the heart of how I would like to analyze our collection of songs in this chapter:

1. The believer has a new *capacity* to give glory to God, and
2. There has been a great explosion of new songs of praise (*content*).

More specifically, *capacity* refers to the skills, dispositions, and acquired know-how that make the content work or function. *Content* refers to the words and music comprising the worship form and its meanings. *Capacity* empowers *content*, and *content* expresses what is unspoken in *capacity*.[5]

Capacity can also be seen as consisting of three components (levels IV, V, and VI), and the same is true of *content* (levels I, II, and III), as shown below in the diagram I have created based on John Witvliet's comments on the levels involved in assessing liturgical change:[6]

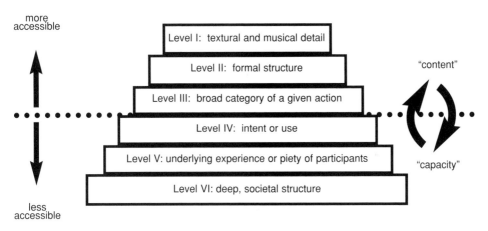

Diagram 1: A Model of liturgical Analysis

In this chapter I will look at our 77 songs using Witvliet's levels IV, V, and VI, what I have called "capacity" for two reasons:

1. Other contributors to this book will be analyzing our sample using levels I, II, and III, even if by other labels than I am using.
2. Most studies of worship forms and meanings concentrate on issues of content and tend to ignore the three levels I have grouped together under the heading *capacity*. As Witvliet remarks, a good deal of liturgical history examines only two levels (form and text detail) apart from the broader considerations at levels IV, V, and VI.

In an earlier book on the theology of church song, I developed a threefold model introducing the terms *kerygmatic* (songs that proclaimed something about God or the gospel), *koinoniac* (songs that functioned to build up the Body of Christ) and *leitourgic* (songs of prayer and praise addressed to God).[7] This model has been widely used and, in fact, forms the basis for one of the chapters in this book. In chapter 6, Woods, Walrath, and Badzinski systematically categorize the function of the 77 songs as *kerygmatic, koinoniac,* or *leitourgic.* To determine if a song fits the *leitourgic* mode better than *kerygmatic* or *koinoniac* modes, the authors rely on discrete words and phrases representative of the different types of *leitourgic* expression (that is, thanksgiving, petition, praise, and adoration). However, in the final analysis, the songs identified as *leitourgic* are not further subcategorized as thanksgiving, petition, praise, or adoration, although the authors of chapter 6 suggest that such analysis holds both theoretical and practical benefits and should be taken up by others. Thus, in this chapter I want to take up the authors' challenge and develop a classification within the *leitourgic* mode in greater detail, using the 77 songs in our sample as illustrative material.

This new model integrates level V (the underlying experience or piety of the participants) and level IV (intent or use) into one unified model. It is hoped that this will encourage other scholars, researchers, worship leaders, and songwriters to reflect more deeply about the nature of worship and worship music in our time. I will conclude this chapter with some practical advice and a suggestion for further research.

I will start with level VI, historical context or "deep, societal structure" as Witvliet calls it, since it is this context that has been the most formative for our sample of songs. Then I will look at our 77 songs through a new model—published here for the first time—of what I have elsewhere called the *leitourgic* mode of Christian song.

Deep, Societal Structure and Our Sample of Songs (Level VI)

As pointed out in my opening paragraph, our sample of songs originated mainly in a global historical context of revival, the Pentecostal/charismatic movement. To understand what drives and has driven the contemporary worship music movement is to understand an unspoken and barely verbalized deep-rooted need that has provided the stimulus for the worldwide revival and, by implication, the songs in our sample.

What deep, societal structures or contexts gave rise to this movement? One of the most perceptive and interesting analyses of Pentecostalism comes from Harvey Cox in his 1996 work *Fire from Heaven.* Cox's basic thesis is that Pentecostalism's amazing success as a movement in barely 100 years is that it has plugged into a worldwide hunger for what he calls "primal spirituality," that "largely unprocessed nucleus of the psyche in which the unending struggle for a sense of purpose and significance goes on."[8] For example, song #50 on our table of 77 songs (see table 1, pages 24-28), My

Life Is in You, expresses the singer's conviction that his or her life, strength, and hope is in God. Song #72, *We Will Glorify*, asserts the lordship of Christ over everything: "He is Lord above the universe." The song mentions, specifically, how Christ is Lord of heaven, earth, and everyone who lives. Here the song touches a deep human need for purpose, significance, and one's place in a God-created universe.

Other scholars agree with Cox, most notably Alister McGrath in his recent work *The Twilight of Atheism* (2004). A major determinant for atheism in any culture, he writes, "is whether a sense of the divine has been eliminated from a culture."[9] McGrath is profoundly concerned that it has been Protestantism that has "encouraged the notion that God was absent from human culture and experience."[10] By contrast, "Pentecostalism declares that it is possible to encounter God directly and personally through the power of the Holy Spirit. . . . It is this form of Protestantism that may be expected to resist erosion by atheism."[11] Liturgical historian James White concurs: "Far from being scandalized by the thought of God making direct intervention in worship, that very concept is a basic premise of Pentecostal worship."[12] This sense of God's manifest presence comes through in song #60, for example, *Surely the Presence of the Lord*: "I can feel His mighty power and His grace / I can hear the brush of angel's wings / I see glory on each face."

What is the relevance of this for the analysis of our song sample? Simply this: the deep, inarticulate cry of our culture, indeed any culture, is the same as David's: "My heart says of you, 'Seek his face!' Your face, LORD, I will seek" (Psalm 27:8 NIV). Deep below new songs, new technologies, new faces, and new voices is the ancient spiritual hunger of man to find God in a real and authentic way. These songs bear witness to that hunger and the conviction that God can and will manifest His presence where two or three are gathered in His name. As worship leaders we need always to remember the deep spiritual needs that drive all of worship and to believe that God can and will meet those needs. All of these songs address those needs in some way or other. The majority of them were created out of a deep hunger for God and speak to that hunger. These needs are inarticulate and sometimes impossible to put into words, but they are real and determinative for worship. For example, song #47, *Lord, Reign in Me*, gives voice to a deep hunger for the sovereignty of God over all of life: "Lord reign in me, reign in Your power / Over all my dreams, in my darkest hour."

After this brief sketch of the deep, societal structures of "primal spirituality" and how the revival recovered that in its music, as seen in our sample, we can now look at the unified model of the *leitourgic* mode, a model of worship music.

As we look at the context of revival that produced the new songs of praise, we notice that a whole new way of thinking about worship has emerged. Worship is now conceptualized as the explicit adoration of God, which should move in a seamless flow of songs of *petition, thanksgiving, praise,* and *adoration* toward increasing awareness of the manifest presence of God. This means that songs to be used in worship now function in a new spiritual *context*, which means that the songs now require new *content*. In fact, all 77 of the songs in our sample fall within the categories of petition, thanksgiving, praise, and adoration.

The full model of the different expressions within the *leitourgic* mode is reproduced below in table 1. The model overviews the contents of this chapter. It is quite compact and contains a lot of information that needs to be digested and unpackaged. I will do this in the remainder of the chapter.

	1. Definition of Song Types	2. Biblical Basis for the Song Types (Waltke)	3. Theological Basis for the Song Types (Moltmann)	4. Attitudes needed to make the song function to potential (Albrecht)	5. Emotions needed to make the attitude function to potential (Edwards)	6. Percentages of Song Types in our sample
Petition (includes confession and intercession)	To move God to act based on the nature of God, the relationship between God and the worshipper and the situation faced by the worshipper, a confession of need.	Petition lament psalms: • address to God • lament to express emotions and move God to act • confidence • petition • praise e.g., Psalm 26	All the terms of doxology (thanksgiving, praise and adoration) crystallize out of the experience of salvation. (So petition must precede salvation, just as salvation precedes the doxological response)	Modes of transcendental efficacy: an attitude participating in pragmatic ritual action. It has practical goals expecting God to answer, giving a hoped-for empirical result	• desire • hope • hatred (of sin) • fear (of God) • grief (over sin) • pity • zeal • compassion	**18%** (14 songs: 5, 8, 9, 12, 14, 16, 45, 47, 52, 53, 56, 57, 58, 61)
Thanksgiving	Expressing gratitude to God for what He has done, the public acknowledgment and confession of benefits received from God through His actions. His works.	Declarative praise: • intention to praise is stated • narrates experience of deliverance • testifies to the Lord's gracious act • may give a homily to the congregation • meaning of declarative praise is to confess in praise e.g., Psalm 33	"In doxology the thanks of the receiver return from the goodly gift to the giver."	Mode of gratitude: an attitude of free, unobligated and grateful acknowledgment for freely given and undeserved blessings received from God's hand.	• gratitude • gladness • happiness • appreciation • awareness of God's grace	**12%** (9 songs: 4, 10, 20, 25, 31, 51, 62, 64, 76)
Praise	The public acknowledgment and confession of one or more of the attributes of God, e.g., His love, mercy, grace, patience, goodness, holiness, etc., which constitute His person rather than His works.	Descriptive praise: • celebrates God's person and his works in general • praises God for his mercy, steadfast love, unfailing love • call to praise • cause for praise • renewed call to praise e.g., Psalm 103	"But the giver is not thanked merely for the sake of the good gift: he is also extolled because he himself is good. So God is not loved, worshipped and praised merely because of the salvation that has been experienced, but for his own sake. That is to say, praise goes beyond thanksgiving. God is recognized, not only in his goodly works but in his goodness itself."	Mode of celebration: rooted in the action and attitude of play. Contains little or no religious bargaining and does not pursue any specific result. There is no ulterior motive, only play-like abandonment	• love • joy • affection • celebration • rejoicing • triumph • exaltation	**43%** (33 songs: 1, 2, 3, 6, 7, 11, 13, 15, 19, 22, 23, 24, 26, 32, 33, 34, 39, 42, 43, 44, 46, 48, 50, 54, 55, 59, 66, 67, 69, 72, 73, 75, 77)
Adoration	The contemplative expression of the supreme worth, beauty, and utter glory of God's being, His essence, rather than His works (as in thanksgiving).	Adoration "One thing I have asked from the Lord . . . To behold the gaze upon the beauty of the Lord. And to take delight in his temple" (Ps. 27:4 composite translation) see also 2 Cor. 3:18	"And adoration, finally, goes beyond both thanksgiving and praise. It is dazzling and absorbed because the beholder is totally absorbed into its counterpart in the way that we are totally absorbed by astonishment and boundless wonder. God is ultimately worshipped and loved for himself, not merely for salvation's sake."	Mode of contemplation: a deep receptivity and a sense of openness to God. Submissiveness toward God is actively cultivated. In the contemplative mode one waits attentively for God.	• love • desire • delight • awe • devotion • adoration • wonder	**27%** (21 songs: 17, 18, 21, 27, 28, 29, 30, 35, 36, 37, 38, 40, 41, 49, 60, 63, 65, 68, 70, 71, 74)

Definitions of Song Types

The definitions of the four *leitourgic* song types are composite definitions that I have put together from various sources, mainly the articles on prayer from *A Dictionary of Christian Spirituality* edited by Gordon S. Wakefield.[13] I have also drawn from works on Old Testament prayer and praise like Patrick Miller's *They Cried Out to the Lord*[14] and Roland B. Allen's *And I Will Praise Him*.[15] Table 2 below summarizes the different praise and worship song types within the *leitourgic* mode and provides examples from the 77 songs in this study. Note that the songs in each table below are identified by their corresponding number in the list of 77 songs that appears at the end of the introductory chapter of this book (see pages 24-28).

Table 2

	1. Definitions of song types	**Illustrations of the song type from the sample**
Petition (includes confession and intercession)	To move God to act, based on the nature of God, the relationship between God and the worshiper and the situation faced by the worshiper, a confession of *need*.	*As the Deer* (#5): may my spirit yield . . . my heart's desire . . . long to worship Thee (desire) *Better Is One Day* (#8): one day in your courts than thousands elsewhere . . . my soul longs and even faints for You . . . One thing I ask and I would seek (desire) *Bind Us Together* (#9): Bind us together (request to God for a unified body of Christ) *Breathe* (#12): I'm desperate for You . . . I'm lost without You (desire, longing for God) *Change My Heart, Oh God* (#14): make it ever true . . . Note: in the chorus, the petitioner's hope is found in the fact that God is the potter and the petitioner is the clay (petition, hope, grief over a hard heart) *Open the Eyes of My Heart* (#53): The petitioner wants "To see you high and lifted up" (desire, hope, zeal for God's person and God's glory)

1. Definitions of song types	**Illustrations of the song type from the sample**
Thanksgiving Expressing gratitude to God for what He has done, the public acknowledgment and confession of benefits received from God through His actions or *works*.	*Give Thanks* (#20): with a grateful heart . . . because God has given Jesus Christ, His Son, for us . . . (gratitude, narrates experience of deliverance, confidence arises out of thankfulness) *He Has Made Me Glad* (#25): this is the day that the Lord has made . . . I will rejoice for He has made me glad (testimony to the Lord's gracious act, joy, gratitude) *The Wonderful Cross* (#62): oh the wonderful cross . . . did e'er such love and sorrow meet (gratitude, thankfulness, deep appreciation, love, joy, deliverance based on the facts of Christ's death for us) *Oh How He Loves You and Me* (#51): He gave His life . . . brought hope from despair (gratitude, thankfulness, deep joy, and reciprocal love for God's salvation in Christ)
Praise The public acknowledgment and confession of one or more of the attributes of God, e.g., His love, mercy, grace, patience, goodness, holiness, etc., which constitute His *person* rather than His works.	*Hallelujah (Your Love Is Amazing)* (#24): Your love is amazing . . . a mountain firm beneath my feet . . . Note: the singers go on to mention how God's love makes them sing (love, joy, and affection for qualities in God's character and person: love, faithfulness, goodness) *Celebrate Jesus* (#13): He is risen and He lives forevermore . . . come on and celebrate (joyful call to praise, let's play in His presence, let's rejoice in His mighty power) *Let There Be Glory and Honor and Praises* (#44): glory and honor to Jesus (public acknowledgment of His person as our Savior, joy, affection, and love for Jesus because of His love for us)

	1. Definitions of song types	**Illustrations of the song type from the sample**
		My Life Is in You (#50): You are my strength, my hope, my life . . . I will praise You (rejoicing in the strength-giving, hope-giving and life-giving attributes of God)
		Trading my Sorrows (#67): for the joy of the Lord . . . yes, Lord . . . His joy comes with the morning (I have joy in Christ, all the promises of God are "Yes" in Jesus, He is a faithful Savior)
Adoration	The contemplative expression of the supreme worth, beauty, and utter glory of God's *being*, His *essence*, rather than His *person* (praise) or His *works* (thanksgiving).	*Father, I Adore You* (#18): . . . lay my life before you. . . . Note: the singers go on to express that they love the Father (docility, gazing on His beauty, delight in God)
		I Stand in Awe (#38): . . . beautiful beyond description (love for God, desire for God, awestruck contemplation of the essence of God)
		Holy Ground (#29): standing in His presence . . . on holy ground (humility and docility in His presence, appreciation for His presence, certain knowledge that God is really here)
		In Moments Like These (#41): singing I love you Lord . . . a love song to Jesus (tender affection, docility in His presence, pouring out one's heart to our Redeemer)
		When I Look into Your Holiness (#74): when I gaze into Your loveliness . . . enthralled in your love (closeness, intimacy with God, contemplation of God's very being and essence)

The Biblical Basis for the *Leitourgic* Song Types

Bruce Waltke's recent essay on the book of Psalms makes it clear that scripture validates songs of petition, thanksgiving (declarative praise), and praise (descriptive praise).[16] Although Waltke does not discuss adoration (what he might call "contemplative praise"), it is clear that it does have a place, an important place, in Old Testament and New Testament worship. This much is evident from the scriptures I have quoted, Psalm 27:4 and 2 Corinthians 3:18. Table 3 below summarizes the biblical basis for each song type within the *leitourgic* mode and provides examples from the 77 songs:

	2. Biblical basis for the song types	Table 3 Illustrations of the song type from the sample
Petition (includes confession and intercession)	Petition/lament psalms: • address to God • lament to express emotions and move God to act • confidence • petition • praise	*As the Deer* (#5): may my spirit yield . . . my heart's desire . . . long to worship Thee (desire) *Better Is One Day* (#8): one day in your courts than thousands elsewhere . . . my soul longs and even faints for You . . . One thing I ask and I would seek (desire) *Bind Us Together* (#9): Bind us together (request to God for a unified body of Christ) *Breathe* (#12): I'm desperate for You . . . I'm lost without You (desire, longing for God) *Change My Heart, O God* (#14): make it ever true . . . you are the potter (petition, hope, grief over a hard heart) *Open the Eyes of My Heart* (#53): I want to see you . . . see you high and lifted up (desire, hope, zeal for God's person and God's glory)

	2. Biblical basis for the song types	**Illustrations of the song type from the sample**
Thanksgiving	Declarative praise: • states intention to praise • narrates exper-ience of deliverance • testifies to the Lord's gracious act • may give a homily to the congregation • confesses in praise	*Give Thanks* (#20): with a grateful heart . . . because God has given Jesus Christ, His Son, for us . . . (gratitude, narrates experi-ence of deliverance, confidence arises out of thankfulness) *He Has Made Me Glad* (#25): this is the day that the Lord has made . . . I will rejoice for He has made me glad (testimony to the Lord's gracious act, joy, gratitude) *The Wonderful Cross* (#62): oh the wonderful cross . . . did e'er such love and sorrow meet (gratitude, thankfulness, deep appreciation, love, joy, deliverance based on the facts of Christ's death for us) *Oh How He Loves You and Me* (#51): He gave his life . . . brought hope from despair (gratitude, thankfulness, deep joy, and reciprocal love for God's salvation in Christ)
Praise	Descriptive praise: • celebrates God's person and His works in general • praises God for His mercy, steadfast love, unfailing love • call to praise • cause for praise • renewed call to praise	*Halleujah (Your Love Is Amazing)* (#24): Your love is amazing . . . a mountain firm beneath my feet. . . . Note: the singers go on to mention how God's love makes them sing (love, joy, and affection for qualities in God's character and person: love, faithfulness, goodness) *Celebrate Jesus* (#13): He is risen and He lives forever-more . . . come on and celebrate (joyful call to praise, let's play in His presence, let's rejoice in His mighty power)

2. Biblical basis for the song types	Illustrations of the song type from the sample
	Let There Be Glory and Honor and Praises (#44): glory and honor to Jesus (public acknowledgment of His person as our Savior, joy, affection, and love for Jesus because of His love for us)
	My Life Is in You (#50): You are my strength, my hope, my life . . . I will praise You (rejoicing in the strength-giving, hope-giving and life-giving attributes of God)
	Trading My Sorrows (#67): . . . trading my shame . . . Yes, Lord, Yes, Lord, Yes, Yes, Lord—in response to His joy and promises to deliver (I have joy in Christ, all the promises of God are "Yes" in Jesus, He is a faithful Savior)
Adoration Adoration: "One thing I have asked from the Lord . . .	*Father, I Adore You* (#18): . . . lay my life before you . . . Note: the singers go on to express that they love the Father (docility, gazing on His beauty, delight in God)
To *behold/gaze* upon *the beauty of the Lord*. And to *take delight* in his temple"	*I Stand in Awe* (#38): beautiful beyond description (love for God, desire for God, awestruck contemplation of the essence of God)
(Psalm 27:4; composite translation); also see 2 Corinthians 3:18.	*Holy Ground* (#29): standing in His presence . . . on holy ground (humility and docility in his presence, appreciation for His presence, certain knowledge that God is really here)
	In Moments Like These (#41): singing I love You Lord . . . a love song to Jesus (tender affection, docility in His presence, pouring out one's heart to our Redeemer)
	When I Look into Your Holiness (#74): when I gaze into Your loveliness . . . enthralled in your love (closeness, intimacy with God, contemplation of God's very being and essence)

The Theological Basis for the *Leitourgic* Song Types and the Progressive Nature of Worship

Some critics are skeptical of the charismatic worship progression from thanksgiving to praise to adoration. Before they dismiss it too quickly, however, the comments of Jürgen Moltmann on what he calls the doxological Trinity should be carefully studied as I have reproduced them here.[17] Here Moltmann explicitly validates the theological "logic" of the progression from thanksgiving → praise → adoration, while at the same time grounding doxology in the nature of God as the immanent Trinity (God in Himself) and the economic Trinity (God for us). What is clear from Moltmann's discussion of the doxological Trinity is that *our* worship (and its natural progression as outlined) and the nature of God as both economic and immanent Trinity mirror each other in a mutually escalating exchange of thanks, love, and adoration.

Diagram 2

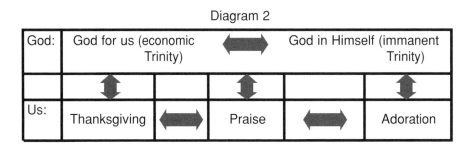

This is a formal, theologically explicit way of stating what Paul stated with Spirit-inspired eloquence in 2 Corinthians 3:18: "But we all, with unveiled face, beholding as in a mirror the glory of the Lord, are being transformed into the same image from glory to glory, just as from the Lord, the Spirit" (NASB).

Table 4 below summarizes the theological basis for each *leitourgic* song type and provides examples from the 77 songs:

Table 4

	3. Theological basis for the song types	Illustrations of the song type from the sample
Petition (includes confession and intercession)	All the terms of doxology (thanks-giving, praise, and adoration) crystallize out of the experience of salvation. (Petition	*As the Deer* (#5): may my spirit yield . . . my heart's desire . . . long to worship Thee (desire) *Better Is One Day* (#8): one day in Your courts than thousands elsewhere . . . my soul longs and

3. Theological basis for the song types	**Illustrations of the song type from the sample**
must precede salvation, just as salvation precedes the doxological response.) (Moltmann)	even faints for You . . . One thing I ask and I would seek (desire)
	Bind Us Together (#9): Bind us together (request to God for a unified body of Christ)
	Breathe (#12): I'm desperate for You . . . I'm lost without You (desire, longing for God)
	Change My Heart, Oh God (#14): change my heart . . . make it ever true. . . . Note: in the chorus, the petitioner's hope is found in the fact that God is the potter and the petitioner is the clay (petition, hope, grief over a hard heart)
	Open the Eyes of My Heart (#53): The petitioner wants "To see you high and lifted up" (desire, hope, zeal for God's person and God's glory)
Thanksgiving	In doxology the thanks of the receiver return from the godly gift to the giver. (Moltmann)	*Give Thanks* (#20): with a grateful heart . . . because God has given Jesus Christ, His Son, for us . . . now let the weak say I am strong (gratitude, narrates experience of deliverance, confidence arises out of thankfulness)
	He Has Made Me Glad (#25): this is the day that the Lord has made . . . I will rejoice for He has made me glad (testimony to the Lord's gracious act, joy, gratitude)
	The Wonderful Cross (#62): oh the wonderful cross . . . did e'er such love and sorrow meet (gratitude, thankfulness, deep appreciation, love, joy, deliverance based on the facts of Christ's death for us)

3. Theological basis for the song types	Illustrations of the song type from the sample
	Oh How He Loves You and Me (#51): He gave his life . . . brought hope from despair (gratitude, thankfulness, deep joy, and reciprocal love for God's salvation in Christ)
Praise	But the giver is not thanked merely for the sake of His good gift; He is also extolled because He Himself is good. So God is not loved, worshiped, and perceived merely because of the salvation that has been experienced, but for His own sake. That is to say, praise goes beyond thanksgiving. God is recognized, not only in His good works but in His goodness itself. (Moltmann)	*Hallelujah (Your Love Is Amazing)* (#24): Your love is amazing . . . a mountain firm beneath my feet . . . Note: the singers go on to mention how God's love makes them sing (love, joy, and affection for qualities in God's character and person: love, faithfulness, goodness)

Celebrate Jesus (#13): He is risen and He lives forevermore . . . come on and celebrate (joyful call to praise, let's play in his presence, let's rejoice in His mighty power)

Let There Be Glory and Honor and Praises (#44): glory and honor to Jesus (public acknowledgment of His person as our Savior, joy, affection, and love for Jesus because of His love for us)

My Life Is in You (#50): You are my strength, my hope, my life . . . I will praise You (rejoicing in the strength-giving, hope-giving, and life-giving attributes of God)

Trading My Sorrows (#67): trading my shame . . . Yes, Lord, Yes, Lord, Yes, Yes, Lord—in response to His joy and promises (I have joy in Christ, all the promises of God are "Yes" in Jesus, He is a faithful Savior) |

3. Theological basis for the song types	Illustrations of the song type from the sample
Adoration	And adoration, finally, goes beyond both thanksgiving and praise. It is totally absorbed into its counterpart, in the way that we are totally absorbed by astonishment and boundless wonder. God is ultimately worshiped and loved for himself, not merely for salvation's sake. (Moltmann)	*Father, I Adore You* (#18): . . . lay my life before you. . . . Note: the singers go on to express that they love the Father (docility, gazing on His beauty, delight in God) *I Stand in Awe* (#38): . . . beautiful beyond description (love for God, desire for God, awestruck contemplation of the essence of God) *Holy Ground* (#29): standing in His presence . . . on holy ground (humility and docility in His presence, appreciation for His presence, certain knowledge that God is really here) *In Moments Like These* (#41): singing I love You Lord . . . a love song to Jesus (tender affection, docility in His presence, pouring out one's heart to our Redeemer) *When I Look into Your Holiness* (#74): when I gaze into Your loveliness . . . enthralled in Your love (closeness, intimacy with God, contemplation of God's very being and essence)

Attitudes and Emotions Needed to Make the Songs Function to Potential

As pointed out above, John Witvliet (the author of our book's concluding chapter) has noted the significance of underlying piety or experience in studying worship. He comments that very often the surface manifestations of a liturgical artifact (for example, a song or a prayer) are studied to the neglect of the underlying spirituality.[18] Worship historian James White is even more direct when he writes that "piety is the essential equipment worshippers bring to church. Subjective as it may be, what one brings to church determines in large measure what one experiences there."[19]

To incorporate this dimension into my *leitourgic* model of song, I have drawn on the work of two scholars. The first is Dan Albrecht in his ethnographic study of the ritual life in three charismatic congregations in California. Albrecht noticed that charismatic rites (as he calls them) needed certain ritual sensibilities to make them "work."[20] It is important to notice that Albrecht distinguishes the rites (what I have called *content*) from the ritual sensibility (what I have called *capacity*). Ritual sensibilities for Albrecht are embodied attitudes that, while not necessarily contained within the structure of the rites, actually animate each of the various rites. He lists seven attitudes, but I believe only three of them (the three I have used in my model: the modes of transcendental efficacy, celebration, and contemplation)[21] are true ritual sensibilities. The others are generic to all Pentecostal/charismatic worship. He also has no ritual sensibility explicitly listed for thanksgiving. For this reason I have created for the category "thanksgiving" my own description of a ritual sensibility I am calling the "mode of gratitude" based on a very insightful discussion by Brian Childs.[22]

The second scholar whose work I draw on is Jonathan Edwards. This philosopher/theologian/pastor is best known for his book *Religious Affections*. Here he makes the startling assertion that "true religion, in large part, consists of holy affections."[23] Edwards goes on to give singing a formational role in the development of holy affections: "The duty of singing praises to God seems to be given wholly to excite and express religious affections. There is no other reason why we should express ourselves to God in verse rather than in prose and with music, except that these things have a tendency to move our affections."[24] Notice the reciprocal relationship between song and affections: song expresses affections; affections excite song.

For my model I have drawn on the lists of religious affections he gives in the early part of his book, concentrating on those he lists at least two or more times and supplementing them with some additional affections to suggest a wider range of emotions. I see a symbiotic relationship between Albrecht and Edwards, which is reflected in table 5 below. Albrecht has identified the general attitude that, as he says, orients and animates the particular rite discussed. The various song types can only be "animated" if the prerequisite attitude is in place. Since Edwards specifies the particular constellations of godly emotions that drive the corresponding attitudes identified by Albrecht, I have placed Albrecht and Edwards next to each other in Table 5 below.

Table 5

	Attitudes needed to make the song function to potential (Albrecht)	Emotions needed to make the attitude function to potential (Edwards)
Petition (includes confession	Mode of transcendental efficacy: an attitude participating in pragmatic ritual work. It has	• desire • hope • hatred (of sin)

and intercession)	practical goals expecting God to answer, giving a hoped-for empirical result.	• fear (of God) • grief (over sin) • pity • zeal • compassion
Thanksgiving	Mode of gratitude: an attitude of free, unobligated, and grateful acknowledgment for freely given and undeserved blessings received from God's hand.	• gratitude • gladness • happiness • appreciation • awareness of God's grace
Praise	Mode of celebration: rooted in the action and attitude of play. Contains little or no religious bargaining and does not pursue any specific result. There is no ulterior motive, only play-like abandonment.	• love • joy • affection • celebration • rejoicing • triumph • exaltation
Adoration	Mode of contemplation: a deep receptivity and a sense of openness to God. A docility toward God is actively cultivated. In the contemplative mode one waits attentively for God.	• love • desire • delight • affection • awe • devotion • adoration • wonder

Percentages of Song Types in Our Sample

Based on the definitions developed and the supplementary material offered in the tables above, I have assigned each of the 77 songs in our sample to one of the four song types. As table 6 below reveals, songs of praise and adoration predominate, a fact that is not surprising given that these songs largely originated within the Pentecostal/charismatic revival. Daniel Albrecht's comments here are very appropriate: "With the advent of the charismatic renewal came a reorientation toward explicit adoration of God. This adoration springs from the newer genre of worship choruses that have emerged and now dominate the congregational music in all three of these churches [the churches studied in his fieldwork]."[25]

Table 6

	Percentages of song types in our sample	Illustrations of the song type from the sample
Petition (includes confession and intercession)	18% (14/77 songs: 5, 8, 9, 12, 14, 16, 45, 47, 52, 53, 56, 57, 58, 61)	*As the Deer* (#5): may my spirit yield . . . my heart's desire . . . long to worship Thee (desire)
		Better Is One Day (#8): one day in your courts than thousands elsewhere . . . my soul longs and even faints for You . . . One thing I ask and I would seek (desire)
		Bind Us Together (#9): Bind us together (request to God for a unified body of Christ)
Thanksgiving	12% (9/77 songs: 4, 10, 20, 25, 31, 51, 62, 64, 76)	*Give Thanks* (#20): with a grateful heart . . . because God has given Jesus Christ, His Son, for us (gratitude, narrates experience of deliverance, confidence arises out of thankfulness)
		He Has Made Me Glad (#25): this is the day that the Lord has made . . . I will rejoice for He has made me glad (testimony to the Lord's gracious act, joy, gratitude)
		The Wonderful Cross (#62): oh the wonderful cross . . . did e'er such love and sorrow meet (gratitude, thankfulness, deep appreciation, love, joy, deliverance based on the facts of Christ's death for us)
Praise	43% (33/77 songs: 1, 2, 3, 6, 7, 11, 13, 15, 19, 22, 23, 24, 26, 32, 33, 34, 39, 42, 43, 44, 46, 48, 50, 54, 55, 59, 66, 67,	*Celebrate Jesus* (#13): He is risen and He lives forevermore . . . come on and celebrate (joyful call to praise, let's play in His presence, let's rejoice in His mighty power)
		My Life Is in You (#50): You are

Percentages of song types in our sample	Illustrations of the song type from the sample
69, 72, 73, 75, 77)	my strength, my hope, my life . . . I will praise You (rejoicing in the strength-giving, hope-giving, and life-giving attributes of God)
	Trading My Sorrows (#67): for the joy of the Lord . . . yes, Lord . . . His joy comes with the morning (I have joy in Christ, all the promises of God are "Yes" in Jesus, He is a faithful Savior)
Adoration 27% (21/77 songs: 17, 18, 21, 27, 28, 29, 30, 35, 36, 37, 38, 40, 41, 49, 60, 63, 65, 68, 70, 71, 74)	*Father, I Adore You* (#18): . . . lay my life before you. . . . Note: the singers go on to express that they love the Father (docility, gazing on His beauty, delight in God)
	I Stand in Awe (#38): . . . beautiful beyond description (love for God, desire for God, awestruck contemplation of the essence of God)
	Holy Ground (#29): standing in His presence . . . on holy ground (humility and docility in His presence, appreciation for His presence, certain knowledge that God is really here)

Conclusion

The key point to emerge from my extension of the *leitourgic* aspect of my earlier model is this: It is easy to learn the words and music of a new worship song. It is another matter entirely to acquire the underlying piety or spirituality that enables the song to function to potential. To acquire this piety is a matter of conversion to Christian faith and a time-consuming commitment to living as a disciple of Christ; it is, in a word, a commitment to sanctification. Here I am referring to an openness to the work of the Holy Spirit as recently discussed by Joel Beeke.

In his comments on the importance of the *Genevan Psalter* in Calvinist piety over the centuries, Joel Beeke highlights the importance of the Holy Spirit: "As a devotional book, it warmed the hearts of thousands. The people who sang from it, though, understood that its power was not in the book or its words, but in the Spirit who impressed those words on their hearts."[26]

We need to see the whole of Christian song, especially CWM, in this perspective, that of the sanctifying work of the Spirit in the life of believers toward greater Christlikeness. Wayne Grudem has recently emphasized the need for Christians to intentionally cooperate with the Spirit's work in their lives, saying that there are no shortcuts by which we can grow as Christians other than "the old-fashioned and time-honored means of Bible reading and meditation (Psalms 1:2; Matthew 4:4; John 17:17), prayer (Ephesians 6:18; Philippians 4:6), worship (Ephesians 5:18-20), witnessing (Matthew 28:19-20), Christian fellowship (Hebrews 10:24-25), and self-discipline or self-control (Galatians 5:23; Titus 1:8)."[27]

What this means is that worship—more particularly in this chapter, singing Christian songs—has to be seen as an integral part of the entire process of Christian sanctification. Songs have the task of contributing to our spiritual growth or movement through the entire "order of salvation" (*ordo salutis*): calling, conviction of sin, repentance, faith, regeneration, justification, sanctification (which actually encompasses the entire order of salvation from beginning to end—see Grudem[28]) perseverance, and glorification. Sanctification is "the continual re-making of the believer by the Holy Spirit, the increasing consecration of body and soul to God. In sanctification, the believer offers himself [or herself] to God as a sacrifice."[29] Here we can see that worship is a master metaphor for the Christian life, understanding worship as comprising what I have called elsewhere[30] *worship I* (the heart of worship, what Jaroslav Pelikan[31] recently called "creed"), *worship II* (the community at worship: "cultus"), and *worship III* (a lifestyle of worship: "code"). (See diagram 3 below.)

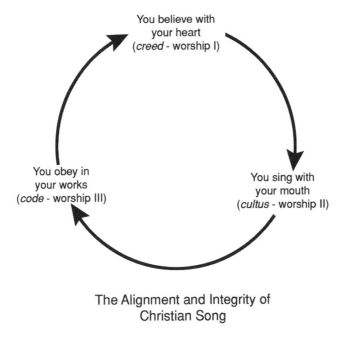

The Alignment and Integrity of Christian Song

There is a saying from John of Salisbury (1120–1180), who was bishop of Chartres and a well-known philosopher, that sums up the concerns I have tried to address in this chapter: "See that what you sing with your mouth you believe with your heart, and that what you believe with your heart you obey in your works."[32] In other words, what John of Salisbury is referring to is the concept of *alignment*: our songs, our hearts, and our lives need to line up in accordance with the gospel of Christ.

Before concluding with a suggestion for future research, let me offer the following three recommendations for pastors, worship leaders, and worshipers as they reflect on the model of worship music I have proposed in this chapter:

1. The key to changing worship songs is changing attitudes. None of us likes change (really). Sometimes it is necessary, sometimes it is not. Again, a prayer for wisdom to know the difference is a good idea. Only make those changes that take yourself and those you lead in the direction of greater Christlikeness and commitment to Him.

2. It is much easier to teach a new song than it is to cultivate the dispositions necessary to make that song function to its true capacity. Always ask yourself, Are the prerequisite attitudes in place for this song to work? If they are not, be prepared to work twice as hard at cultivating appropriate attitudes as you have to work in teaching the song as a song.

3. Above all rely on the Holy Spirit to inspire and develop in you and others the dispositions, capacities, and abilities necessary to make the songs and worship "work." Be prepared to teach on it and live out these attitudes in life and heart. Remember it is always "caught" rather than "taught." You can only lead people where you have been yourself. All of this takes time, effort, dedication, suffering, and prayer.

Finally, the application of Witvliet's model to analyze contemporary worship music has many fruitful possibilities. Some extensions to his taxonomy will be needed, however. Currently Witvliet sees the six levels as independent. My opinion is that the levels are actually interrelated in a dynamic way and that the closer the levels come to alignment in a given instance, the greater the communicative and transformative power of a given song. That is the kind of "Aha" experience the hymnologist Erik Routley was talking about when he described an ordinary Christian as saying of a certain song, "That is what I wanted to say, but I am grateful to whoever put the words in my mouth."[33]

CHAPTER 8

Praise the Name of Jesus: Are All Praise and Worship Songs for the Congregation?

Bert Polman

Introduction

Modern worship music in Western Christianity displays a rich variety of practices. On any given Sunday you may find services in which the congregation sings primarily traditional hymnody and the choir sings classic anthems; other congregations retain traditional hymnody but their choirs also sing contemporary choral music. There are "traditional" services and "contemporary" services, shared by the same congregation, while other churches feature "blended" services that combine traditional and contemporary elements into one liturgy. Some churches continue to rely on the organ and piano as primary accompaniment instruments, while others have accepted small instrumental ensembles to animate their singing. Still other congregations incorporate "global" songs or modern, classically oriented hymns into their worship, while others have abandoned classic hymnody altogether in favor of singing exclusively contemporary worship songs. Finally, some churches continue to use hymnals, whereas others have replaced hymnals with a computer system that projects song lyrics on a screen. What a rich variety!

As editors Woods and Walrath explain in our book's introduction, Contemporary Worship Music (CWM) is a broad category of church music that includes modern White gospel hymns and modern Black gospel songs, as well as classically oriented modern hymnody, the mini-hymns from the Taizé and Iona communities, and worship songs from the Third World.[1] The largest groups of songs within CWM are those known as Praise and Worship (P-W) songs, often associated with praise teams as primary leaders. Rooted in artist-oriented Contemporary Christian Music (CCM), P-W music has swept through Western Christianity since the early 1970s and quickly has become a global worship phenomenon.[2]

Traditional church music in Western Christianity has consisted primarily of congregational song, on the one hand, and of music sung by choirs and soloists on the other. Composers understood the difference between these two large categories of church music, and publishers marketed their music separately for congregations and for choirs. When P-W music began to appear, it was marketed as congregational music, even though much of it was composed by CCM artists whose primary experience was with small ensembles, not with congregations. These artists were accustomed to rehearsing music prior to performance and would work out the interpretation of complex rhythmic patterns and extended formal structures with their soloists and small teams of instrumentalists. But congregations are, by nature, unfamiliar with any experience of rehearsing their songs prior to singing in worship. After some three decades of P-W history, we could ask ourselves how successful the CCM artists have become in making the transfer from small ensembles (who rehearse the nuances of performance) to larger congregations (who do not rehearse).

Does all P-W music work well for congregations, or is it true that some of it works better as presentational music performed by praise teams alone? As I have said, there is room in the church for both congregational music *and* for choral music, for folk-like music that is readily amenable to communal singing *and* for the praise offerings that only trained musicians can produce in small ensembles. It is my thesis that some P-W songs have the stylistic characteristics we associate with congregational hymns, and that other P-W songs have the stylistic features of choral or solo music. I think it will be helpful for congregations and for those who lead church music to continue to appreciate the differences in style and function between these two large categories of church music, especially as the modern P-W repertoire is marketed entirely as congregational music.

While it is true that much P-W music comes from the CCM tradition of performance music and that some church members may object to P-W music as being "too much performance-oriented," I want to emphasize once more that the church has always had room for fully communal congregational singing *and* for the musical gifts of trained singers in choral ensembles who "perform" more complicated music. I am assuming that the singing of P-W songs will most frequently involve a praise team who "performs" either as a leader/accompanist to congregational singing or as a soloist ensemble in its own right. So I am interested in examining P-W music to determine which songs are suitable for congregational singing and which are more appropriate for singing as solos by praise teams, and to use various stylistic characteristics as the criteria for the distinction.

In light of the foregoing, working with the list of the 77 most popular CWM songs as reported by CCLI, I plan first to determine which of these songs most accurately represent the genre of P-W. Then, once I determine which songs among the 77 are most representative of the P-W genre, as a hymnologist, it is my more important intent to examine the remaining songs on the list with a view to ask the following primary question: *Which of these P-W songs are best suited for communal congregational singing (even if led by praise teams) and which are more appropriately sung by praise teams and their soloists alone, and on what grounds do I make such distinctions?*

Background

Though congregations in Western Christianity may sing psalm tones, canticles, prayer responses, settings of the liturgy or Mass, and other nonmetrical music, much congregational singing has consisted, traditionally, of hymns, that is, hymn texts sung to hymn tunes. In hymns, "relatively short musical structures" (hymn tunes) are united with "regular stanzaic poetic textual structures," and performed so that "stanza by stanza repeats the musical structures."[3]

In most churches, congregations tend to consist of those who are musically literate and those who are musically nonliterate, and of those who are good singers and those who are only average or even poor singers, all combined into one assembly of singing believers. By the nature of their life, congregations do not habitually rehearse, but acquire and retain their hymnic repertoire largely as an oral tradition, much like folksongs. This means, as my hymnology teacher, the late Erik Routley, emphasized repeatedly, that "singability" and "memorability" are crucial qualities for the composition and reception of hymn music. These two qualities come to expression in specific musical features of hymns such as melody, rhythm, harmony, and overall structure or form.[4]

In addition, as a hymnologist, I have always understood that much worship music came from the nave, that is, from the congregation, in the form of hymns, but that other worship music emanated from the choir loft, from musicians who took care to rehearse their more difficult music such as anthems, arias, and cantatas and perform them for the congregation. As Paul did in his explanation of different gifts in the body of Christ (1 Corinthians 12), traditional church musicians have always encouraged the "simple gifts" from the congregation and augmented that music with more elaborate offerings from well-trained performers, always claiming that the *whole* was a congregation's best composite "sacrifice of praise" to God.

However, the P-W tradition of singing hails initially not from the folksong-oriented world of congregational music but from the domain of Christian popular music with its emphasis on solo artists and/or small ensembles. As Robb Redman explains,

> Contemporary Christian Music (CCM) is a name applied to music meant *for solo or ensemble performance, not congregational singing.* CCM recordings, including worship music, are generally "artist-oriented." Moreover, CCM artists give their versions of songs an idiosyncratic and personalized treatment. Music is performed in keys and tempos that are comfortable for the artist; such settings do not always work for churches [emphasis mine].[5]

To put it another way and return to my architectural analogy once more, P-W came into the church via the choir loft at first (usually now renamed the "stage"), not through the nave, that is, the congregation's place. But once inside the church and its liturgy, P-W songs were held up as the best models of "sing to the Lord a new song," which the body of Christ was to perform in their worship of God with one congregational voice. P-W leaders encouraged entire congregations to sing these new worship songs along with their praise teams to foster "full, conscious, and active participation"[6] in the communal worship of God. They did so regardless of whether all of their songs were equally suited for congregational singing or whether some were more suited to performance by a small ensemble that actually rehearsed and could master the intricacies of some of this new music. And even if individual P-W musicians sometimes recognized the difference between truly congregational music and small ensemble or soloist music, this kind of discernment was functionally discouraged due to the fact that the commercial institutions that publish and promote P-W songs were eager to claim the entire congregation as their market!

When P-W appeared around 1970 and soon took over a prominent place in Western church music, various tensions arose, tensions often expressed as "church music (or worship) wars" between those who favored "traditional" worship and those who favored more "contemporary" styles.[7] Much of that tension is the result of stylistic preference by individual persons or groups of people who tend to idolize their own musical tastes. But there is also an issue here of what music works well for congregations and what music is more suited for smaller ensembles (such as choirs, praise teams, and soloists). And it is *that* issue that will be the focus of the rest of this chapter.

Method of Analysis

My method of analysis consisted of two stages. Given that the list of 77 songs used throughout the essays in this volume is essentially a list of the most popular CWM in the United States, my first task was to refine the current list by focusing on those songs I considered most accurately representative of the P-W genre. As a hymnologist, I wanted to narrow the field among the 77 based on my understanding of the stylistic criteria for identifying this genre. This I did in Stage 1.

In Stage 2, after I established the working list of songs among the 77 that were truly representative of the P-W genre, I examined each one to look for features that could either make them well suited for congregational singing or more appropriate for singing only by praise teams (in the same manner that anthems or other choral music would be sung only by church choirs, and not by the full congregation).

Stage 1: Praise and Worship Songs

To determine which songs were not representative of my understanding of the P-W genre, I applied four basic criteria (and I realize that not everyone will agree with these criteria):

1. Since many observers of contemporary church music agree that P-W songs appear only after the very late 1960s or early 1970s, songs with earlier copyrights were excluded from further examination. Applying this criterion, I eliminated the following five songs from the original list of 77: *His Name Is Wonderful*, *This Is the Day*, *Thou Art Worthy*, *Thy Lovingkindness*, and *Turn Your Eyes upon Jesus*. Three of these are scripture

songs, a subgenre that is important in the prehistory of P-W music, but whose initial performances with guitar predate the P-W performance practice with a full praise team.

2. Songs that are strongly associated with White gospel music (in the tradition of Ira Sankey or Homer Rodeheaver, with the Gaithers as a modern representative) or with Black gospel music (in the tradition of Thomas A. Dorsey, with Andraé Crouch as a modern representative) were also dropped from consideration because both of these traditions have long histories that predate P-W, feature performance practices that are different from P-W, and publish their respective repertoires through companies not associated with the P-W tradition. This led to the elimination of *Because He Lives*, *Bless His Holy Name*, *Oh How He Loves You and Me*, and *There's Something about That Name*.

3. Any songs associated with the "explosion" of modern classic hymnody (by British authors such as Fred Pratt Green, Brian Wren, Timothy Dudley-Smith, and Erik Routley—and their counterparts elsewhere in English-speaking Christianity, such as Carl Daw Jr., Jaroslav Vajda, Sylvia Dunstan, and Shirley Erena Murray) were also excluded because such hymns have a different *ethos* than P-W songs and do not require the praise team performance practices associated with P-W. This meant that Wren's *How Can We Name a Love* was dropped from further analysis.

4. Finally, songs that were P-W *arrangements* of classic hymns (as opposed to authentic new P-W compositions) were also excluded. This led to the omission of *Joy to the World* and *The Wonderful Cross*. The "refurbishing" of classic hymns by some P-W performers is commendable. However, classic hymns tend to have more complex theological lyrics than most P-W songs and predate the rock musical style in the melodies and rhythms of traditional hymn tunes. Applying the mannerisms of P-W performance to a classic hymn is a fascinating venture, but it does not make such hymns authentic P-W songs.

To put it more positively, I retained on the list only those songs that in the recording and publishing industry were strongly associated with CCM artists who have produced "worship" songs. I kept only those songs whose performance was strongly associated with praise teams, headed by named P-W artists.

After applying the four criteria above, the following 12 songs were culled from the list of 77 used in this book on the grounds that they did not fit as true P-W songs, either chronologically, stylistically, or by association (see table 1):

Table 1

Song Title	Description
Because He Lives [1971]	modern White gospel hymn
Bless His Holy Name [1973]	modern Black gospel song
His Name Is Wonderful [1959]	gospel song that predates P-W
How Can We Name a Love [1975]	modern classic hymn
Joy to the World [1719/1836]	arrangement of a classic hymn
Oh How He Loves You and Me [1975]	modern White gospel song

The Wonderful Cross [1707/1824]	arrangement of a classic hymn
There's Something about That Name [1970]	modern White gospel song
This Is the Day [1967]	Scripture song that predates P-W
Thou Art Worthy [1963]	Scripture song that predates P-W
Thy Lovingkindness [1956]	Scripture song that predates P-W
Turn Your Eyes upon Jesus [1922]	old gospel song

Stage 2: Congregational Versus Soloist Performance

I used four criteria in my examination of the remaining 65 songs to determine whether they were better suited for congregational singing or more appropriate for soloist and praise team performance:

Range and Tessitura

Traditional hymn melodies have often been within the range of an octave, or only slightly beyond an octave. If a melody's highest and lowest pitches are an octave and a half apart, then it is not suited for congregational singing, although it may be quite workable with trained solo or choral voices. Thus the range of *I Love You, Lord* makes this melody congregational, but the extended range of the American national anthem is a challenge for congregations.

Further, congregational singing requires not only a modest range of pitches but also a comfortable tessitura (that is, the majority of the melody's pitches must be around the middle of the average person's voice range). Melodies that have either high tessitura (the chorus of *Great Is the Lord*) or low tessitura (*Holy Ground*) may require that they be transposed down or up to make them comfortable for congregational singing.

Rhythms

Like folksongs, most hymn tunes have dependable metric structures in which consistent rhythmic patterns of accents are applied. In other words, the beat and the rhythmic accents do not change within the song. Some traditional hymn tunes such as Orlando Gibbons's melody *SONG 34* or Johann Crüger's *SCHMÜCKE DICH* will exhibit some shift in rhythmic accents, a musical practice known as syncopation. However, congregations tend to be uncomfortable with *excessive* syncopation, and certainly object to excessive *and* inconsistent syncopation. In fact, when faced with a syncopated pattern such as in Example 1 below many congregations will often straighten out the rhythmic structure in their actual singing as in Example 2.[8] Complicated rhythmic and syncopation patterns, however, are perfectly appropriate for soloists or small ensembles (such as praise teams) who take the time to rehearse the intricacies of such rhythms (e.g., *Blessed Be Your Name* or *God of Wonders*).

Example 1

from "Blessed Be Your Name" [chorus]

Bles-sed be the name of   the Lord.

Example 2

from "Blessed Be Your Name" [chorus]

Bles-sed be the name   of the Lord.

Instrumental "Flourishes"

Hymn tunes that congregations sing typically consist of four to eight phrases of melody, each of which has a defined cadence, or ending, but which are sung from the beginning of the stanza to its final cadence (ending) in a consistent manner. There may be brief instrumental interpolations (or "flourishes") *between* stanzas (as in *Shine, Jesus, Shine*), but not *within* stanzas in this congregational practice.

On the other hand, concert arias, anthems, or popular songs may contain breaks in their melodic phrases, during which the instrumental accompaniment comes to the foreground and the voices momentarily cease. Compositions such as *Celebrate Jesus* and *Holy Is the Lord* thrive on the constant interplay of voices and instruments, on the dialogue between voices and instruments that requires voices to start and stop numerous times within a melody line. Such interplay is a common feature of popular songs (whether secular or Christian), and it works because soloists and ensembles who perform such music take the time to rehearse these nuances carefully.

Formal Structure

The most common structures of hymns are those that contain either one or several stanzas, or those that contain a number of stanzas that alternate with a refrain. Similar structures are found in the folksong tradition and in P-W songs such as *All Hail King Jesus* and *Our God Reigns*. These are the two patterns that large bodies of people such as congregations appear to be able to sing easily (remembering that such groups of people contain trained and untrained singers, those who are musically literate and those who are not).

In the popular song traditions from Broadway and contemporary rock music, however, a song may have stanzas, a refrain, a bridge section, and often an alternate ending or coda. Soloists or small ensembles negotiate these more complicated forms through rehearsal and knowledge of such larger patterns. The more extended formal pattern of *Better Is One Day* (two verses, a chorus, a bridge, an altered chorus, and an ending) may mystify congregations.

Results

After applying the four criteria to the remaining 65 P-W songs in Stage 2 of my work (i.e., range and tessitura, rhythm and syncopation, instrumental "flourishes," and formal structures), I determined that almost two-thirds of these songs (65%) were definitely suited for congregational singing. These songs are listed in table 2. The remaining group of songs (35%)—in table 3—was judged to be more appropriate for singing primarily by praise teams and their solo voices.

Table 2
P-W songs suitable for congregational singing

All Hail King Jesus	*Jesus, Name above All Names*
Arise and Sing	*Let There Be Glory and Honor and Praises*
As the Deer	*Lord, Be Glorified*
Awesome God	*Lord, I Lift Your Name on High*
Bind Us Together	*Majesty*
Change My Heart, Oh God	*More Precious Than Silver*
Emmanuel	*My Life Is in You*
Father, I Adore You	*Open Our Eyes*
Give Thanks	*Our God Reigns*
Glorify Thy Name	*Praise the Name of Jesus*
Great Is the Lord	*Sanctuary*
He Has Made Me Glad	*Seek Ye First*
He Is Exalted	*Shine, Jesus, Shine*
Here I Am to Worship	*Shout to the Lord*
How Majestic Is Your Name	*Surely the Presence of the Lord*
I Exalt Thee	*We Bring the Sacrifice of Praise*
I Love You, Lord	*We Have Come into His House*
I Stand in Awe	*We Will Glorify*
I Will Call upon the Lord	*What a Mighty God We Serve*
I Worship You, Almighty God	*You Are My All in All*
In Moments Like These	*You're Worthy of My Praise*

Table 3

P-W songs suited for praise teams (soloist performance)

Above All	*Holy Is the Lord*
Ah, Lord God	*How Great Is Our God*
Better Is One Day	*I Could Sing of Your Love Forever*
Blessed Be Your Name	*I Give You My Heart*
Breathe	*Lord, Reign in Me*
Celebrate Jesus	*Open the Eyes of My Heart*
Come, Now Is the Time to Worship	*The Heart of Worship*
Draw Me Close	*Trading My Sorrows*
Forever	*We Fall Down*
God of Wonders	*When I Look into Your Holiness*
Hallelujah (Your Love Is Amazing)	*You Are My King (Amazing Love)*
Holy Ground	

Discussion

First, judging some of these P-W songs to be suitable for congregational singing and others for performance by praise teams is only one important decision. As the first seven chapters of this book have explained, a worship leader must consider several factors in addition to music such as lyrical quality and theological appropriateness. Along these lines, let me also affirm that a few of these P-W songs are theologically or poetically so deficient that I would not want a congregation or a praise team to sing them, regardless of their respective musical merits. A judgment on the congregational suitability of *Draw Me Close*, and *When I Look into Your Holiness* becomes irrelevant when there are good reasons never to sing these songs in Christian worship. This is not the place to defend my convictions on these songs[9] but simply to point out that there are other issues at stake beyond whether a P-W song is truly congregational or not.

Second, some P-W songs may have stanzas that are so syncopated that they are more suitable for soloists or praise teams, but their refrains might be rhythmically more accessible to congregations. Thus these judgments are not always clear-cut: I have determined that *Above All* and *Forever* are more suited to be sung by praise teams, but will readily concede that the chorus sections of both of these songs could be sung by congregations, if a soloist takes the more rhythmically challenging stanzas.

Third, the long history of church music in Western Christianity has shown that some congregations readily sing non-hymnic portions of the liturgy (e.g., psalm tones, musical responses, sung litanies, etc.), and can do so well, under capable leadership. Thus it is possible that good leadership will enable an individual congregation to sing some of the P-W songs that I have initially categorized as more suitable for solo or small ensemble singing. I have certainly heard *Better Is One Day* and *Come, Now Is the Time for Worship* sung in congregations with a large student attendance, but I suspect this is still an unusual occurrence from what one may expect generically.[10]

And that leads me to a fourth consideration. Like folksongs, traditional hymnic repertoire is often learned initially by rote hearing and singing. Many nontrained congregational singers have nevertheless acquired a rudimentary ability to read hymn music by visually connecting the written music from the hymnbook page with what they are hearing and singing. Today, however, the prevailing use of CDs among the younger generation means that they are hearing many of these P-W songs solely by rote; they are hearing and imitating complex rhythmic patterns by rote that would astound a traditional hymn singer who looks at the musical score. Similarly, the prevailing use of projected lyrics can simplify a congregation's following of the formal design or structure of a song, such that having a "bridge," for example in *Better Is One Day*, is no longer a complicating issue. That these technologies are changing the practices of Western church music is definitely clear, but to what extent the differences between music from the nave and music from the praise team platform will be eroded as a result of modern technology is a matter for further study and discernment in local congregations.

Finally, the list of 77 songs used throughout this book is America-based. The CCLI agency also tracks similar data in other English-speaking countries such as Canada, Britain, South Africa, Australia, and New Zealand. Discarding duplicates, the composite data produces some 150 songs for the same time period (1989–2005). It would be an interesting study to examine this larger group of global P-W songs and determine if similar proportions prevail among those judged to be most suited to congregations and those more readily assigned to soloists and praise teams.

Conclusion

P-W songs have become an important segment of contemporary Christian worship. It is certainly clear that the Spirit of God is blowing renewal through the modern Christian church worldwide, and that, concomitantly, a mighty explosion of new worship songs is available in worship today. As a hymnologist, I am excited to be alive in an era when the fertility of hymnwriting abounds as much as it does today. The repertoire of Christian hymnody has always operated on an anthology concept, keeping the best of the old hymns and always open to the best of the new songs.[11] And by all accounts, at least some P-W songs appear to be taking their place in that anthology. Stuart Townend and Keith Getty's *In Christ Alone* is probably the best example of a P-W song that will be known by later generations, I suspect, as a "classic" hymn![12]

The origins of P-W music in the tradition of the artist-oriented CCM world have required, however, some adjustment by P-W composers and performers toward the limitations inherent in congregational singing. That some two-thirds of the P-W songs examined in this study actually qualified as truly congregational songs is in itself a notable achievement, a significant testimony to the ability of P-W composers and performers to discipline their soloist inclinations and be true servants of congregational music.

That one-third of the songs examined in this study were judged to be noncongregational is therefore not surprising either, given their historical origin. What is surprising is the implication of industry interviews and CD promotions that *all* P-W music is congregational. I hope that the P-W movement will mature sufficiently to recognize that composing and performing true congregational songs requires humble musical characteristics, and that it is perfectly acceptable to compose more complicated musical settings for soloists and praise teams (similar to what composers have always done in their music for church choirs), but they should be marketed to praise teams, not to congregations.

Finally, I have noted that some P-W songs are ambiguous in performance practice, that is, their stanzas may be suited for soloists, but their refrains are accessible to congregations. The tradition of gospel hymns has a similar phenomenon: Often the stanzas were sung by soloists such as Ira Sankey or George Beverly Shea, but the assembled congregation would sing the chorus parts. A hymn concertato offers the same principle: Several stanzas of the hymn are sung by the congregation, but some stanzas might be sung in a more polyphonic setting by the choir. Given the flair for syncopation among P-W composers, I would hope to see more P-W songs that clearly earmark the stanzas (and bridges) to be sung by soloists on the praise team, but make the musical characteristics of the refrains eminently "singable" and "memorable" by congregations. In the meantime, the responsibility falls to the worship leader to make such clarifications obvious to praise teams and congregations in the interest of facilitating communal music performance and participation. This, after all, is the reason for congregational singing in public worship.

WHEN THE MUSIC FADES: THE ARTISTIC WORTH OF WORSHIP SONG MELODIES

GUY JANSEN

Introduction

Three years ago I met a respected denominational leader who thought that congregations, not music leaders or pastors, should choose the songs for corporate worship. I was just beginning to see wisdom in this comment when he added that music was only a vehicle for the words selected and that musical worth did not matter. When I raised a mild objection about musical values and excellence in all parts of God's world, he was not interested. Even the possibility of choosing the musically better over the musically worse did not appeal to him.

This church leader's curious and forthright stance against artistic standards prompted me to reconsider my own long-standing views. I thought of the Apostle Paul writing to the Philippian church about the "lovely," "commendable," and "excellent" in life (Philippians 4:8-10). Yet in my experience not many seem to care about excellence in worship music. Does it not matter if we sing musical garbage? Is it true that "an aesthetically inept song remains inept however scriptural the words might be"?[1]

In some circles, there has been a tendency to dismiss all popular-style worship songs because of an assumed lack of musical merit. At the same time, others have claimed that because music is so influential in corporate worship, the rhythms, instrumental accompaniments, tunes, and other musical aspects should be considered *equally* along with the lyrics when making assessments of suitability.

A number of authors who write about songs and hymns extol the need for quality, for example, "excellent music"[2] and "great songs."[3] The greatest challenge for standards of worship music excellence has come from Calvin College professor John Witvliet, for us to develop a clearer, more precise, and more consensual statement about aesthetic quality in hymnody. A theoretical approach that simply repeats platitudes that hymns should be tasteful or maintain excellence is not specific enough to function well in conversations with mega-churches or other populist forms of religious expression.[4]

This need to be clearer about aesthetic quality applies as much to CWM as to hymnody. To paraphrase Witvliet, we have to try to define more precisely and objectively what "good" worship music looks like.

In short, the problem of the musical worthiness of CWM songs has never been tackled in depth even though there has been quite a lot of criticism about the music. I therefore wanted to know how the 77 CWM songs stack up against standards of high musical quality. In determining musical quality, music scholars typically look at many musical elements and principles in combination: timbre (tone color), dynamics, rhythm, melody, harmony, texture, form (structure), overall expressive impact, and style. Given space limitations I could not analyze all relevant musical factors. Of all these musical characteristics I have selected one that seemed most relevant: melody.

Why melody? As with much other music, CWM appears to be viewed through the lens of melody. In discussing it, singers often talk about the melodic element first and, indeed, more about this than anything else.

Second, while some rock styles emphasize rhythm and instrumental textures, generally it is the tune that wins popular appeal. Composers aim to create melodies that people will respond to and sing after they hear just one verse; a good composer will seek "musical intelligence within a deep simplicity."[5] Songwriter Tommy Walker commented perceptively in 2005, "In modern music, the rhythms and the grooves allow us to get away with melodies that really have little to them. . . . Simple is usually better. The problem is that worship CDs are beginning to sound the same."[6]

Finally, in music of the church, home, and theater, melodies have always had a subtle function of communication. Familiar melodies have seemed to empower people, uplifting them, enriching their lives. Put another way, as experienced songwriter Dan Schutte says, "Melodies capture people."[7]

In light of the foregoing, the central research question thus became, *How do melodies of the 77 songs reflect characteristics of high musical worth?*

Background
Musical Criteria and Intuition

For centuries music philosophers tried to find bases for distinguishing between the meritorious and the meretricious, and between the mediocre and the maudlin. In recent times few people have attempted the work of finding criteria for making musical judgments. Alan Walker claims that criticism only explains something a person already knows on an intuitive level. In *An Anatomy of Musical Criticism* he argues that we do not have critics with standards: We can only have music with standards that critics may observe.[8]

It is increasingly recognized that as part of an appropriate process in making judgments on musical quality, one should rely on the intuitive responses of experienced, trained musicians for advice. Sympathy with the particular musical style being studied is a key factor. There are persuasive voices, for example, F. E. Maus in *The New Grove Dictionary*, who favor the perceptive "insider" calling the shots, this on the basis of genre-specific or style-specific understandings. They advocate noting "the pleasure of the qualified."[9] The literature on worship songs is conspicuously silent about the theme of who is most qualified to make musical judgments.

Even at the more obvious level of providing helpful, practical tips for song selection, few writers have contributed schema, checklists, or other plans by which to check suitability or musical worth of CWM. Let me mention briefly three approaches.

First, Sally Morgenthaler provides the most complete and adequate formula for testing musical quality in worship songs. After dealing with "the more technical side of songwriting," she then suggests a "compositional checklist" for "evaluating" worship music.[10] To uncover attributes such as "attractive" and "singable," she lists the four factors of structure, melody, chords, and rhythm as perspectives. Unusually, Morgenthaler gives an example of a song fitting each factor. She is one of the very few commentators prepared to name names (those titles considered good songs).

Second, Terry Bocklund McLean's music evaluation process is based on the same (limited) number of factors: form, melody, harmony, and rhythm.[11] However, in her Evaluation Work Sheet (found in appendix D in *New Harmonies*) additional simplistic factors are introduced. Points are required to be awarded for (a) the presence of a bridge or ramp (but these features often make the song more difficult for a congregation to sing) and (b) a built-in key change. (Actually, the mannerism of modulating to another key can sometimes suggest an absence of imaginative thinking about how to proceed.)

Finally, a work group in The Evangelical Lutheran Church in America, in providing a set of music principles "for discerning the suitability of music," lists several categories different from Morgenthaler and McLean. Their two criteria relating to quality are (a) the music should support and match the text and not get in its way, and (b) if the melody uses repetition it should do so "consistently and artfully," and if syncopation is used it should do so "in a natural (artfully predictable) way."[12]

The Inherent Difficulties Remain

Apart from isolated and incomplete offerings such as the three referred to above, and some general description of, structural analysis of, and informed comment about CWM material, there is no known rigorous examination of the musical merit of worship songs. The famous "test of time" criteria is sometimes trumpeted as the ultimate tool of appraisal, but we know that not all good music lasts, some great music gets overlooked, and some poorer music survives because of nonmusical influences. In any event, selection decisions need to be made long before stable doors are unlocked, musical horses bolt, and new repertoire becomes part of a church's regular diet.

I have long thought that assessment of musical worth is often avoided because of its inherent difficulties. It is seen as an imprecise science similar to qualitative assessment in other fields. The late Don Hinshaw, musician, editor, and publisher, said, very honestly, that "gut reaction" was something he had to consider when choosing music to be performed or published. Importantly, not only the place of intuition remains but also the subjective nature of the exercise is plain for all to see. This pervasiveness of subjectivity must be openly acknowledged and welcomed.

Technical and Artistic Criteria of Melodies

For reasons explained in this chapter's introduction, of all the musical elements available I chose melody as the focus of this study. Within the element of melody, one can distinguish between technical and artistic criteria. Technical criteria deal with the more mechanical issues of "singability" and accessibility for members of a congregation. They include comfortable melodic range, vocal expectations appropriate to congregational singing, and melodies that move well for amateur singers rather than being "soloistic." The corporate worship of God needs to *involve* those who choose to attend; it is about participation. Without carefully crafted, singable melodies, participation is more difficult.

The artistic criteria refer to issues of aesthetic quality and standards of value. Artistic criteria are more open to debate than technical criteria when it comes to evaluating music. Compared to the straightforward scope and nature of the technical criteria, the artistic criteria are fraught with difficulty in their application. If readers applied technical criteria themselves to all 77 songs, we would likely all come to very similar conclusions, but readers would likely find the subjective nature of the artistic criteria far more demanding to apply. Here there is a need for experienced, trained ears and a sensitivity to style.

Even the best musical minds find the legitimate appraisal of other people's melodies challenging, and they are often reluctant to claim special insight. In a senior music class at Victoria University of Wellington we once asked Professor Douglas Lilburn, New Zealand's finest composer, "What makes a good melody?" He said he did not know. This modest reply probably meant that he was not about to articulate an immediate response to a difficult question. We were sure, though, that *intuitively* he knew very well what a good melody was. I now need to use my musical intuition and some broadly accepted criteria to find which are the good (and not so good) melodies in the list of 77 worship songs.

Note that the distinction between the two classes of criteria (technical and artistic) is made only for the purposes of clarifying thoughts on the difficult issues of qualitative assessment. In reality the two classes cannot be easily separated; sometimes hard-to-see artistic criteria are connected to more easily observed technical ones. Nevertheless, it is extremely helpful to concentrate on only one characteristic (such as melody) at a time, and to relate both technical and artistic criteria to that. The task ahead, in assessing the melodies of 77 songs (in their many different musical styles) is daunting enough. It would be well nigh impossible to justify artistic decisions if several elements were being considered together.

And even though it would be ideal to consider both technical and artistic criteria of melodies at the same time, given space limitations in this chapter I could not report on an analysis using both sets of criteria. Thus, in light of the special difficulties surrounding the application of artistic criteria, I have devoted this chapter to explain and give examples of artistically good melodies found in the 77 songs.

Method of Analysis

In the light of the importance of melody in assessing the quality of CWM, I applied five artistic criteria to each of the 77 songs. The criteria were assembled partly as a result of wide reading in the aesthetics of music before and during my time at the University of Queensland. They were heavily influenced by reflecting upon my intuitive assessment of hundreds of worship songs and by detailed discussions with fellow musicians. One criterion (no. 5) borrows heavily from Leonard B. Meyer's concept of delayed gratification,[13] and Alice Parker, in a recent book, reinforced for me the notion of inevitability.[14]

Each melody is rated according to the five criteria and then assigned a grade of A, B, or C in terms of overall artistic quality. The outcome of the application of these five criteria is reported in tables 1, 2, and 3 in the Results and Discussion section.

For musical scores of the 77 songs, I used those obtained for me by a colleague. I studied them in conjunction with commercially available recorded performances chosen by other colleagues. Where there were significant differences between print and recorded versions I sought to establish likely "common practice." In four instances I had no recorded version.

Artistic Criteria of Melodies

(1) Criterion No. 1: *Basic melodic idea, "hook," or motif with inherent musical worth and originality.*

(a) Was there was a hook (an arresting or catchy melodic idea), motif, or other musical idea that was *not* essentially derivative, "all been heard before," trite, or formulaic? In a typical rock melody, as Michael Campbell points out, a short, clearly delineated riff (melodic idea) will comprise between two and seven notes. Such melodic material has to be weighed, compared, and lived with before its worth can be established. Among the songs with trite, formulaic hooks was *What a Mighty God We Serve.* Of the 77 songs, many had artistically compelling hooks. Some of these follow in (b) through (d).

(b) Especially on the first hearing, is there a spark of lovely or noble freshness, a germ of substantial newness and vitality in the melodic cell(s)? This can range from the subtlety of a little phrase bending back on itself in a surprising and appealing fashion, to startling melodic leaps, challenging and beautiful in their context.

Examples of songs with a good germ of an idea are *Better Is One Day, Forever, The Heart of Worship,* and *Glorify Thy Name.* On occasion an excellent musical idea is indissolubly linked with a chord or chordal progression assisting in the creation of a wonderful melody: *Draw Me Close.*

(c) Is the musical material interesting to an experienced, trained musician? By "interesting" I mean that our sense of curiosity has been roused, even excited, causing us to become personally involved and engaged. Is the hook absorbing, engrossing, stimulating, thought-provoking, or unusual? In encountering an "interesting" melodic idea or rhythmic figure, our curiosity has been piqued, we begin to wonder what is coming next, and we ponder the new direction in which we are being led. "Interesting" hooks were evident in *Shout to the Lord* (with its strong off beats on "Lord," "earth," and "sing"), *Breathe,* and the verse of *You Are My All in All.* Ones that were not "interesting" (in fact were quite boring) included the simplistic *Trading My Sorrows,* as well as *Holy Is the Lord; Ah, Lord God;* and the verse of *Hallelujah (Your Love Is Amazing).*

(d) Is there genuine newness and worth rather than just memorability? While many fine melodies may quickly or ultimately become memorable I am not asking for a merely "memorable" musical idea, one that sticks in the mind or lasts a long time. I can give an excellent reason for why not. The now very dated Singspiration tune *It Is Summertime in My Heart* (not in the final list of 77) with its catchy chromatic twists and turns is memorable; indeed, one finds it rather too difficult to forget, but it quickly wears out, becoming vacuous and trivial. In the 77, examples of hooks with little genuine newness and worth included the formula-driven *We Will Glorify,* with its melody stuck on the third degree of the scale until the last two bars, and *You're Worthy of My Praise*—in spite of its (unusual) use of the flattened seventh.

(2) Criterion No. 2: *Ideas developed inventively, with unifying devices and sufficient variety.*

(a) Have the hook(s), motif(s), or musical idea(s) been developed inventively with appropriate use of the compositional devices of repetition, imitation, variation, and contrast? For example, *Jesus, Name above All Names* uses too much repetition, to the neglect of other devices, with the static tune returning too often to the same note. In *Emmanuel,* even a trace of inventive relief would have been artistically rewarding; its single motif—a dotted quarter note—is repeated unfailingly.

(b) Does the song fail to "gain traction," or is it lame, *either* because it has (i) technique but no creative spark (or so little spark as to be inconsequential), *or* (ii) sincerity, passion, and zeal, but no semblance of craft? An example of a song without either creative spark or craftsmanship is the innocuous *We Bring the Sacrifice of Praise.*

Craftsmanship is a key to artistic songwriting, building, as it can, unity and variety within a consistent writing style, giving greater musical satisfaction. Sally Morgenthaler says, "Good worship songs do not just happen. They are built that way."[15]

(c) Is there sufficient repetition within the melody so that the tune can be remembered from one singing to the next? Sometimes repetition subtly morphs into the device of imitation. A particular kind of imitation is the sequence (a "copy cat" phrase), which is such a foundational aspect of worship songs that one is aware of it at every turn. An example of sequence follows in (d).

(d) Are the devices of imitation and variation handled in a balanced manner? Henry Smith's *Give Thanks* is an example of good musical sequences. The attractive seven-note musical cell that accompanies the words "Give thanks with a grateful heart" is heard twice, the imitation flowing with the movement of the words. There is pleasing imitation too, in the middle section of the song (from "And now let the weak say"), but the pitches have been changed enough (introducing welcome variety) to stop the melodic line from becoming boring. Although it is not the most imaginative of melodies, it is still well constructed.

(e) Is there sufficient contrast within the melody (appropriate to style and length) to retain the listener's attention? Music leader David Montgomery says that the repetition in Martin Smith's *I Could Sing of Your Love Forever* (long motifs four times in both verse and chorus) would be fine if the piece were sung just once or twice, but he fears that some leaders of worship appear to take the words of the song literally. Despite the unwritten rule that a theme should not be repeated exactly more than three times, a melody needs to be viewed as a whole, on its own terms and in context.[16] Another example of good contrast is in *Shout to the Lord* where an excited, slightly faster chorus follows a low-set, reverent stanza.

(f) If the music is a melody-driven style (rather than accompaniment-driven), can you bear to listen to the tune *apart from the words* several times without tiring of it? Is it a vibrant, unique, freestanding, and structured melody that flows freely? An example of a melody that fails to meet these standards is *God of Wonders*: An unpleasant four-note melody that goes nowhere is followed later by a tag that begins with "Hallelujah," the melody of which barely survives—even *with* its accompaniment.

(g) Has the songwriter made friends with the element of surprise: an unexpected interval, an unusual modulation, a note that will necessitate a little-used harmonic progression? Are there imaginative flashes, small but telling decisions that push the tune "out of the ordinary" and away from the charge of being formula-driven, stilted, or, at best, mediocre? An example of this element of surprise is found in *Above All* as it transitions into the chorus. The last note of the verse is a bottom A on the unexpected chord of A. The first note of the chorus is an octave away—a pleasant surprise full of exploding tension on the first word of the chorus, "Crucified." Features like these can involve us deeply as we repeat the song. Compare this piece to the unsurprising and artistically dead *We Bring the Sacrifice of Praise*.

(3) Criterion No. 3: *Structural shape and phrasing with a sense of tension and release.*
(a) Does the melody have a discernible, musically satisfying outer shape that relates well to its internal phrases? Here we might examine a long introduction, a bridge or ramp, or a lengthy coda. Do not look for symmetry or classical balance in such melodies. They must be assessed on their own terms. Two songs that have irregular forms that are not successful are *Trading My Sorrows* (it only holds together through its three-chord ground bass), and *Ah, Lord God*, with its two bizarre final sections destroying the unity of the whole.
(b) Does the tune use natural, speech-like rhythms reflecting "the cadence and inflection of vernacular American speech" (a trademark of rock melodies, especially since 2000)? This stylistic factor applies to *I Could Sing of Your Love Forever, Better Is One Day*, and *Blessed Be Your Name*, and should be remembered when assessing such melodies. In constructions using riffs, phrasing centers on very small sections of a tune. The hearer "listens through" all the gaps in the melodic line, for example in the verse of *Hallelujah (Your Love Is Amazing)*, and a new sense of phrasing is discovered.
(c) Can the melody actually be phrased in some fashion, to realize the song's potential "forward movement and energy flow"? A rock melody may feature jagged melodic contours, but phrasing can still be detected and clarified by noting the melody's rising and falling, by observing the natural inflection of syllables in common speech, and the emphasized word-meanings. An example of this is *Come, Now Is the Time to Worship*.
(d) Are the larger intervals (leaps within a melodic line) expressive, generating emotional energy? Leaps can add special character to a melody, and there are distinguished examples in many musical genres and styles—for example, the falling major 9th at the very opening of Andrew Lloyd Webber's *All I Ask* from *Phantom of the Opera*; the tune continues *within* the interval just negotiated. Among the 77 songs, the beginning of the melody of *Breathe* is perceptibly enriched by vocal leaps of a 4th and a 5th, and the melody of *Above All* begins with two upward leaps appropriate to the meaning of the song, which immediately distinguishes it from many lesser melodies. The verse of the beautiful *Draw Me Close* has more leaps than all its stepwise movements and repeated notes together. Other examples among the 77 are *Here I Am to Worship, Shout to the Lord*, and *Forever*.
(e) Is there a sense of creative tension and its subsequent release? Moving a melody toward the climax of a phrase or section (the "money note" in popular parlance) often creates a great intensification of feeling. Using upward-moving sequences and thickening the texture by adding further melodic parts can also foster this. Reversing those techniques can achieve the relaxation of tension. A telling example of creative tension, melodically and harmonically, is in *Lord, Reign in Me* at the long held note on the last word "am" in the phrase "You are the Lord of all I am." *I Stand in Awe* creates tension as it moves from an incantational quality at its opening to a compelling chorus with a rising 6th and a falling 5th interval. Release comes

with a repetition of the chant-like opening. Another example is *The Wonderful Cross*.

(4) Criterion No. 4: *A "fittingness" between lyrics and tune in temperament, style, and affect.*

(a) Does the tune fit the text, supporting it, giving it greater life, and embracing word accents in a natural manner, or does it call attention to itself, detracting from the merits of the words? John Witvliet suggests that poorly chosen music can trivialize a text.[17] For example, the melody of *Ah, Lord God* detracts from its words. There is a mismatch between a jolly tune reminiscent of an advertisement and our thinking about the Sovereign Creator. Similarly, the text of *What a Mighty God* is plagued by a tune more suited to *Snow White and the Seven Dwarfs*!

(b) Is the "affect" (the single most dominant emotion) of the text matched and enhanced by the "affect" of the melody? Don McMinn states that vocal music is primarily logo-genic, that is, it should relate to, and arise from, words. For example, the melody of *I Love You, Lord* features sustained notes on key words and three lifts in pitch to match the meaning of the heartfelt text.

(c) Has the melody been "stylized" in a way without regard for its integrity? Examples of such modified melodies are *As the Deer*, written in a folk idiom but now sometimes inappropriately stylized as a rock item, and the simple folk masterpiece, *I Love You, Lord*, given soft rock treatment. A song that is unusually flexible (in speeds and styling) is *Lord, I Lift Your Name on High*.

(5) Criterion No. 5: *Rather than predictability, a sense of inevitability in the melody's progress, with a compelling intensity and an acceptance of delayed gratification.*

(a) Is the melody so predictable and simplistic in melodic direction and rhythmic figuration that a listener can *predict* the next phrase almost exactly, as well as accurately guess the song's ending? One such song with a predictable melody is *What a Mighty God*. Another is *We Will Glorify*. Others where the melody is not predictable or simplistic are the chorus of *Because He Lives*, *When I Look into Your Holiness*, and *Above All*.

(b) By the conclusion of the song, has the flow and form of the melody sounded "inevitable," but not entirely predictable? What this means is that there is a sense of "Yes, of course, it had to be like that!" after it has finished. Expectations set up by the first notes have been met, and an elegant musical "logic" has become plainly evident. Songs that demonstrate this are *Glorify Thy Name*, *Turn Your Eyes upon Jesus*, and the English folk tune for *How Can We Name a Love*. This latter song has a sense of expectation set up by its cadences, and repetition in its graceful second line completes a melody of great shapeliness. A song where there is no such sense of inevitability is *Ah, Lord God* because of its ill-fitting final sections.

(c) Does the melody exemplify a tendency toward instant gratification or to the more mature principle of delayed gratification? Leonard B. Meyer claimed that aesthetic value was slightest when musical goals are reached in the most immediate ways. In the most recent song of the 77, *How Great Is Our God*, it is a shame that the composer *started* the song with the notes G – C, considering that much of the rest of the melody depends upon exactly the same notes with its rising 4th interval. One feels that all the compositional bullets were shot at the beginning. However, in *Open the Eyes of My Heart*, which has a nice sense of goal-directed shape, the composer holds his fresh chorus ammunition until the message of the verse has been absorbed. Another mature melody is *Glorify Thy Name*. A weak, immature melody is *Celebrate Jesus*.

(d) Is there a compelling intensity in the melody as it grows and leads to a conclusion? Is there a degree of passion and depth of feeling (not bland or shallow)? Intensity is not the same as a higher dynamic level or volume of sound, and it can be strong, exquisite, excessive, or quietly concentrated. A simple instance of this is in the structure of the song *Lord, Reign in Me*; in measure seven at "my only aim" the melody is suddenly held back by two beats, giving a small but definite feeling of urgency and weight to the thought behind it. *The Wonderful Cross* begins with a quiet intensity, using a drone in the bass to heighten the powerful effect of the slow-moving Isaac Watts melody, and builds to a vigorously passionate intensity with a contemporary feel in the chorus.

Results and Discussion

As a result of applying the five artistic criteria to the 77 songs, and gaining an overall assessment of artistic merit, I was able to apply the grades of A, B, or C to each melody. These ratings follow in tables 1, 2, and 3 with the songs in alphabetical order in each table. Songs with Grade A appear in table 1, Grade B in table 2, and Grade C in table 3.

Grade: A

Songs in table 1 earned the grade of A because of their generally high artistic quality. The best songs featured a well-crafted, appealing melody built on a superior hook or motif and a good match with the words. Subtle links between initial and later strains of a melody were noticed, as well as nice structural variety, and leaps that gave melodies some "air." Some pieces seemed very simple, such as *Seek Ye First; Father, I Adore You; Turn Your Eyes upon Jesus*; and *I Love You, Lord*, but I actually found them to be *simply profound*. It is exciting to see excellence continuing in the worship song genres, and one can give thanks for such impressive artistry. Some of these superb melodies may not be used as widely as one might think or wish because they may be linked with inadequate texts. A pity, but that was understood from the beginning. The study sought only to discover the quality of each melody as a separate entity.

	Table 1	
	Category A	
Above All	His Name Is	Majesty
As the Deer	Wonderful	Open the Eyes of My Heart
Because He Lives	I Could Sing of	Seek Ye First
Blessed Be Your Name	Your Love Forever	Shout to the Lord
Draw Me Close	I Love You, Lord	Turn Your Eyes upon Jesus
Father, I Adore You	I Stand in Awe	The Wonderful Cross
Forever	I Worship You,	When I Look into Your
Glorify Thy Name	Almighty God	Holiness
Great Is the Lord	Joy to the World	You Are My King (Amazing Love)

Grade: B

Songs in this category (see table 2) had substantial artistic worth but were distinctly deficient in one or more areas. For example, there may have been little coherent connection between phrases (*Breathe*), or pure repetition may have taken the place of (even a little?) development (*Here I Am to Worship*). On occasion, a melody in this category was disappointing because after an excellent opening idea there had been no inventive growth (*The Heart of Worship*). Sometimes the melody was quite weak with the song being built through textural layering, instrumentals, and vocals (*How Great Is Our God*). Perhaps some of the lesser songs in this grade grouping have survived because of the enthusiasm of music leaders, others have been seen by congregational clientele to have some good qualities apart from the melodies, and still others have filled a niche or a gap in worship programming. Maybe they were the only reasonable pieces available at the time.

	Table 2	
	Category B	
Arise and Sing	Here I Am to Worship	Lord, Reign in Me
Better Is One Day	Holy Ground	More Precious Than Silver
Bind Us Together	How Can We Name	My Life Is in You
Breathe	a Love	Our God Reigns
Change My Heart,	How Great Is Our God	Praise the Name of Jesus
O God	How Majestic Is Your	Shine, Jesus, Shine
Come, Now Is the	Name	Surely the Presence of the
Time to Worship	I Exalt Thee	Lord
Give Thanks	I Give You My Heart	The Heart of Worship
God of Wonders	I Will Call upon the	This Is the Day
Hallelujah	Lord	Thy Lovingkindness
(Your Love Is	Let There be Glory and	You Are My All in All
Amazing)	Honor and Praises	
He Is Exalted	Lord, I Lift Your Name	
He Has Made Me Glad	on High	

Grade C

The musical merit of the melodies in table 3 was questionable. Some were certainly saved by the harmony, instrumental backing, the words, or other aspects. However, for other pieces, "when the music fades" and all is stripped away to single, unadorned melodic lines, the relative paucity of imaginative musical thought and the lack of artistic hard work is laid bare. Not even time will heal those tunes, for example, *Ah, Lord God* (unfortunate in its scansion of the text and structure), *Lord, Be Glorified, Sanctuary* (poor word settings), and *We Will Glorify* (melodically poverty-stricken).

<table>
<tr><td colspan="3" align="center">Table 3
Category C</td></tr>
<tr><td>*Ah, Lord God*</td><td>*Lord, Be Glorified*</td><td>*We Bring the Sacrifice*</td></tr>
<tr><td>*All Hail King Jesus*</td><td>*O How He Loves*</td><td>*of Praise*</td></tr>
<tr><td>*Awesome God*</td><td>*You and Me*</td><td>*We Fall Down*</td></tr>
<tr><td>*Bless His Holy Name*</td><td>*Open Our Eyes*</td><td>*We Have Come into His*</td></tr>
<tr><td>*Emmanuel*</td><td>*Sanctuary*</td><td>*House*</td></tr>
<tr><td>*Holy Is the Lord*</td><td>*There's Something*</td><td>*We Will Glorify*</td></tr>
<tr><td>*In Moments Like*</td><td>*about That*</td><td>*What a Mighty God We*</td></tr>
<tr><td>*These*</td><td>*Name*</td><td>*Serve*</td></tr>
<tr><td>*Jesus, Name above*</td><td>*Thou Art Worthy*</td><td>*You're Worthy of My*</td></tr>
<tr><td>*All Names*</td><td>*Trading My Sorrows*</td><td>*Praise*</td></tr>
</table>

Conclusion

In the final analysis, an investigation such as the one presented above may have an important practical purpose: to aid in the selection of songs that discerning listeners would more readily accept and, by implication, encourage artistically poorer pieces to be used less.

It must be stressed that these results are solely research findings on the *melodies* of the 77 songs. Any particular song considered as a musical whole (a "gestalt") might score quite differently from the rating above. In addition, it must be remembered that the texts were not involved in the grading process, apart from considering the fittingness of the words/melody match.

It also needs to be pointed out that the study has been conducted in somewhat of a vacuum. There has been no church context, with the myriad of influences and factors that a regular church setting would bring. Every church fellowship is a unique environment, and contextual factors are critical. Thus, in addition to all the criteria listed in this chapter there are many other factors that might mitigate against choosing a particular song for a particular service:

(a) unsuitability for the theme of the day; (b) an unaccepting congregational attitude because of a bad experience with the song; (c) a congregation's level of experience with contemporary music making the song inappropriate at the present time; (d) an insufficient number of worshipers to carry the song (or too many for a fast piece); (e) wrong duration (length) for the song's proposed place in the service; (f) instrumentalists unable to cope with the accompaniment; (g) lack of leadership to introduce it effectively; (h) too little rehearsal time to prepare; and (i) a decision to leave it for another service, for example, a multigenerational gathering.

Sing to the Lord a New Melody?

What kinds of newness was the psalmist thinking of when he exhorted us to "Sing to the Lord a new song"? Should we be seeking to be creatively *new*—even cultivating a tiny flash of melodic genius—and not merely making a tune to carry another worthy set of words? There is no real dichotomy between originality (or a source of inspiration) and craft. (Note how Bezalel, the artist, in Exodus 31:3, besides being thoughtful and reflective on his art, was Spirit-filled and skilled as a craftsman.) God, the generous Creator, the essence of newness, loves to see creative brilliance and flair. When the common building blocks of tones are arranged and rearranged in new ways with careful boldness, aesthetic sensibility, and nuance, then a winsome, obedient gift is the result. God must be delighted.

"And the Greatest of These Is Love"

Framing discussions about choices of music for corporate worship are the invasive questions of taste, personal preferences, consumerist influences, social background, and ideology. In some churches everything seems to be up for discussion, and yet nothing seems to stay on the table. Attitudes toward those who do not share similar views are fragile at best, and charges of "dumbed-down ditties" or "that traditional stuff," lie just below the surface of an uneasy truce. Yet music leaders have the freedom and responsibility to inaugurate a climate of accepting love toward everyone else in the church music fraternities. Would that we could look away from discord (sometimes born of a species of arrogant ignorance) to reconciliation and unity! Any of us, with Christian motivation, may think we know the best direction for the future of music in worship, but the practice of love and a humble servanthood is far more important than any of that. Nearly sixty years ago, C. S. Lewis wrote about musical High Brows and Low Brows in the church, saying that they assume far too easily the spiritual value of the music they want.[18] John Frame suggests, "It is important for both sides to put away the flame throwers and speak to one another with the wisdom and love of Christ."[19]

In the end, purely musical considerations should not get in the way of a comprehensive appraisal of the theological, liturgical, and pastoral needs of worshipers when deciding on songs for gathered worship. The Holy Spirit chooses to work in a great many different ways, and a rigid set of music rules is the last thing needed by any community of faith. Authenticity and genuineness is highly prized by the latest (Y) generation and many others. Baloney disguised in excellence is being rejected. If my efforts assist, in some small measure, to develop greater understanding and a sense of musical discrimination and discernment in the selection of contemporary worship songs, I shall be pleased. My hope is that the technical and artistic music criteria offered in this chapter will become filters through which musicians can pass new, potential worship songs that are not on the list of the 77 analyzed in this study.

WHEN I SURVEY THE WONDROUS CROSS: THE MUSICAL STYLES OF THE TOP 77 SONGS—A HISTORICAL-CRITICAL ANALYSIS

MARGARET BRADY

Introduction

This past year, I took informal surveys at the academic worship and music conferences I attended. During coffee hour, I asked several participants whether they spent much time critically analyzing the lyrics or music of contemporary worship music. One replied, "What is there to analyze? It's all choruses." Another said, "It's throw-away music; it's not worth the time to study it." Even from the podium at plenary sessions, there were occasional references to "the little ditties," accompanied by half-smiles and rolled eyes.

I also spent two weeks in a seminar on African-American worship and music, led by a gifted musician who held a doctorate in church music and organ performance, but could also play everything from rhythm and blues to gospel from any era. Several times during coffee hour, musicians approached him, asking if they could have a lesson with him to learn how to play gospel music. In class, he responded:

> That's like asking someone to teach you classical piano in one hour. And which "gospel" are they talking about? Studying gospel music is like studying any other kind of music. You need to know its historical and musical roots. How does it relate to other music of its time? The Saturday night blues often becomes Sunday's good news, but with subtle differences. You need to listen to recordings of the best in that style and practice, practice, practice.

The conversations described above outline some challenges involved when studying, and identifying, the musical genres of the 77 songs. First, the music is considered by most authors to be all one style and therefore not requiring further stylistic study. Few writers delineate different styles within CWM. In *The New Worship*, Barry Liesch offers two broad categories: hymns and choruses, even while saying that choruses can represent different styles.[1] Marva Dawn, criticizing CWM in *Reaching Out without Dumbing Down*, offers genre or style names that are instructive but have little to do with music, concluding with "clever, casual, and trivial."[2] Greg Scheer offers a comprehensive review of CWM, dividing CWM into the following categories: Scripture Song (1971–1977), Praise Chorus (1978–1992), Praise and Worship (1993–1998) and Emerging Worship (1999–present).[3]

Second, many consider the 77 songs to be "throw-away" music, or music that is used briefly and then discarded from a church's repertoire. Much of higher education does not value other popular music either, so there is little research or teaching skills being developed for it.[4] But it is difficult to analyze new music without a historical perspective. Without hindsight, we do not know the evolution of the musical movement or its duration. We also do not understand its relationship to other music of its time.

Finally, like the perception that gospel piano accompaniment can be mastered in an hour, the 77 songs are considered by many worship scholars to be so simple musically that it would not be necessary to identify their stylistic characteristics or to develop good performance techniques. But closer examination using historical musical form and analysis may indicate the opposite. As Katherine Charlton notes in *Rock Music Styles: A History*, "To listen critically does not mean that one must try to decide whether the music is pleasing or not, but rather to analyze exactly what one is hearing."[5] This kind of listening and practicing is vital to authentic performance of any style, including the styles of the 77 songs.

If there *are* different styles in these 77 songs, would studying the historical and musical roots of the 77 give us insights into their styles today? More practically speaking, would such an understanding of different styles among the top 77 CWM songs identified in this book raise the level of their presentation and performance in our congregations by relating them to popular music styles and developing skills within those styles?

Method of Analysis

Using a historical-critical method, I developed a process for identifying the musical style of the 77 songs on our list. To begin, I grouped the songs into decades based on the copyright dates supplied by the CCLI. (See table 1 at the end of this chapter.) The earliest copyright dates appeared in the 1950s (1950–1959). As a result of inaccurate copyright dates, two songs were removed from the study.[6] Then, beginning with the songs with copyright dates in the 1950s and continuing through the 2000s (2000–2004), I employed the following steps in an attempt to identify the musical styles of the remaining 75 CWM songs.

Musical Elements

First, I analyzed the musical elements that were used to create the popular secular song styles during each decade. I relied upon Michael Campbell's[7] definitions of the following musical elements: rhythm, melody, harmony, instrumentation, texture, and form[8] and considered how they were expressed during each decade. To help identify these musical elements, I examined the musical scores from the remaining 75 songs on our list. The unique combination of the musical elements is what defines the particular musical styles, or subgenres, within "popular" songs during a particular decade.

Musical Style

Second, I determined that five musical styles were present in varying degrees throughout the decades between 1950 and 2000. I defined each of these genres in terms of their distinctive musical elements as follows:

1) The first style, *folk music* refers to music written or sung in the manner of the folk revival of the late 1950s and early 1960s. While traditional Appalachian and Southern folk songs were sung, others were composed and performed in a similar style: verse/chorus song form with "pure, unadorned singing," 2- to 3-chord harmony (or harmony limited to two or three chords), and acoustic guitar instrumentation sometimes enhanced by recorder or dulcimer.[9]

2) The second style was *country music*, a commercial form of the music of white Southerners, which began with the advent of commercial radio in the early 1920s. In the 1950s and 1960s, songs were written in verse/chorus form with "nasal" twang, 2- to 4-chord harmony, and acoustic guitar, string bass, and drums instrumentation, sometimes enhanced with fiddle, steel guitar, and dobro. In the 1970s, 1980s, and 1990s, country fused with other styles to make hybrids such as country rock, which had the hard-driving beat of rock and the addition of the electric guitar, but the twanging vocals, harmony, and other instruments of traditional country.[10]

3) The third style, *rock music*, emerged out of the 1950s, combining Black gospel, rhythm and blues, and country. Rock songs from the 1960s were written in verse/chorus form, used 3- to 4-chord harmony, and emphasized vocal harmony in 2 or 3 parts. Instruments included lead and rhythm electric guitar, electric bass guitar, drum set, and possibly keyboards. In the 1970s to the present, other forms of rock style developed. *Hard-rock* style is characterized by loud dynamics, 4- to 6-chord harmony, a strong beat, fast tempo, aggressive vocal styles, and prominent guitar lines. *Soft rock* is more closely related to popular song characterized by sweeter singing styles, slower tempo, a softer dynamic level, more complex chords, and the possible addition of acoustic guitar and orchestral instruments.[11]

4) *Popular song* of the 1950s and 1960s refers to songs that resemble Broadway show tunes and ballads, have complex chords, and are accompanied by full orchestra or band. The melody is the most important element, with smooth movement between steps and rhythm in natural speech patterns. Melodic idea is repeated again and again and sung in a sweet, straight-forward manner. The songs and singing style were called "Tin Pan Alley,"

named after songs written in the 1920s and 1930s that were pleasing and easy to remember. After rock dominated the 1960s, popular song resurfaced, retaining its traditional harmony and a dominant melody but with the addition of a gentle rock beat.[12]

5) Finally, James Goff adds *Southern Gospel* as a category that was helpful in describing the popular music styles of each decade. Southern Gospel is a varied field with singing styles ranging from traditional four-part harmony quartet singing to a blend of country and bluegrass. It uses the 2- to 3-chord harmony of country music, and instrumentation varies from a single acoustic guitar or keyboard to a rhythm band. It has a gospel feel in its Southern roots and creation for congregational singing.[13]

Note that each decade often displays more than one of these genres of secular popular music, particularly as we near the end of the twentieth century, although it is safe to say that in each era one style is predominant. One aspect of my research was to note if there was existence of multiple pop styles in a given decade of secular music that was mirrored by the *Contemporary Worship Music* of that same period. In other words, in a specific decade, was the most popular Christian worship music exclusively of one style or of more than one style of popular music?

Historical Roots

The first two steps led to a third step in my historical process, which involved connecting the popular secular music styles of each decade with the actual CWM songs of the same time period. For example, early rock and roll (*The Beatles, The Rolling Stones*) dominated the pop music charts of the 1960s. CWM of that same era, however, was largely reflective of Southern Gospel style, demonstrating a lack of connection between the pop music culture of that day and worship music culture of the church.

Musical Form

Lastly, two important terms need to be operationally defined before we discuss the results of the historical process described above. In my analysis of styles of CWM, I differentiated between two main musical *forms*, the chorus and the song, as they appeared during each decade.

A *chorus* is a short, 8- or 16-measure tune that may or may not have originated as the "chorus" or "refrain" of a larger hymn, gospel song, or popular song. Unlike a gospel song, it has no "verses" or "stanzas" to precede each singing of it. When performed it is simply repeated as many times as is felt to be appropriate by those singing it. A secular counterpart to it might be the "campfire" chorus.

A *song* will be defined as having both verses (stanzas) and a chorus. When a song—in its simplest form—is performed, it is sung in a progressive sequence such as verse one, chorus, verse two, chorus, verse three, chorus, and so forth. It has many secular counterparts in popular music in all of the seven styles mentioned above. However, both choruses and songs can appear within any musical style in any decade.

Results and Discussion

1940s–1950s

After World War II, American popular music was celebrated on Broadway and in big bands. Into the 1950s, streams of popular music included folk (Pete Seeger), country (Hank Williams), African-American gospel soloists and quartets (Mahalia Jackson, the *Soul Stirrers*), rhythm and blues (Muddy Waters), and rockabilly (Elvis Presley). Popular song contained verse and chorus, with the melody still originating from the Tin Pan Alley tradition, but emphasizing the chorus.

There is evidence of these popular styles in church music during this same time period. In 1945, Youth for Christ International, established in Winona Lake, Indiana, built on the foundation of Billy Graham's preaching and Homer Rodeheaver's new gospel songs. Graham became one of their most famous evangelists, leading enormously popular rallies and utilizing new music of the day. "In the same era that Fats Domino found his 'thrill' on *Blueberry Hill*, Christian teenagers at Youth for Christ rallies lobbied for a new musical language in which to express and experience the thrill of knowing Jesus."[14]

If we relate the popular musical styles of the decade to my analysis of the remaining 75 CWM songs, there are only two pieces from the 1950s used in the CCLI list. *Thy Lovingkindness* (1956) is a strong representative of Singspiration, a type of chorus written for revival meetings in the early 1930–1940s. Only eight measures long, it uses 3-chord harmony and stepwise melodic movement limited to five notes. *His Name Is Wonderful* (1959) exemplifies Bill Gaither's signature style: Southern Gospel harmony with popular song melody. The first section is a traditional chorus followed by a bridge (a musical section that provides a connection between other sections) and a repeat of the chorus's last line.

Thus, we can conclude that there was some crossover from secular popular song style of this era into that of the CWM of that time period, although my limited sample of two songs could not be considered conclusive evidence of any widespread trend.

1960s

The 1960s were a time of tremendous change and upheaval for established institutions and traditions in the United States. In popular music, some rock emphasized dissatisfaction with the status quo (*The Rolling Stones*). Other groups, like *The Beatles*, took rock music and stretched the boundaries. Folk music continued to be popular, including traditional Appalachian music reinterpreted (Joan Baez) and original music with a folk sound (*Simon and Garfunkel*). A wider range of popular song, including the music of Broadway and film musicals, was prominent on the radio. Country music grew in popularity through hybrids. Harmony often consisted of only 2-4 chords, based on the first, fourth, or fifth degree of the scale.[15]

In the Christian world, the Second Vatican Council of 1962 encouraged the Roman Catholic Church to compose new music for worship in the vernacular language and instruments of their people. "In England the *20th-Century Light Music Group* introduced light rock music to the church. . . . In New Zealand *The Garratts* began to compile the scripture songs that had been developing in Pentecostal circles."[16] In the United States, Roman Catholic folk masses were composed with a soft acoustic guitar accompaniment. A "gospel-folk sub-genre developed, incorporating the harmonic and melodic styles common to historic Anglo-American religious folk songs and the new secular-folk style of the 1960s."[17]

There were few changes in predominant musical styles from the 1950s to the 1960s in the 77 songs. Among our list of 77, four were published during the 1960s. The chorus form remained dominant, and the music reflected Southern Gospel practice. *Thou Art Worthy* (1963) is rooted in the 1950s; it has a longer chorus form and slower tempo, and uses 3-chord harmony. *This Is the Day* (1967), from New Zealand, uses chorus form and 3-chord harmony. Parts of the melody echo each other, reminiscent of camp songs from Youth for Christ.

The Gaithers provide another chorus form during this decade in the Southern Gospel tradition with *There's Something about That Name* (1970), expanding the melody and harmony with chromatic (moving by half-steps) movement. In *Because He Lives* (1971), they change to using a Southern Gospel song form with three verses and a chorus. The melodic range is increased, as is chromatic movement in melody and harmony.

Thus, despite the continued popularity of folk music and the rise of harder rock during this decade, the songs in the 1960s represented a strong Southern Gospel feel.

1970s

There were two main currents in rock music of the 1970s: back-to-basic hard rock and the return to melody in soft rock. Country-rock, a fusion of country and 1960s rock, had an American sound precisely because it mixed rock, Black, and country influences. Popular song contained elements of Tin Pan Alley style such as clear form, traditional harmony, and dominant melody, but added a gentle rock beat.[18]

During the early 1970s, a group of musicians in California began integrating rock and roll into church services and concerts. Maranatha! Music released the album *The Everlastin' Living Jesus Concert* in 1971, and performers like Larry Norman toured. It "wasn't until 1974 when Maranatha! Music released the *Maranatha! Praise* album that worship music and evangelistic music began to split into two distinct branches with their own fledgling markets."[19] Among our 77 songs, this decade offers greater variety in musical styles and forms. The 23 songs include one gospel song, one hymn, two folk songs, eight popular songs, and eleven choruses.

Andraé Crouch provides the only gospel song of the 77 songs during this decade. *Bless His Holy Name* (1973) has a chorus/verse/chorus form and uses triplets and chromatic harmonic movement. When performed, the pianist adds many more chord progressions to give more of the gospel song style of the 1970s.

Hymnwriter Brian Wren makes a unique contribution to the collection in *How Can We Name a Love* (1975). Wren wrote new lyrics to a traditional English melody adapted by Franklin Sheppard in 1915. Hymn lyricists often set their words to old hymn tunes. Nevertheless, this melody in particular fit in well with the folk revival of the 1960s.

The next two pieces are influenced by folk music. *Father, I Adore You* (1972) is a round (voices start at different parts of a song and sing them simultaneously). *Seek Ye First* (1972), another folk song from *Maranatha! Music*, uses a simple acoustic four-chord accompaniment.

The following eight songs during this decade sound like 1950s popular songs and Broadway show tunes. *Our God Reigns* (1974) combines a popular song melody with a Singspiration-period chorus. *Oh How He Loves You and Me* (1975) also sounds like a popular song with an upward scale movement in the melody. *Arise and Sing* (1976), *Ah, Lord God* (1976), *I Exalt Thee* (1977), and *Give Thanks* (1978) are written like popular songs from the 1950s with a distinct verse and chorus, even though there are no additional verses. *We Have Come into His House* (1976) has three verses and a common last line. Its slower tempo also adds to the popular song effect. *Bind Us Together* (1977) is written in ABA, a common popular song form. In contrast to the other songs and choruses of this decade, this one emphasizes harmonic movement typical of 1970s popular song.

The chorus form during this decade had grown from eight measures to sixteen or more and had melodic characteristics similar to those of popular songs of the 1950s and 1960s. *All Hail King Jesus* (1974, 1981) has a strong triumphant impact similar to an anthem. Beginning the piece on the second beat of the measure and using triplets (three notes per beat) gives it increased energy. *Jesus, Name above All Names* (1974), another contribution from New Zealand, uses triplets to provide a lilting feel to the simple chorus form.

Emmanuel (1976), *Glorify Thy Name* (1976), *He Has Made Me Glad* (1976), *Open Our Eyes* (1978), *Praise the Name of Jesus* (1976), *Let There Be Glory and Honor and Praises* (1978), *Surely the Presence of the Lord* (1977), and *I Love You, Lord* (1978) are all variations on a standard chorus form, which may differ in the lines repeated and the frequency of the repetition. While their melody and harmony have 1950s popular song characteristics, there is a new use of sequences (melodic line repeated, starting on a different note). The harmony for *Lord, Be Glorified* (1978) is more representative of 1960s rock music; the seventh chord (a chord built on the seventh note of the scale) is lowered and the key changes ascend chromatically.

So with the possible exceptions of the Andraé Crouch gospel song and the two folk songlike choruses, the most popular CWM of the 1970s was still firmly entrenched in the popular music styles of the 1950s and 1960s.

1980s

The 1980s marked a conservative trend in popular music. Soft rock rose in popularity, blending an emphasis on melody and clear forms with an understated rock rhythm. Both heavy metal (*Metallica*) and a back-to-basic rock movement (Bruce Springsteen) flourished. As for country, "there was broad support for virtually the entire spectrum of country music from updated versions of traditional styles (Willie Nelson), countrypolitan (Kenny Rogers) to rock-country fusions (Linda Ronstadt)."[20]

During the 1980s, CCM artists were focusing their energies on both concert performance and church performance. Amy Grant, Michael W. Smith, Twila Paris, and Rich Mullins recorded performance songs that were used in church services; they also sold instrumental tracks of these songs so that they could be performed exactly as they had been recorded. Music from the Vineyard movement was also influential, primarily using soft-rock music to keep their music "relevant in both style and quality to the cultures in which they live."[21]

There were a total of 24 songs in our list of 77 published during the 1980s: eleven choruses, six popular songs, four popular songs that crossed over from CCM, one hymn, and two soft-rock songs. It is remarkable that in the 1980s seven new choruses were written in the style of 1950s popular song. *In Moments Like These* (1980), *More Precious Than Silver* (1982), *Sanctuary* (1982), *We Will Glorify* (1982), *Holy Ground* (1983), *We Bring the Sacrifice of Praise* (1984), and *What a Mighty God We Serve* (1989) are all written in chorus form with melody and harmony from 1950s popular music. Four additional pieces could actually be called extended "choruses" since the first section of each comprises only one "verse" followed immediately each time it is sung by the same "chorus" or refrain. Nevertheless, stylistically, *I Worship You, Almighty God* (1983), *My Life Is in You* (1986), *I Stand in Awe* (1987), and *Celebrate Jesus* (1988) reflect the harmonic characteristics of the 1960s and 1970s, that is, they use 2- to 4-chord harmony.

Popular song forms were widely used that reflected 1970s musical style. For example, the harmony and rhythm of *Majesty* (1981), *I Will Call upon the Lord* (1981), *When I Look into Your Holiness* (1981), *Change My Heart, Oh God* (1982), *You Are My All in All* (1984), and *As the Deer* (1984) used major sevenths (chords holding onto the seventh note of the scale instead of resolving to the eighth note) and syncopation (rhythm that emphasized the off beat). Such musical elements were common during the 1970s.

There are several songs written by CCM artists that also appear on the list during this decade. Michael W. Smith's *How Majestic Is Your Name* (1981) and *Great Is the Lord* (1982). Rich Mullins's *Awesome God* (1988), and *He Is Exalted* (1985) by Twila Paris also demonstrate sophisticated popular song construction beginning the melody with the 8th, 7th, and 5th degrees of the scale, which is indicative of 1980s melodic technique.

Graham Kendrick's *Shine, Jesus, Shine* (1987) represents a new generation of hymns we see in the 1980s. The melody flows smoothly and hints at folk style, while the harmony is more complex than the typical 1980s pop song. *Shine, Jesus, Shine* was embraced by supporters of historic hymnody and worship bands and traveled the world through missions conferences.

The two remaining songs, *You're Worthy of My Praise* (1986) and *Lord, I Lift Your Name on High* (1989), provide a transition into the next decade by bringing soft rock into the church. *You're Worthy of My Praise* has the syncopated rhythms and harmony of 1980s soft rock, but it also has an echo that is reminiscent of Youth for Christ music. *Lord, I Lift Your Name on High,* another soft-rock piece, holds the CCLI's highest rating from the past fifteen years.

Although much of the CWM of the 1980s is still lagging stylistically behind the contemporary popular music of its day, there are signs that it is catching up. A significant minority of these songs is only ten years behind (1970s), and the last eight of this group are actually truly contemporary to this decade. This appears to mark an important milestone in the creation and use of CWM.

1990s

In popular music, alternative (*Red Hot Chili Peppers*) and grunge rock (*Nirvana*) emerged from garages onto the radio and recordings. Rock had a message, as evidenced by *U2*'s music. The blues (Stevie Ray Vaughan) and the singer/songwriter (Tracy Chapman) experienced resurgence in popularity. Country music in all its hybrid forms continued to thrive. World music was available to the masses through new and emerging forms of media. "Pop" music was not very popular. Rap became dominant, with its emphasis on rhythm and beat instead of melody.[22]

In many churches, a revolution had taken place. Churches focusing on evangelism or on retaining their youth looked to the example of megachurches such as Willow Creek Community Church. Popular music, drama, PowerPoint, and video became part of new "contemporary" services offered in addition to more traditional forms of worship. Other churches attempted to "blend" the music with their hymnic tradition. Hillsong Church in Sydney, Australia, modified its mission to develop new worship music communicated through recordings and their annual conference.[23]

There were a total of 14 songs in the list of 77 that were published during the 1990s. For the first time in several decades, no new choruses appeared in the 1990s. The transition to popular song and rock was complete. Musical bridges (e.g., "Holy, holy, holy") from such songs as *Open the Eyes of My Heart* became important as vehicles for improvisation that could be extended at will by the leaders. While acoustic guitar accompaniment was still popular in the 1980s, all of the repertoire for this decade was written for electric instruments and amplified sound.

Two distinct musical styles emerged during the 1990s. The first was "the slick, radio-ready pop style forged by Darlene Zschech and Hillsong, marketed in large part by Integrity Music."[24] Zschech wrote *Shout to the Lord* (1993) strictly for congregational use. The melody, harmony, and form of *Shout to the Lord* seem like a pop ballad from the 1990s, as does another by Hillsong, *I Give You My Heart* (1995). Hillsong now presents its new collection of soft-rock worship songs for the congregation and hard-rock songs for youth meetings at its annual conferences, which in 2006 attracted over 30,000 participants from 71 countries. *Draw Me Close* (1994), another contribution from Vineyard composers, was written in the same soft-rock style, as were *Breathe* (1995) and *We Fall Down* (1998). Finally, the lyrical melody of Paul Baloche's *Above All* (1999) blends beautifully with 1990s pop-song harmony.

The second style of CWM from the 1990s was "heartfelt guitar-driven rock. Martin Smith and his band *Delirious?* pioneered their sound with their hit *I Could Sing of Your Love Forever* (1994)."[25] *Better Is One Day* (1995), *The Heart of Worship* (1997), and *You Are My King (Amazing Love)* (1997) are good examples of rock ballads with a slower tempo. They also include a bridge that can be repeated as needed. *Open the Eyes of My Heart* (1997), *Come, Now Is the Time to Worship* (1998), and *Lord, Reign in Me* (1998) have a fast, driving beat and bridge. *Trading My Sorrows* (1998) is so closely associated with the opening bass riff that it literally cannot be performed without a bass player who is up to the challenge.

Contemporary Worship Music had finally come of age; the majority of the composers of the 1990s were actually writing worship songs in the current musical styles of the day. The dominant instrument was no longer keyboard or acoustic guitar but electric guitar. It was during this decade that *Christianity Today* acknowledged the significance of this music by publishing "The Triumph of the Praise Songs: How Guitars Beat out the Organ in the Worship Wars."

2000s

By the end of the 1990s, pop music had become increasingly fragmented. In an interview with Michael Campbell, he noted that in our present popular culture, "there isn't a common repertoire that everyone knows and there's no common harmonic language. The rhythms have become progressively more active. The sound world has become more aggressive and has let go of melody. The only place where one consistently finds tuneful melody is country."[26]

While many churches continued with services in their historic traditional, contemporary, or blended formats, a new movement became popular. The "Emerging Church" movement offered services that mixed ancient and current influences in multisensory worship.[27] For example, to adapt to these changes, Willow Creek developed a service called "Axis" aimed at but not limited to Gen X, using participatory multimedia and a variety of original, alternative, and world music.[28] The "Passion" movement produced music and worship events aimed at evangelizing college students; their music became widely used in churches and reached the CCLI lists in the late 1990s and early 2000s.

The eight songs in our list from 2000–2004 represent several trends. *Hallelujah (Your Love Is Amazing)* (2000), written by Vineyard musicians, is a guitar-driven rock song, but its form is altered; verses are sung by a soloist/worship leader while the chorus is sung by the congregation. Tim Hughes's recording of *Here I Am to Worship* (2000) begins with a string quartet, adds the piano, and then the band enters. At different points of *God of Wonders* (2000), one can hear the first line of the traditional hymn *Holy, Holy, Holy* by Reginald Heber ("Holy, holy, holy, Lord God almighty"). Weaving old hymns with new refrains comes to fruition in *The Wonderful Cross* (2000), where Chris Tomlin sings Isaac Watts's *When I Survey the Wondrous Cross* over open chords with a sustained bass note. After the verses, he inserts the rock chorus "Oh, the wonderful cross."

From 2001 to 2004, two members of the "Passion" movement dominated the CCLI lists. *Forever* (2001) was written in verse/chorus order with only 4-chord harmony and no bridge. *Holy Is the Lord* (2003) includes a verse, pre-chorus, chorus, and bridge. *How Great Is Our God* (2004) won the Dove Award for best song and CD. The marriage of melody, rhythm, and lyric flows well and comes together in a "U2-like praise anthem."[29] Matt Redman composes in a variety of styles, whichever happens to be most popular at the time. In *Blessed Be Your Name* (2002), he thickens the texture of each verse by adding instruments. He builds tension with a melodic line that ascends to a climactic bridge. These techniques are new to the 2000s.

Music most likely to appear on future CCLI lists may come from David Crowder, also from "Passion." *O Praise Him* (2004) leans toward alternative rock, with a multi-section form in random order. When interviewed about the song, Crowder said, "There's one song on our recent CD that I tried to at least give a feel of a hymn. . . . That is not very present in a lot of new songs, modern, contemporary songs."[30] In 2004, these "Passion" musicians produced a CD called *Hymns: Ancient and Modern*, the majority of which are old hymns arranged in new ways.

In the 2000s, recording labels are taking an active role not only in music but also in planning worship services. Membership in worshiptogether.com includes a weekly free song download, online instruction and videos, e-mail newsletters with links to new Bible studies, featured worship leaders, new music, conferences/training seminars, and access to the discussion lists.[31]

At the time of this writing, halfway through the first decade of the twenty-first century, it is premature to try to guess what history will say about CWM in this decade. Nevertheless, there are some hints embodied in the first five years. If present trends continue, the key word for this decade may be "diversity." The digital communication revolution has impacted every area of life, including that of worship music. On the one hand, affordable computer technology has placed within the hands of almost every musician and composer the tools to not only create new songs but to record, publish, and distribute them around the world at virtually no cost. This has led to an explosion of new sources of music that is independent of the traditional recording and distribution companies.

At the same time we see these same musicians accessing "world music" of almost limitless stylistic variety. Many of the songs written in this decade are exhibiting a fusion of musical characteristics that go beyond a single style. As this section of the chapter demonstrates, it is already becoming difficult to categorize this new music. One would expect that it will only be more so in the future and that we may need to develop a different methodology for use beyond this point.

Conclusion

Reviewing the different decades showed many similarities between popular music and the 77 songs. Different versions of folk, popular song, Southern Gospel, and rock and roll were present in both popular music and the 77 songs. Worship music trends responded to popular music but until recently were consistently behind them.

There were also notable differences between popular music and the 77 songs. The chorus form, while produced with different musical influences, was not dominant in popular culture, but stayed in this repertoire well into the 1980s. The recent trend in the 2000s of incorporating historic hymnody into current song is a sampling unique to CWM.

I think that identifying the different genres of the 77 songs is a step toward healthy conversations between those who think CWM is all choruses and those who think CWM should be used exclusively. Using nonmusical terms like "clever, trite, and trivial" to describe CWM is not productive. Musical analyst Peter Van der Merwe, in *Origins of Popular Style*, wrote about the challenges of describing popular music: "Very often, a name refuses to be just a name and acquires laudatory or pejorative overtones. The great trouble with loaded terms is that they lead to endless arguments about definitions and applications, which are really disguised squabbles about values."[32]

When comparing classical and popular music, Van de Merwe found that many people held the classical term as a value of higher quality, even to the point of stating that it was both the right and best music. Popular music held the opposite value. As Harold Best warned in *Music through the Eyes of Faith*, there is a danger in assigning moral value to sound.[33] There is also danger in valuing certain genres over others. It is possible that these misplaced values have led to many of the worship wars still savaging churches today. If church musicians of all backgrounds carefully studied each other's music in a spirit of cooperation, they might also find common ground in the pursuit of congregational participation and musical excellence.

I think identifying the music genres of the 77 songs could also be helpful to music and worship leaders. Understanding characteristics particular to each genre could help them coach church music volunteers in performance skills for congregational songs. As the gospel musician from the African-American Worship and Music Seminar described at the opening of this chapter said, each genre has its own performance skill set; musicians will need to develop their skills by listening to great performers along with practicing individually and in groups. It may also be helpful to perform according to the specific strengths of each genre, by emphasizing the lush melody in soft rock or the driving beat in hard rock. Awareness of these characteristics and their use may improve the accompaniment of congregational singing.

In the future, I hope churches might use a more broad-minded approach to selecting music in which leaders would choose music sensitively, combining familiarity of the genres with knowledge of the background and needs of congregations. Integrating increased understanding of CWM with a knowledge of traditional hymns, African-American repertoire, folk, and global worship music would provide a varied and representative repertoire for their congregations.

Finally, given the rapidly expanding world of musical styles and options, the lone church musician/worship pastor would benefit from an advisory team approach to music selection and planning. This is particularly important in church settings that cater to college ages and young professionals, who actively keep abreast of world music trends. A team of music-loving laypeople could broaden the horizons of the worship leader in the musical selection process while freeing the leader to focus on the numerous other aspects of his or her job. In strengthening their musical foundations and broadening their musical horizons, worship leaders will find a greater ability to serve God and their churches well.

Table 1
1950s

1. *Thy Lovingkindness* 1956
(Southern Gospel chorus)

2. *His Name Is Wonderful* 1959
(Southern Gospel chorus)

1960s

1. *Thou Art Worthy* 1963
(Southern Gospel chorus)
2. *This Is the Day* 1967
(folk chorus)

3. *There's Something about That Name* 1970 (Southern Gospel chorus)
4. *Because He Lives* 1971
(Southern Gospel song)

1970s

1. *Father, I Adore You* 1972
(folk round)
2. *Seek Ye First* 1972 (folk song)
3. *Bless His Holy Name* 1973
(gospel song)
4. *How Can We Name a Love* 1975 (folk hymn)
5. *All Hail King Jesus* 1974, 1981 (1950s pop chorus)
6. *Jesus, Name above All Names* 1974 (1950s pop chorus)
7. *Our God Reigns* 1974 (1950s pop song)
8. *Oh How He Loves You and Me* 1975 (1950s pop chorus)
9. *Ah, Lord God* 1976 (1950s pop song)
10. *Arise and Sing* 1976 (1950s pop song)

11. *Emmanuel* 1976
(1950s pop chorus)
12. *Glorify Thy Name* 1976
(1950s pop chorus)
13. *He Has Made Me Glad* 1976
(1950s pop chorus)
14. *Open Our Eyes* 1976 (1950s pop chorus)
15. *Praise the Name of Jesus* 1976 (1950s pop chorus)
16. *We Have Come into His House* 1976 (1950s pop song)
17. *Bind Us Together* 1977 (1970s pop song)
18. *I Exalt Thee* 1977 (1950s pop song)
19. *Surely the Presence of the Lord* 1977 (1950s pop chorus)
20. *Let There Be Glory and Honor and Praises* 1978 (1950s pop chorus)

21. *Give Thanks* 1978
(1950s pop song)
22. *I Love You, Lord* 1978
(1950s pop chorus)

23. *Lord, Be Glorified*
1978 (1960s pop chorus)

1980s

1. *In Moments Like These* 1980
(1950s pop chorus)
2. *Majesty* 1981
(1970s pop song)
3. *How Majestic Is Your Name*
1981 (1980s pop song)
4. *I Will Call upon the Lord* 1981
(1970s pop song)
5. *When I Look into Your Holiness*
1981 (1970s pop song)
6. *Change My Heart, Oh God*
1982 (1970s pop song)
7. *Great Is the Lord* 1982
(1980s pop song)
8. *More Precious Than Silver* 1982
(1950s pop chorus)
9. *Sanctuary* 1982
(1950s pop chorus)
10. *We Will Glorify* 1982
(1950s pop chorus)
11. *Holy Ground* 1983
(1950s pop chorus)
12. *I Worship You, Almighty
God* 1983 (1960s pop chorus)

13. *We Bring the Sacrifice of Praise*
1984 (1950s pop chorus)
14. *As the Deer* 1984
(1970s pop song)
15. *My Life Is in You* 1984
(1960s pop chorus)
16. *He Is Exalted* 1985
(1980s pop song)
17. *I Stand in Awe* 1987
(1960s pop chorus)
18. *Shine, Jesus, Shine* 1987
(hymn)
19. *You're Worthy of My Praise*
1987 (soft-rock song)
20. *Awesome God* 1988
(1980s pop song)
21. *Celebrate Jesus* 1988
(1960s pop chorus)
22. *Lord, I Lift Your Name on High*
1989 (soft-rock song)
23. *What a Mighty God We Serve*
1989 (1950s pop chorus)
24. *You Are My All in All* 1990
(1970s pop song)

1990s

1. *Shout to the Lord* 1993
(1990s pop song)
2. *Draw Me Close to You*
1994 (1990s pop song)
3. *I Could Sing of Your Love Forever*
1994 (1990s rock ballad/song)
4. *Above All* 1999
(1990s pop song)
5. *Better Is One Day* 1995
(1990s rock ballad/song)
6. *Breathe* 1995
(1990s pop song)
7. *I Give You My Heart* 1995
(1990s pop song)

8. *Open the Eyes of My Heart*
1997 (1990s rock song)
9. *The Heart of Worship* 1997
(1990s rock ballad/song)
10. *You Are My King (Amazing Love)* 1997
(1990s rock ballad/song)
11. *Come, Now Is the Time to
Worship* 1998 (1990s rock song)
12. *Lord, Reign in Me* 1998
(1990s rock song)
13. *Trading My Sorrows* 1998
(1990s rock song)
14. *We Fall Down* 1998
(1990s pop song)

2000s

1. *God of Wonders* 2000
(2000s rock song with hymn)
2. *Hallelujah* (*Your Love Is Amazing*)
2000 (2000s rock)
3. *Here I Am to Worship* 2000
(2000s rock ballad/song with strings)
4. *The Wonderful Cross* 2000
(hymn with 2000 rock chorus)

5. *Forever* 2001
(2000s rock song)
6. *Blessed Be Your Name* 2002
(2000s rock song with extended bridge)
7. *Holy Is the Lord* 2003 (2000s
rock song with pre-chorus and
extended bridge)
8. *How Great Is Our God* 2004
(2000s rock anthem)

DISCIPLESHIP AND THE FUTURE OF CONTEMPORARY WORSHIP MUSIC: POSSIBLE DIRECTIONS FOR SCHOLARSHIP, SONGWRITING, AND PUBLIC WORSHIP

JOHN D. WITVLIET

But speaking the truth in love, we must grow up in every way into him who is the head, into Christ, from whom the whole body, joined and knit together by every ligament with which it is equipped, as each part is working properly, promotes the body's growth in building itself up in love. (Ephesians 4:15-16)

The authors of this volume have taken on the risky challenge "to speak the truth in love." It is a risky venture because when the ligaments and muscles of the Body of Christ grow and are knit together, there is often a bit of pain involved. As in a good physical workout, part of the pain comes from identifying areas of weakness and needed growth. Part of the pain comes through the exercises designed to address those concerns—in this case the exercise of painstakingly analyzing texts and melodies, and then making theological and pastoral judgments about them. And part of the risk comes because the topic of this volume, our worship and its music, is so closely bound up with our personal identities, our sense of self. Constructive engagement with the music of worship touches a profound point of vulnerability.

I am honored to contribute to this volume in part because of the combination of generosity and courage that its contributors share. Each one cares deeply about the students with whom they are entrusted; each wants nothing more than to lovingly challenge them to a life of worship that is both passionate and well-grounded. Each one appreciates the significance of this music. Each one is also willing to take the risk of constructive criticism, all for the sake of the strength of the Body of Christ.

167

After reflecting on these essays, readers may well be feeling a little muscle burn, though hopefully the kind one experiences after a good workout. In fact, by now readers may well be grateful, provoked, perplexed, or inspired—perhaps all at the same time. A few of you may be songwriters surprised to see your song commended or called into question. A few of you may be scholars, teachers, or students, eager to contribute a new method for analysis in addition to those used in these studies, or eager to protest the categorization of a song in one of this volume's charts. Some of you may be pastors grateful for a set of questions to pose to your worship team or for data to confirm a hunch about the strengths or weaknesses of the music that you most love or that you most question. Many of you may be worshipers who are now surprised that there is this much to say about the songs you regularly sing or are convicted about a missing ingredient in your musical diet.

Now that we have arrived at the end of these ten chapters, it is time to pull back, to set our gratitude, questions, perplexity, and inspiration in the context of a larger horizon. It is time to assess what we have learned and to consider how best to apply it. But as we do, we must remember that the whole point of this exercise is nothing less than to "test everything; hold fast to what is good" (1 Thessalonians 5:21), and to "grow up in every way into [Christ]" (Ephesians 4:15). Our goal is nothing less than Christian discipleship.

In what follows, I will first summarize and briefly reflect on what we can learn from the essays in this volume in the areas of both text and music of CWM. For both the texts and music, I will point to topics or motifs that unite the essays of this volume and are worthy of further reflection.

Second, I will reflect on a series of topics that future studies could profitably probe to complement the work of this volume. I will point to several areas of current academic reflection that have much to teach us about CWM and provide endnotes with resources both for students who want to pursue research on a given question and for other practitioners or interested readers who would like to follow up a given theme.

Finally, I will conclude with a list of practical applications for scholars, songwriters, and worship leaders. People who are studying this book together—perhaps in a pastor's or songwriter's peer learning group, a church small group, or college or seminary class—may profit from working together to adapt this list of applications in ways that best fit your current needs.

Summary and Reflections
Reflections on Chapters 1–7: Essays on CWM Texts

The majority of essays in this volume attend to the texts of CWM songs. Overall, these essays point to both recurring strengths and weaknesses of song texts, along with some indications of promising developments that may over time mitigate some of the perceived weaknesses.

- In chapter 1, Lester Ruth observes that CWM songs are strong at creating a shared affective experience. He also points out that very few songs establish the kind of explicitly Trinitarian piety or approach to worship that best promises to ground and sustain a deep affective experience over time.
- In chapter 2, Jenell Williams Paris observes that many CWM songs have developed a language of intimacy in worship, but also that they over-rely on the American romantic ideal for conceptualizing the love of God.
- In chapter 3, Keith Drury reports on the mixed reviews of lyrics given by young singers of this music, with a particular concern for the response of young male worshipers. He reports on the positive responses to CWM lyrics by many, but also worries that the songs have privatized the imagery of intimacy and overly focused on the humanity of Jesus.
- In chapter 4, Jay Howard studies the lack of a social justice vision in CWM, observing the lack of a prophetic voice in the texts of this literature as a whole, despite a few notable exceptions to the general rule.
- In chapter 5, Wendy Porter concludes that CWM texts say little about human pain and suffering, giving support to Michael Card's recent conclusion that lament is indeed the "lost language" of contemporary Christians.
- In chapter 6, Robert Woods, Brian Walrath, and Diane Badzinski describe different functions of CWM texts and observe the relatively high and growing percentage of songs that function in a priestly mode to shape the prayers of the people before God. Indeed, a unique feature of CWM, regularly celebrated by its promoters, is that it not only invites people to sing *about* God but *to* God.
- In chapter 7, David Pass extends the theme set forth in chapter 6, analyzing the types of priestly prayers that these songs express. He observes a notable balance among expressions of petition, thanksgiving, praise, and adoration. He also establishes the significance of adoration or glorification of God, in which we are "totally absorbed by astonishment and boundless wonder," as a key strength of this literature.

Considering these essays together is especially important for readers of this volume. For example, Jenell Williams Paris's and Keith Drury's concerns about the overuse of romantic imagery may be another way of reinforcing Lester Ruth's concern about the lack of explicit Trinitarian language, in that when the language of love is used in an explicitly Trinitarian way, it tends to be far less likely that singers would confuse it with American romantic ideals. Moreover, Wendy Porter's concern about the lack of lament fits naturally with David Pass's affirmation of the strong emphasis on adoration in these texts. And Robert Woods, Brian Walrath, and Diane Badzinski's learning about the significance of priestly, prayer-oriented texts magnifies Jay Howard's worries about the lack of a prophetic voice in CWM texts. Overall, there is enough evidence here in the first seven chapters to feed the hunger of both CWM's critics and defenders, and I suspect that this volume will be used to support both cases.

A Pattern for Future Analysis

These essays also set a pattern for future work. Students could take the same 77 songs and analyze them in terms of any number of other theological themes or motifs:

- Which of God's divine attributes do they celebrate, and which do they leave out? Do they focus more on God's power than God's beauty, more on God's mercy than on God's justice—or is it the other way around?
- Which biblical images for the atonement do they refer to or imply, and which do they leave out? Do they focus on the cross as a sacrifice? A conquest? A ransom? An example?
- Which biblical metaphors for baptism or the Lord's Supper do the songs feature, and which do they leave out?
- Which biblical motifs about heaven and the afterlife do they depict? Which do they omit?

Nearly every major Christian doctrine could be a worthy subject for study.

In all of this theological analysis, it is crucial that we draw on the richest and most biblical of Christian theological traditions. Often the power and beauty of a given theological theme is found not simply in a single word or concept, but in the surprising ways scripture redefines that word. For example, Christian theology has long distinguished several attributes of God: God is loving, merciful, all-powerful, beautiful, wise, just, omnipresent, eternal, incomprehensible, infinite, invisible, and unchangeable or constant. The remarkable contribution of the best Christian thinking about the divine attributes, however, is not simply this list but the claim that in God's being all these attributes perfectly cohere. In contrast with human experience, in which we might be inclined, for example, to think of love and justice in tension with each other, that tension is not a part of divine life. In God's being, love and justice perfectly cohere in a way that forever redefines these terms and how we apply them to our descriptions of the human life. If this is the case, however, simply locating terminology about one or more of these attributes in the song list will be insufficient. We will also need to attend to the nuances of its presentations (as indeed several of our authors have done).

I think of the importance of nuance in light of a comment I once overheard from a parent reflecting on the experience of sending children to a camp where a number of CWM songs were sung: "I worry about my children singing all those Divine Rambo songs." Indeed, the biblical notion of divine power is hardly that of a raw-fisted "Divine Rambo God" eager to exert force over against creation. A more biblical understanding of divine power celebrates the unlimited capacity of God's power, but also notices the particular ways in which that power is expressed, including the remarkable self-sacrificial way it is expressed on the cross. As a result, analysis of this particular theological theme would—as only one example—require not only looking for references to divine power in the 77 songs but also examining the level of nuance in treating it.

The Implicit Balanced-Diet Thesis

A common, if implicit, assumption of each of the ten chapters is that our worship music should consist of a balanced diet of theological themes, images, and ideas, as well as emotions. This is an assumption that I wholeheartedly endorse.[1] We need to sing the whole gospel, the message of the whole Bible, the experience of every dimension of Christian living, not just the parts that most resonate with our own particular subculture.

At the same time, I would point out that the "spiritual dieticians" of the church's song—those who most worry about the church's balanced diet—have historically not been songwriters but instead those who edit published collections of songs, as well as those who choose music on a local level.

For traditional Protestant worship over the past century, published hymnals have been one of the church's primary ways of working to establish a balanced musical diet. Most hymnals are structured with sections on each major area of Christian doctrine and life, with sections on creation and providence, the life of Jesus, the work of the Spirit, the ministry of the church, and the life to come (though each hymnal organizes songs in different and often imaginative and theologically significant ways). Hymnal editors and selection committees then labor to present some songs in each area of Christian doctrine and life, instead of a *lot* of songs in *one* area.

But while hymnal editors usually generate a structure that holds them accountable to balance, contemporary song publications have only rarely done so. The vast majority of contemporary music publications offer songs that are mostly alike, with no attempt to sort them by theological themes or corresponding liturgical actions. The imbalance our authors have described is, I would suggest, one of the direct effects of the ways that songs are disseminated—primarily through the Internet, recordings, radio, and (mostly) homogenous printed musical collections.

At the same time, having a balanced published collection of songs does not ensure a balanced diet for a congregation—any more than having a balanced diet of choices in a local grocery store ensures that a given family will eat healthy food. The ultimate arbiters of a balanced diet of songs, themes, biblical teaching, and types of prayer are those who plan and lead worship in local congregations. It is very possible, for example, that a given local church might choose a majority of its songs (say 75% of them) from the list of 77 used in this volume, but that a pastorally alert song leader would instinctively realize that songs from this list need to be balanced by more songs of lament, social concern, and Trinitarian piety, and thus choose less well-known songs that address these themes to round out the congregation's diet. It is also possible that a wise pastor would instinctively realize the relative strengths and weaknesses of this literature and choose preaching themes to complement the strengths and mitigate the weaknesses of this body of music.

But note that I say only "it is possible." Further research would be needed to learn how common this is—research into the range and balance of music used in particular congregations over time. I have had several students who have done this on a limited basis. They frequently report discovering significant missing elements in their congregation's diet (e.g., "we have not sung a song of confession in a year," or "we have sung many songs about heaven, but none about the new heavens and new earth"). I suspect that widespread studies of congregational diets would feature the same kind of mixed reviews as the textual essays in chapters 1 through 7: There would be wonderful models of leaders who either instinctively or intentionally offer their congregations a balanced diet of themes, and there would be a significant number of congregations whose overall diet of theological and scriptural themes would be imbalanced in a pastorally significant way.

Reflections on Chapters 8–10: Essays on CWM Music

This volume also extends a conversation about the music of CWM, with much-needed attention to the rhythms, melodies, harmonies, and texture of these songs.

- In chapter 8, Bert Polman, in distinguishing praise and worship songs suited for soloistic performance from praise and worship suited for congregational singing, helps us articulate the experience that many of us have had of trying our best to sing along with a new song, confidently led by a worship team, only to find ourselves unable to sing because of some aspect of the song's rhythm, harmony, or structure.
- In chapter 9, Guy Jansen takes the brave step of evaluating the musical quality of our 77 songs. He walks us through a process of trying to make the implicit criteria we use to evaluate songs more explicit. Songwriters whose material has been questioned may be helped to know that Guy is a very amiable, encouraging, and generous person, whose comments in person always come with a generous twinkle in his eye!
- In chapter 10, Margaret Brady clarifies that CWM songs speak very different musical languages and arise out of different musical movements, songwriters, and social contexts. Just like sixteenth-century Lutheran chorales might feature remarkable stylistic differences depending on their author, composer, or city of origin, so too these 77 songs reflect the imprint of not only different songwriters but also of different recording companies and musical traditions.

The Theological Significance of Musical Form

One topic that is mentioned briefly in all three chapters in the second part of our book strikes me as especially important and worthy of further study. This is the topic of musical form, that is, the way a given piece of music is organized or structured. Students of classical music in the West spend a number of semesters of their college study learning to recognize various musical forms: concerto form, rondo form, theme and variations form, a passacaglia, and so forth. Music comes to us in a myriad of forms, and, most often, composers have worked within a well-established form. Their creativity, then, is expressed not primarily in coming up with a new outline or structure for a piece of music, but rather in how they work within an established form.

What is less often discussed is what each form *means*—or, to say it in a different way, what each form or musical structure is good at. Theme and variations form, for example, is especially good at giving a composer the opportunity to demonstrate creativity, while giving an audience the delightful experience of trying to listen for the main theme through (usually) an ever-growing complexity of harmony, countermelody, and rhythm as the variations on the main theme progress. Symphonic form rests on the assumption, now generally proven by modern psychologists, that we respond favorably to music we recognize. So after introducing a melody to its audience, symphonists take their audience on a journey through various subsidiary melodies and keys, all of which—in part—set up the return of the opening melody, inviting audiences to experience that familiar melody in new and compelling ways. The moment of recognition of the original melody is often a moment of significant musical satisfaction or surprise. Symphonies that do not achieve that satisfaction or surprise are often quickly forgotten.

Forms also matter in worship music. Repetitive Taizé choruses (music from the Taizé community in France that has been sung worldwide), as well as some CWM worship songs, are well suited to capturing an emotion and then helping worshipers dwell in or "center" on that feeling over time. In contrast, a ballad (whether a hymn or CWM song) is good at telling a story. A traditional four-stanza hymn, in turn, is effective at presenting the development of a theological idea, unpacking the beauty of a metaphor, or juxtaposing multiple ideas or metaphors in ways that create new meaning. Michael Hawn offers one of the best analyses of liturgical forms to date, unpacking the value of both *cyclical* and *sequential* musical forms for the life of faith.[2]

What is needed is further classification of various song forms of CWM, along with descriptions of particularly noteworthy examples of how the *musical* structure (not just the textual structure) of a song contributes to a song's meaning. Such an analysis may well help us understand why some songs simply do not work: perhaps they try to unpack a complex theological idea in a refrain form, or they try to help us dwell in a particular emotion in an overly complex structure. Also, as in formal studies of the music of Bach or Beethoven, this analysis may point to some delightful exceptions to the general rule, in ways that open up new ideas for songwriters.

To extend the "balanced-diet thesis" of the earlier section, I would suggest that one value worth pursuing for both songwriters and worship leaders would be to develop a balanced diet of musical forms in worship. The well-balanced Christian life is strengthened through intensely felt and shared experiences, well-told stories, and well-developed ideas. Likewise, it can be strengthened by music that pursues each of these three aspects. That, in turn, may call for using music with different structures. We need both cyclical and sequential musical forms in worship. When a music leader acquaintance of mine recently mentioned to me that she likes to choose three multiple-stanza hymns and three choruslike refrains for each worship service, she was expressing a kind of well-tuned pastoral instinct that affirmed this balanced-diet approach.

Note: I am not saying worshipers need to be aware of the musical forms of the songs they sing in worship, any more than they need to be aware of the particular homiletical theory espoused by the preacher they listen to. I am saying that formal or structural music analysis is yet another tool that can help those of us who write, choose, and lead music to better understand what we are doing as we lead people into mature Christian worship over time.

Complementary Areas of Study and Lines of Inquiry

The essays of this volume can be a catalyst for a great deal of future study and for rethinking the practice of both songwriting and worship leadership. But future work can also push beyond the topics addressed here into some largely uncharted territory. In what follows, I offer a brisk tour of multiple academic disciplines, each of which I believe has much to contribute in helping us better understand CWM. Mindful of the many students who are likely to use this volume, I will describe the diversity of approaches in terms of a tour from one classroom or academic discipline to another—though you certainly do not have to be a student to engage in these wide-ranging conversations.

Descriptions of Performance Practices

Let us begin in a music classroom, perhaps in a course on music in worship or perhaps in a general music analysis or musicology class. In addition to studies of musical scores (as in chapters 8–10), we also need insightful descriptive studies of "performance" practice. What happens when various congregations actually sing these songs? Consider a few of the questions an alert worship musicologist or music critic might ask about CWM:

- Are there contrasting and recognizable patterns or types of musical leadership that emerge among various kinds of congregations?
- When a musical score is unfriendly to a congregation, what do musicians instinctively do (or what could they do) to enable congregational participation?
- Are there performance practices that unwittingly undermine some of the strengths of a given musical form or genre, or mitigate various weaknesses? Performance practice can either heighten or obscure the connections of a given song to its secular counterparts. Musicians can make a rock song sound more folk-like, a country-and-western song sound like Black gospel (and vice versa), and a traditional hymn sound like a rock song. What patterns and meanings emerge from these kinds of crossover interpretations? What, to name only one fairly common example, are the pros and cons of singing *Lord, I Lift Your Name on High* to a Caribbean beat? What does that change in style do to its original cultural associations, and what do those cultural associations do to our worship?

- What is the effect of amplification and acoustics on these songs? For example, could it be that in designing a band-friendly worship space some architects make genuine congregational singing very difficult—the very kind of congregational singing that CWM may have been originally designed to promote?

Those who reflect on these questions will be acting a little bit like musical anthropologists, closely observing how the leadership of a song affects its meaning for a congregation.

Liturgical Context

From a music class, we move next to the worship classroom. A second pressing area to probe is the liturgical context in which these songs are used in actual worship services (and here I use the term "liturgical" to refer to all types and styles of worship services, for all types and styles of services take on some kind of shape or develop some set of expectations over time). In worship, as in other areas of artistic expression, context makes a big difference. For wedding rings, the setting in which we place a diamond is almost as important as the diamond itself. Similarly, a frame can make or break how we perceive a painting. The same is true for CWM.

At least two factors typically set the context for a CWM song in worship. The first are the worship leader's actions, words, and gestures that immediately precede or follow the song. Congregations can experience that very same song very differently if it is introduced one week with the words, "Here's a fun song to try," and the next week it is introduced with "We come before God in prayer as we sing. . . ." In fact, it may be that these "framing words" are the most important factor in whether a congregation experiences a song as *kerygma*, *koinonia*, or *leitourgia* (to use the categories of chapter 6).[3]

Relatedly, one of the most important results of the growth of CWM is the changing leadership structure for worship leadership that it frequently produces. When churches embrace CWM, they usually also embrace a praise or worship team in some form as a primary group of worship leaders. Often, the leaders of praise or worship teams are the ones who are also asked to direct the congregation through a significant portion of a worship service—in ways that choirs or organists never did. The "framing words" that they speak between songs gives them not just a musical but also a pastoral role that significantly shapes how the congregation will experience these songs.

The second part of what sets the context for a given song is the overall shape or form of worship. CWM actually serves as a primary musical genre in worship services with very different overall forms or structures. For example,

- In a Charismatic Anglican Eucharistic service or in a contemporary service at a Lutheran church, the majority of music may come from CWM, but the service will likely be structured according to the (similar) historic pattern of the *Book of Common Prayer* or the *Lutheran Book of Worship*, with its emphasis on scripture reading, preaching, communal prayers, and the Lord's Supper. Here the music functions to fill in what some observers have called the "soft spots of the liturgy," the transition points between preaching, prayer, and the Lord's Supper.

- In a charismatic temple-model service, CWM serves to lead a congregation on a journey from the outer courts of praise, through the gates of thanksgiving, eventually into the intimate worship of the holy of holies.[4] Here music is not merely filling the "soft spots" of the liturgy; it *is* the liturgy. It does not merely accompany the sacrament or ordinance; the music itself is perceived to be sacramental, the primary way that the congregation encounters God.

- In a Willow Creek–style seeker service, CWM may function primarily to create a comfortable bridge into the service rather than be intended to generate a direct encounter with God. Its goal may be to prepare those present for the teaching or preaching time, which will present the Christian gospel in a compelling way. In this service, CWM may well be used in a presentational, rather than a participatory, way.

- And then there are all sorts of combinations and hybrids of these services, including several of the most well-known examples of "Emerging" or "Emergent" worship. For example, two recent volumes of service plans suggest how to plan a coherent, flowing service of text, song, and prayer, using mostly CWM, but also drawing, in an intentional but unannounced way, on the historic structure of Western liturgy.[5]

Each of these service structures is based on a different theology of how we encounter God's presence. Each has a different sacramental sensibility. The historic Western pattern of worship is based on the notion that God meets us primarily through the reading and preaching of scripture and the celebration of the Lord's Supper. Charismatic services are based on a theology that asserts that we encounter God through Spirit-led prayer, which is often sung. Seeker services, like the revivals that preceded them, stress that we encounter God especially in conversion. Hybrid services draw on several of these theological motifs.

Each of these traditions is more complex than I can describe in this limited space. But the point remains: The structure of the service, and the implicit theology that this structure reflects, is a significant determining factor in how congregations experience the music of CWM. Future studies could helpfully describe how this plays out. How might worshipers in congregations with different liturgical patterns (different outlines to their worship service) describe their experience of the same piece of music?

Theology of Worship

"Theology of worship" is a topic for consideration not just in courses about worship, but in any broad course about theology.[6] "Theology of worship" refers to what worshipers think they are doing as they participate in worship and how that can be deepened and enriched by scriptural teaching. Nearly all theologies of worship assume that worship has something to do with an encounter between God and human beings. But theologies vary widely in how they picture or describe this encounter.

A particularly poor and unbiblical theology of worship might conceive of worship as an act of obeisance that we render to a divine tyrant, or as an act of manipulation through which we try to persuade a god to do something for us. (In the Old Testament, look at the worship of Baal for examples of these and other poor substitutes for Christ-centered worship.) In contrast, a biblical theology of worship might speak of worship as the renewal of promises that we make before God; as a means of grace through which God nourishes, challenges, and comforts us; and as a token or symbol of lifelong obedience, to work with only a few relevant biblical concepts.

On this point, two of the essays in this volume are particularly suggestive. Lester Ruth (chapter 1) is not merely calling for a lot of Trinitarian references in song. His concern is more fundamental: Do worshipers (including songwriters and leaders) conceptualize worship in Trinitarian terms? As they worship, do they conceive of God as one who simultaneously receives, prompts, and perfects our worship? Are they aware that genuine worship is impossible without the mediation of both Jesus and the Spirit?

Similarly, Keith Drury's chapter 3 not only probes gender differences in response to song texts. He also raises the fundamental question of whether worshipers think of themselves as expressing their own personal worship or as expressing the worship of the entire community. Are they primarily engaging in a private action, albeit surrounded by a group of other people, or are they engaged in a corporate action?[7]

In this area of the theology of worship, two further kinds of studies are needed. First, we need descriptive studies of the theology of worship implicit in much of CWM, and what theology of worship its advocates and songwriters actually work with. In addition to the songs themselves, one of the best sources for helping to understand better and then describe the theology of worship in CWM is the growing body of testimonial volumes by songwriters and producers, including books by songwriters and recording artists Matt Redman, Gerrit Gustafson, David Crowder, Darlene Zschech, and Louie Giglio.[8]

Second, we need continuing work that articulates in accessible ways the range of biblical images and motifs that can deepen how we conceive of faithful worship. Some of the best sources for thinking prescriptively about a biblical theology of worship are a growing number of books by pastors and theologians who are eager to help worshipers live in and imagine a biblical concept of worship more deeply.[9]

Central Metaphors of Historical Interpretation

From the worship or theology classroom, we move next to the history classroom to imagine how CWM might be analyzed in a course on the recent history of Christianity. A great deal of historical research is done not only in gathering data and artifacts but also in probing how best to tell the story of a given movement. Fortunately, we now have enough published histories of CWM that we can begin a conversation to compare and contrast the various ways we have of telling its story, the various metaphors we use to describe it. We can thus work on both history and historiography.

The introduction to this volume picks up on arguably the most frequent metaphor for describing the history of CWM, that of warfare. It is a metaphor that describes worship committee meetings of the 1980s or 1990s (and some still today) that fought over whether or not to sing the music analyzed in this volume. It is a metaphor that spins out related terms so that we have winners and losers, battles in the trenches, scars, and worship-related post-traumatic stress disorder. Yet while the war metaphor grabs the headlines, it also obscures much of the worship picture. For instance, it can easily suggest a greater degree of "conquest" than is the case. War is typically conceived of as a winner-take-all matter. Thankfully, the same is not the case in worship: All kinds of local ethnic musics remain and flourish in spite of the growth of CWM. Worship may be more like a river than a battle in that it does not end, and in that the primary tributaries that feed into it do not "conquer" other practices as much as they displace them at points of turbulence, only to find themselves swept into a broader stream that itself may experience turbulence when a new source is introduced.

Other ways of telling the story stress the possibilities for renewal found in this music. Robb Redman's *The Worship Awakening*, for example, gives us a morning-time metaphor that speaks of the joy and freshness that much of this material gives to many. He offers a balanced account of the recent worship movements, taking care to speak of both charismatic and liturgical renewal in a variety of traditions. Yet, while the "awakening" metaphor highlights enthusiasm for CWM, it also can too quickly dismiss everything that preceded it as, well, "sleepy." It can prevent us from seeing the vibrant world of gospel song (Black and White), classical hymnody, choral and organ music, and folk and ethnic music that shaped worship in the 1960s, 1950s, and before.[10]

Still other ways of telling the story either relegate CWM to a sidebar in their recent histories or refuse to make a judgment about CWM.[11] Thus, volumes with titles like *The Changing Face of Jewish and Christian Worship in North America* may have little if anything to say about CWM, a reminder that the church is very large and very complex and that the significance and assessment of a phenomenon depends a great deal on one's perspective.[12]

In assessing the best way to tell the history of CWM, one crucial method will be to situate it in terms of both a much larger history of worship music in North America[13] and a much larger social history of Christian worship.[14] These histories are each filled with charismatic song leaders, folk musics of local and national influence, influential economic forces, and controversies over propriety and taste. This history helps us appreciate both how remarkably influential CWM is and how it is not unprecedented. Also much needed are in-depth studies of a greater range of worship practices across Christian traditions, from journalistic accounts to academic monographs.[15] Attention to these in-depth studies in a range of traditions can work to pull us back from the precipice of unbridled optimism or pessimism about CWM and remind us of the importance of those who, in every time and place, took care to "test everything and hold fast to what is good."

Social-Cultural Location: Race, Ethnicity, Gender, and Generational Identity

We move next to a social science classroom, where CWM might be discussed by sociologists, psychologists, and economists. I would suspect that the first thing many sociologists would observe about this book is that it is nearly exclusively focused on Anglo worship traditions: the authors of the essays in this volume are all Anglo, as are—with only a few exceptions—the songwriters of the 77 songs. Yet CWM plays a fascinating, and barely understood, role in the vibrant cultural mosaic of North America. The following are only some of the questions that could be profitably asked in this area:

- What are influences between Black and White musical styles and genre? Are the same kinds of crossovers that were present in the secular side of pop music also present in the church?
- "Praise and Worship" is a major genre in discussions of Black worship practices. Does it mean the same thing in that context as it does in most Anglo contexts?[16] What are the unique contributions of Black songwriters to "praise and worship" music?
- What are the similarities and differences in the reception of CWM and hip-hop worship, which is a significant topic of recent discussion?[17]
- CWM has a particularly strong influence in the Korean community. What particular strengths and insights do Korean CWM leaders bring to this area?[18] What about its influence in other Asian and Asian-American communities?
- Some Latino and Hispanic worship music traditions resemble some of CWM, and some CWM songs have crossed over into Latino and Hispanic traditions.[19] What is the most accurate way to describe these relationships?
- What role does CWM play in promoting unity (or disunity) within and among multicultural congregations, in which people from different races and cultures worship together?[20]

A similar set of questions could be asked about the sociological dynamics of the generations. Much has been made in church growth literature about the differences of the Baby Boomers and Busters, of Gen X and Y. At some times, CWM has been presented as the musical tool for better engaging a Boomer or Buster audience. At other times, its use is universally recommended for all generations. This advice could helpfully be substantiated by more precise analysis of both the perceptions and spiritual needs of each generation.

- How has CWM been received by members of various generations? How does this differ from one part of the country to the next? From one denomination to the next? From one culture to the next?
- Further, how has CWM promoted or inhibited intergenerational community? How, for example, has this movement shaped the attitudes of the church toward its older members? And is CWM as popular in the newest generation of youth as it was for the generation that is now not quite so young?

Many of the same questions could also be asked about gender, about men's and women's experiences, perceptions, and contributions. For example,

- To extend the question Keith Drury's essay probes in chapter 3, how do men's and women's perceptions of this music differ?
- Why are there so few women songwriters in the group of 77?
- Are there differences among gender perceptions depending on the denominational or theological outlook of a given community?

Without asking questions about race, ethnicity, generational identity, and gender, it is altogether too easy to universalize one type of experience, to assume that the story of White, suburban, 20- or 30-somethings is the only story that needs to be told. All of this commends future work by social historians, sociologists of religion, developmental psychologists, and practical theologians. Both large-scale surveys of overarching trends[21] and in-depth ethnographic analyses of particular communities[22] have much to teach us about the complex ways that this literature shapes and is shaped by various social and cultural contexts.

This work represents more than just academic interest. Alert Christian leaders work best when they are immersed in the prayerful study of scripture and also deeply invested in sensing what is going on under the surface in their community. One pastor calls this loving attention to the social context of the congregation an "ethnographic disposition."[23] Asking questions like these can help pastors genuinely attend to the spiritual needs of their communities.

Economics

One of the obvious but largely unexplored areas for further questions in the CWM field is that of its economics.[24] Indeed the term "worship industry" is commonplace in North American Christian periodicals, though it is a befuddling concept for other Christians worldwide. The sales of at least 4 million albums a year generates upward of $50 million in income per year, in addition to the millions of dollars generated through royalties, the direct sale of music, and CWM-related conferences and festivals. Note that the data analyzed in this volume was compiled from a copyright license company (an entity generated by business interests), and one that engages a staggering 136,000 congregations in the United States alone. Some of the best primary sources to help us understand CWM may turn out to be stock reports and market analyses from major publishing companies.

All of these forces represent nothing less than an economic juggernaut. The income generated through all this activity and the expenditures of funds on advertising create a powerful economic force that inevitably lifts up certain songs and artists and sidelines others. When a worship-related company grows, its own spiritual and theological perspective becomes influential. When it falters, that spiritual and theological perspective may be hidden. There is great power in this economy—for both good and ill.

In raising this topic, it is important to remember that *every* approach to worship has its economic dimensions. The pipe organ industry, for example, is supported by the 20,000-member American Guild of Organists, an impressive array of pipe organ builders, professional journals, conferences, and advertisements.

Further, it is very important to maintain balance in thinking about economic issues. It is impossible, after all, to escape economic realities. (The influence of this very book is directly tied to advertising budgets and other market realities.) It is important to stress that the worship industry serves the church and individual Christians in profound and promising ways, making resources available to diverse audiences and encouraging talented young artists to hone their craft. Still, the scope and aggressive nature of worship-related marketing invites us to ask ourselves some tough questions:

- Does a market-driven industry tend to reinforce cultural preferences rather than challenge them? Does it over time reduce or enhance the "saltiness" of Christian witness (cf. Matthew 5:13)?
- What are the implications of having an economic market make celebrities out of worship leaders? Name recognition can be a very good thing, giving voice to people with pastorally significant or prophetic things to say. I think of Michael Card's timely and significant work on lament as one good example.[25] But might it distract us from the deeper virtues of worship? Celebritizing worship leaders (which can also happen with preachers, writers, and other religious figures) is at minimum a cause for concern. I, for one, am grateful for every album I find that is marketed not with a photograph of the artist (taken to resemble other celebrity photos in the entertainment industry) but with a description of its content.
- Does the "worship industry" create a skewed impression of Protestant worship life in North America? Suppose that CWM accounts for half the songs sung in Protestant congregations, but accounts for 80–90% of worship-related advertising. (These numbers are simply illustrative guesses.) Could that advertising create the impression that CWM is more widespread than it is and unwittingly lead to the marginalization of other ethnic music? Could the economics of the worship industry quietly work to erode the mosaic of ethnic musics in Protestant congregations over time?
- Could all of this suggest that when one worships well through producing good

music that one of the chief rewards will be financial? Does this industry create a culture in which leading worship in a congregation is seen as a "stepping stone" to the "higher" goal of becoming a recording artist? Could all of this unwittingly suggest that it takes money to worship well?[26]

- In spite of the protests of its advocates, might the close association of CWM with the entertainment industry cause some of the entertainment industry's values to creep over into worship? (Indeed, on the day I am finishing this essay, *Christianity Today.com* featured an announcement about the top worship albums of the year, prominently listed under the heading "Entertainment." The majority of North American students I know well would look at this and see no incongruity, while some international students I know are utterly perplexed by it.)

Once again, asking all these questions is not designed to take away the joy of a budding young songwriter who has just landed his first recording contract or the sense of calling that an advertising executive might sense about her work in a large Nashville music company. Rather, they are simply questions we need to continually ask ourselves in the Christian community in relation to every part of church life. Asking them is one way we keep our wits about us in the middle of a consumerist culture. They help us discern a way forward that truly serves to build up the Body of Christ.

Communication and Rhetoric

Our list of classrooms is growing: music, worship, theology, history, social sciences, and economics. Add to that also classes in communication and rhetoric. The CWM phenomenon represents a fascinating example of how communication works in our culture— both locally between worship leaders and worshipers, and more generally between the producers of songs and those who use them. The rhetoric of CWM subtly shapes our view of God, the world, and the nature of salvation in Christ, as well as the emotional landscape and community relationships that shape our lives. When experts in communication and rhetoric continue to think about CWM, a wide range of instructive questions may emerge:

- How has CWM interacted with technology? How is it explicitly or implicitly shaped by technological use?[27] More specifically, how have the many various approaches to presenting song texts (e.g., in print, projected in simple style, projected along with moving images) shaped the experience of the music?
- How has this music reflected or created a more oral culture in the church? Has CWM helped make worship more or less word-centered? More or less visual?
- What do the rhetorical and linguistic characteristics of CWM convey? How, for example, do we account for the persistence of so much archaic (King James) language in so-called contemporary music? Why do churches that remove visual symbols from worship spaces and simplify their message for seekers sometimes

sing music with very complex biblical metaphors? (I once attended a seeker-friendly service at which we sang the songs *Emmanuel* and *Lion of Judah*, songs whose metaphors were easily as obscure as the visual symbols and other elements of worship the leaders of the congregation worked so hard to explain or simplify.)

- How could we better understand the range of formal to more casual rhetoric through the CWM literature? Has CWM made worship language more or less metaphorical?
- Has CWM contributed to the growth or the diminishment of Christian virtues in communication?[28]
- How does the worship space shape the communicational dynamics of the worship event? What kind of participation does the space enable? How do the communication dynamics of the service change by moving around the furniture or changing the placement of the musicians?

Pastoral and Congregational Care

Finally, we move out of the social sciences and humanities into the classrooms of Christian ministry. How does CWM look through the eyes of those ministry specialists who do not focus primarily on music, but bring other central ministry-related questions to the front of their teaching and thinking?

One body of literature and academic subdiscipline that may be among the most important for students of CWM to explore is that of pastoral care. It might be said this way: Willow Creek has helpfully challenged all churches to rethink worship in light of evangelism. What is also needed is to rethink worship in light of the church's ministry of pastoral care.[29]

- Has CWM helped the church embrace persons with cognitive disabilities?[30]
- Especially in light of Wendy Porter's analysis in chapter 5, how has CWM changed funeral practices? How has it changed the church's response to natural disasters and national crises? Some churches that typically use CWM nearly exclusively revert back to hymns in times of grief or crisis. Others have revamped their approach to funerals and memorial services, singing praise and adoration even in context of grief and pain. What are the implications of this for pastoral care?[31]
- How has this changed the practice of the Lord's Supper? Has it helped make the Lord's Supper less penitential and more celebratory?
- How has this genre been received differently in churches of different sizes and cultural locations?[32] Does it reinforce the perception that large churches are "cutting edge" and thus culturally desirable in ways that undermine the ministries of smaller congregations? Does it tend to promote the idea that suburban rather than urban or rural congregations are paradigmatic examples of the ideal?

- How has this changed the church's position toward culture, as well as how people in the church perceive the church's position toward culture? While it arguably aids some churches in being relevant to culture, does it unwittingly dampen the church's countercultural stance?[33]

All of these questions drive toward assessing the local reality of a given congregation. And it is in local congregations where the multiple, sometimes contradictory, meanings of CWM (or any worship trend or phenomenon) need to be sorted out. In one congregation, the use of CWM may well represent the spiritual awakening of a congregation once caught in a spiritually deadening approach to worship. In another, it may represent the throwing away of a rich and vital tradition of multiple musical styles in favor of homogeneity. In one congregation it may allow young, creative musicians to participate in worship for the first time. In a congregation across the street, it may lead to the dismissal of a wise veteran musician. In one congregation, it may contribute to an evangelistic vitality, creating a climate of hospitality and openness to guests, seekers, and strangers. In another it may, in fact, narrow the range of ethnic and cultural streams of music featured in a given service, and thus unwittingly limit a congregation's multicultural hospitality.[34] (And sometimes, many of these things happen simultaneously within one congregation.) So much depends on the history, context, and community established in a local congregation. This explains, in part, why both the critics and fans of CWM find so many anecdotal experiences to confirm their point of view. It also explains why patient congregational studies are such an important dimension of both recent scholarship and training for ministry.[35]

Christian Education, Youth Ministry, Formation, and Spirituality

One of the most pervasive themes in recent writing about worship across the traditions centers around the metaphor of "formation." The basic idea is that worship not only expresses our faith and prayer in a particular moment, but steadily and quietly forms us over time to embrace certain views and practices.[36] In other words, worship is one of the spiritual disciplines through which the Holy Spirit works to form us into the image of Jesus.[37] This literature asks, for example, whether worship is forming a community to become more hospitable. It also thinks about how congregations form their children and youth not only to embrace Christian beliefs, but also to engage faithfully in Christian practices over time.

As one example, the topic of CWM and children's ministries raises a fascinating and constructive set of questions. CWM has contributed to the restructuring not only of congregational worship practices but also of congregational education programs and curricula. In many evangelical congregations, CWM has displaced older hymns in worship, and also traditional children's songs in educational ministry. The natural question here is *How adequate is CWM for forming children in faith?*[38] This question may generate very different answers in different contexts. In some congregations, CWM may have functioned to reduce the gap between children's programming and worship, thus enabling the participation of children in worship. At the same time, it may have displaced a body of songs that were (arguably) stronger at linking biblical stories with present experiences of faith. Children's ministries typically stress biblical literacy as a key goal, introducing children to many more Old Testament narratives than are typically featured in evangelical worship. (Think of how many full Old Testament stories have been central to the worship of your congregation.) Over time, curriculum specialists in many traditions have looked for songs that correspond with these narratives, finding them in existing bodies of music—African-American spirituals are especially strong in naming Old Testament narratives—and commissioning new compositions when necessary.

CWM, however, features very, very few references to specific biblical stories. We would have to search long and hard for a list of CWM that included references to Adam and Eve, Noah, Abraham and Sarah, Moses and Aaron, Deborah, Daniel, and Ezekiel. Now it would be very unfair to assume the CWM songwriters have tried to exclude these references. Still, one unwitting consequence of how this material has been used may be to subtly displace songs with more narrative specificity in at least some children's ministries.[39] If specific biblical narratives are crucial for forming the theological imagination of young children, as many have argued, then one important goal for CWM artists in the future might be to write music to fill in these gaps.

When moving from children's ministries to youth ministry, we enter an area of strength for CWM. Youth culture has, no doubt, been the driving force behind the growth of CWM. In many congregations, CWM has been introduced through youth ministries, "youth Sunday" worship services, and worship teams led by young people. In some contexts, CWM has changed the focus of youth ministry itself, suggesting to youth leaders the importance of leading youth ministries not only focused on service projects and fellowship events but also on common worship.[40]

At the same time, a good deal of recent work in youth ministry has explored how seemingly countercultural approaches may be most effective for genuinely helping today's youth. Mark Yaconelli, for example, calls for "contemplative youth ministry." Carol Lytch commends high-accountability, high-participation congregations as the most effective for helping youth establish identity, a sense of belonging, and genuine spiritual growth. Kenda Creasy Dean calls for youth ministry marked by passionate commitment to Christ and the church, as reflected through both intimacy and awe.[41] All three of these authors (as well as a variety of others) call for worship practices that are deeply engaging and theologically robust, and that do not pull back from any of life's most challenging questions. Youth ministers could profitably explore what kinds of music will be best suited to the kind of countercultural formation these authors describe. Should, for example, youth ministry seek out a greater number of songs that are more contemplative?

Beyond children's and youth ministries, spiritual formation extends into other areas of church life as well. Indeed, formation happens across the life cycle. It is especially important in ministries to seekers and new church members. There is never a time in which we are not being formed. The questions to probe are always *What is forming us? And is it adequate for forming us fully in the image of Christ?* These are the questions the CWM songwriters, worship leaders, and worshipers will need to continue to ask in the years to come.

This completes our tour of classrooms across the disciplines. Worship music majors in Christian colleges should be able to write papers on worship practices in many different courses! And those of us who are songwriters, pastors, worship industry executives, and other interested worshipers have many questions to ask as we explore new ways of "growing up in every way into Christ." Growing up into Christ often happens in powerful and compelling ways when we engage in some "cross-training" in the disciplines and areas of inquiry outside of our usual area of expertise. The twinkle in the eyes of our book's editors is there because they are raising more questions than they set out to answer. Some of these questions can be probed on the basis of the data analyzed here. Some will require other methods and questions, though they can helpfully begin here.

Next Steps

Based on these questions, I close now with a brief list of possible action steps for scholars, songwriters, and worship leaders.

A Call to Scholars and Students

1. Take worship music seriously as a subject for further study.

The phenomenon described in this book is culturally, economically, and spiritually significant. It is a topic worthy of more attention from thoughtful scholars in a range of disciplines. As this volume's introduction points out, we need voices in many different parts of the church that can continue to move us beyond the "raves and rants" that alternately laud and lambaste this material, and engage us in a more balanced and honest way. There is a particular opportunity here for faculty at Christian and church-related colleges, as well as seminaries and divinity schools, whose faculty and students bring to their work a deep interest in vital and faithful worship as well as the scholarly tools from a variety of disciplines to help us understand this phenomenon from many points of view.

2. Propose and refine complementary methods of study.

The interdisciplinary study of Christian worship is a relatively new subfield in most Christian traditions. It is almost brand new for evangelical Christians. Scholars have struggled for many years with exactly what methods best help us understand the eucharistic prayers of the early church or best help us understand the diversity of Protestant worship expressions.[42] Over time, methods are clarified and honed in ways that help students see more clearly what is going on under the surface in a given area of study. This book is a beginning point for attempts to study the contemporary worship phenomenon. Its particular strengths are inviting scholars to consider a range of examples, rather than relying on anecdotal experiences. Another strength is that it risks going beyond description of the phenomenon to making judgments about it. But much more work can be done across the disciplines to help us see deeply into what CWM means for living the faithful Christian life today.

3. Beware of the inevitable danger of studying worship.

The danger in studying worship is that once we start asking all the questions that I have posed above, we will never be able again to worship. Indeed, the effect of all this can be to leave us in a permanently analytic mode, never satisfied with the way things are.

Of course, this danger is not unique to worship leaders. Musicians or dancers sometimes suffer from not being able to enjoy a musical performance because their attention is constantly drawn to wrong notes. Butchers, bakers, and candlestick makers can suffer the fate of never being able to simply enjoy a dinner out because they have heightened awareness of how their cut of meat, dinner roll, or environment decorations may or may not meet certain standards. In the Body of Christ, we each take responsibility for asking questions about specific areas of interest, precisely in order to deepen the experience and enjoyment of others.

Further, asking questions about our area of expertise can also—as it might for the musician, dancer, butcher, baker, and candlestick maker—lead us to a deeper appreciation and joy of the best examples in our craft. The fine (if rare) examples of songs about the Trinity, justice, and pain noted in chapters 1 through 5 seem sweeter to us after reading these chapters. Another advantage of multidisciplinary inquiry is that we can discover many different ways to appreciate music. For example, some songs that at first seem musically weak appear to be much more nuanced and interesting after we learn about the social or cultural environment in which they were first written and sung. Often, interdisciplinary study has the effect of tempering our unconsidered judgments, both the positive and negative.

Still, it is wise for all of us who engage in constructive criticism of worship songs to learn to turn down our analytic mode, especially as we worship. Biologists who study butterflies in laboratories do well to step back from (or look through) their scientific precision as they enjoy a nature walk in a national park or read appreciative poetry about the beauty of butterflies. And those who engage with CWM do well to step back from (or look through) their analytical questions to enter, in a biblically childlike way, into the simple joy of God-centered worship.

A Call to Songwriters

1. Write songs to fill in the gaps in the literature.

There are many strategies of songwriting for worship. Many songwriters generate songs out of a desire to capture a powerful and immediate experience of prayer, thought, image, or melody that springs to mind in context of everyday life. Many of the testimonies about the writing of early Vineyard songs, for example, speak of this mode of songwriting.

Some songs emerge because a community commissions them. Songwriters may be approached to write a new song for a baptism, wedding, or church anniversary. In this case, the Bible texts or context of those celebrations contribute to the themes and musical gestures used in the song.

But other songs in the history of the church have been written when songwriters set out to fill the gaps of the church's literature. Some songwriters, for example, have taken the Psalms as their guide and prioritized the writing of musical settings of the Psalms that a given congregation or tradition did not yet sing. Other songwriters have purposely prioritized writing songs for particular occasions in the life of the church for which the church's repertoire was a bit thin.

This volume clearly suggests areas in which new texts and music are needed: songs about pain, songs of confession, and Trinitarian songs. The good news is that some of this work has already begun. Matt Redman's intentionality about Trinitarian texts comes to mind as a particularly important example. It is also very gratifying to see a recent wave of albums coming out on the Psalms.[43]

2. Write for congregations, not just praise teams or soloists.

As Bert Polman in chapter 8 has taught us, there is ample room for both the music of specialists and the song of the congregation. Each is an art to be cultivated.

But congregational song is a particularly challenging (and rewarding!) art that needs to be further cultivated. Writing music that can be sung well by people with no musical training and that addresses texts and themes of varying degrees of complexity is as challenging an artform as there is.

There is no simple prescription for learning this art. One place to begin is simply by listening carefully to how congregations sing and to what is going on when they really sing well. As you listen, peel away in your mind the sounds of your praise team (or, for that matter, your pipe organ), and really listen to how people are singing. Technically savvy leaders might actually record a worship service using separate tracks for the congregation and musical leadership so that each could be examined apart from the other. For many it will be revealing indeed to listen to the congregation's voice. Some of the congregations with the most impressive praise teams will actually have the poorest engagement in singing by the congregation. Others will be surprisingly strong.

Over time, you will notice which rhythms a congregation tends to adjust to subconsciously and which types of phrases constantly trip them up, as well as which kinds of musical and textual repetition energize a congregation and which kinds tire them.

3. Do not neglect the craft of songwriting.

So many areas of labor in God's creation invite us into a world of both spontaneity and craft. Architects generate imaginative ideas for new buildings through a flash of insight and then scrupulously compare their insights with other approaches and hone their ideas through multiple drafts of a building design. Engineers think of a new way to construct a bridge but then carefully calculate the strength of a given set of materials in order to ensure that the bridge will not collapse under stress.

The same possibilities for both spontaneous insight and artful craft are significant for songwriters, poets, and preachers. Some of the best sermons, songs, and prayers have emerged from people alert to both moves. A preacher carefully studies a text and prepares an outline, then receives a spontaneous and creative idea about reworking the approach, then analyzes the new approach to ensure that it speaks to all generations in the congregation, and then prays for a spontaneous energy in delivering it to a waiting congregation.

One challenge we have in church is that we have theologized about spontaneity, associating it with the Holy Spirit. We say things like "I'm glad that we did not plan that part of the worship service, so that the Spirit had some room to work." This is theology of the Holy Spirit that assumes that the Spirit mostly works in the "gaps." It can lead to the notion that the Spirit works *only* through spontaneity. But that hardly does justice to the breadth of the Spirit's work. The Holy Spirit is the one who formed order out of chaos in Genesis 1 and later set a crowd on fire for the gospel at Pentecost in Acts 2. The Holy Spirit inspired the spontaneous sermons of Peter and Paul in Acts, but also some highly refined acrostic poems in the Psalms (e.g., Psalm 34).

In CWM songwriting, I would propose, we need to celebrate the spontaneity but also hone the craft of songwriting.[44] We need to pray for the Holy Spirit to work in us through both modes of creative work.

Textwriters, when you come upon a key theme for which a song is needed, try your hand at writing three different texts to address the theme. Then ask which text has the best combination of both nuance and accessibility. Ask in which text people are likely to find the most meaning after singing it twenty times.[45] Then, keep your best song and set the others aside.

Songwriters, when you come upon a fine text for songwriting, try to produce three different melodies to which it could be set. Listen to real people try to sing them. Try them out for a period of time. Learn to recognize which kinds of musical gestures tire over time, and which ones cause congregations to trip up when they sing them.

One particular craft for textwriters is to relearn some lessons from Poetry 101. High school poetry classes teach students to analyze different patterns of syllabic stress. Two of the most common are *iambic* and *trochaic*. Iambic poetry alternates unaccented and accented syllables, beginning with an unaccented syllable (such as the line "how *sweet* the *name* of Je-sus *sounds*"). Trochaic poetry alternates accented and unaccented syllables, beginning with an accented syllable (such as the line *Hark!* The *her*-ald *an*-gels *sing*). Iambic poetry tends to work better for songs that are gentle, quiet, reflective, or even sweet. Troachic poetry tends to work better for texts that are strong, assertive, and confident. (These two particular examples demonstrate this!) To be sure, no one in the congregation has to be aware of what stress pattern they are singing. Nonetheless, the artful, creative songwriter can draw on this insight—and many others from Poetry 101—to shape and hone a song into something that better serves to reinforce a song's message.[46]

A Call to Worship Leaders and Pastors

1. Take seriously your role as the spiritual dietician for your congregation.

The primary contribution of this volume is its assumption that congregations need a balanced diet. Ultimately, the problem of an imbalanced spiritual diet of song texts is not the responsibility of songwriters, but of the people who choose music for particular congregations. If songwriters produce 100 new Trinitarian songs in response to Lester Ruth's chapter, it will do no good unless you choose to sing them. To get some perspective on our role as spiritual dieticians, consider the following facts.

First, most congregations—even the best singing among them—rarely know more than 200 songs very well (a number that includes Christmas carols, hymns like *Amazing Grace,* and children's songs like *Jesus Loves Me*). Many congregations barely know more than 50.

Second, we have access to a nearly limitless supply of worship Psalms, hymns, and spiritual songs. The total number would easily exceed 200,000, and most of us have ready access over the Internet to at least 20,000. This means that if you are a worship leader in a very good singing congregation, then you have the luxury of choosing the very best .01% of all worship songs for your church. You will (inevitably!) choose not to sing over 99% of these songs.

The numbers mean two things. First, our choices count a great deal. The limited capacities of our congregations mean that each choice we make is very important. Second, we have the luxury of being very, very picky. We have a lot of material from which to choose. That means that we never need to feel that we must settle for a second-rate text or piece of music. Given all the music available to us, finding music that is strong musically, textually, pastorally, and contextually is arguably easier than ever before, if only we are willing to work at it.[47]

2. Balance generally appropriate music with choices that specifically address the themes and texts of a given service.

In most churches where *We Bring a Sacrifice of Praise* is sung, for example, it is generally appropriate to the service. It is, after all, a song about worship, and it features a pervasive biblical image, that of "sacrifice." It is nearly impossible to think of a service in which that text would be inappropriate. But this same song would take on new significance in a service based on Hebrews 13:15, the scripture text on which it is based. In such a service, a congregation might experience that song very differently if it were chosen as the opening song of the service (in which case they might sing it pretty much like any other week) than if it were sung immediately following an insightful and inspiring expository sermon on Hebrews 13:15. Following the sermon, the congregation could sing the same text with much deeper appreciation.

I would like to suggest that in CWM there is an underuse of music that is specifically chosen to fit the text of the teaching or preaching of the day. Though it would take another article to defend this thesis more fully, I would further suggest that this is, in part, why so many CWM texts focus on the same themes, leaving so much of scripture uncovered.[48] Note that I am not suggesting that every song in worship needs to fit the theme of the service. I certainly do not want to have congregation members constantly asking themselves the question, *How does this song fit?* when they could instead be actually praying the song before them. What I am suggesting is that most services could benefit, particularly after the time of teaching or preaching, from a song that would probe the specific biblical theme more fully. And if worship leaders started looking for this kind of song on a weekly basis, that would, over time, create a powerful incentive (including an economic incentive) for songwriters to expand the textual and musical palette from which they work.

3. Address the weaknesses of your congregation while staying strong in areas of your congregation's giftedness.

This book has featured discussions of both the strengths and weaknesses of CWM's 77 most sung songs. They may be, on the whole, quite strong in expressing glorification or adoration and quite weak in expressing a longing for justice. That descriptive sentence may also fit many congregations. Whether that sentence describes your congregation, or whether the exact opposite would be more apt, one take-home lesson from a book like this is to resolve both to appreciate your congregation's strengths and to address its weaknesses.

Many reform movements in the church overcorrect for imbalances. Efforts to pursue justice unwittingly undermine private prayer. Efforts to pursue evangelistic effectiveness end up undermining the love and knowledge of Christian doctrine. It is healthier for us as the Body of Christ to pursue multiple strengths at the same time. The fruits of the Spirit, after all, are not given to us as a multiple-choice exercise. We need, then, to learn how to ask questions like *How can our worship stretch people both emotionally and cognitively? How can we continue to do what we are good at, while working at our areas of weakness?*

For those of you convicted by the essays in this volume, realize that it will take some time before songs are written to address some of the gaps identified here and some more time before the best of them become well-known and well-loved. In the meantime, think of ways that the themes addressed here—justice, pain, lament, the Trinity—can be reflected in your preaching or your choice of scripture readings. I could even imagine a provocative preaching series entitled "Important Christian Themes We Rarely Sing About." And as you address these concerns, do not neglect areas of prior strength!

A Call to Worshipers: Grow up in Every Way into Christ

Ultimately, however, the music studied in this volume becomes significant not primarily when it is studied or analyzed, but when it is sung and lived. Part of this happens when the notes and chords on a leadsheet become melodies and harmonies carried by the breath of the people who sing them in all sorts of real worshiping communities. And part of this happens when the songs are whistled and hummed as people in these communities wake up and go to sleep each day. Indeed, the songs of worship in any style take on some of their greatest significance when they become the soundtrack for the faithful Christian life.[49]

If this is so, then each of us can be helpfully challenged to consider how this music shapes our discipleship to Christ. One way to conceive of Christian discipleship is as prayerful cultivation of each of the fruits of the Spirit: love, joy, peace, patience, kindness, generosity, faithfulness, gentleness, and self-control. Each of us can ask how our musical lives, including the music through which we worship, is forming these fruits in us.[50]

Let me concede one fact: Academic analysis, and essays with lots of endnotes, tends to do better for self-control than for joy. Books like this are only one part of a Christian discipleship program. They are dependent on and derived from the actual singing, whistling, humming, and praying of the music they study. So while we have much to gain by asking deep questions and following up on intriguing endnotes, may it never keep us from singing the songs of God's people.

The wonder of the fruits of the Spirit is that each of these virtues is meant to fit together and enhance each other, so that, for example, love and joy may deepen patience and kindness, and generosity and self-control may foster faithfulness and gentleness. May God's Spirit attend each of you who have journeyed through this volume—singers, songwriters, worship leaders, pastors, teachers, scholars, and worshipers—so that through your efforts to "test all things and hold on to what is good" you will find not only new faithfulness and generosity in your work but also genuine peace and joy.

Notes

Introduction

1. George Barna, *Music and the Church: Relevance in Changing Culture* (Waco, Tex.: Baylor University, 2002), http://www.barna.org/FlexPage.aspx?Page=BarnaUpdate&BarnaUpdateID=126 (accessed August 7, 2005). "Describing the national research conducted by his company for the Billy Ray Hearn Symposium on Christian Music, held at Baylor University in Waco, Texas, Barna indicated that the coverage afforded the 'worship wars' has exaggerated the scope of the problem while ignoring the real issues regarding worship. 'The major challenge,' according to Barna, 'is not about how to use music to facilitate worship as much as it is to help people understand worship and have an intense passion to connect with God.' Citing various findings from three recent nationwide surveys he directed on the issue, Barna noted that relatively few churches have intense musical battles but most churches have too few people who truly engage God in worship."

2. Don Hustad, *Jubilate II: Church Music in Worship and Renewal* (Carol Stream, Ill.: Hope, 1993), 285.

3. Michael Hamilton, "The Triumph of the Praise Songs: How Guitars Beat out the Organ in the Worship Wars," *Christianity Today* 43.8 (1999): 28–35. Hamilton suggests that the main reason for "the recent avalanche of change in worship life generally, and in congregational singing particularly . . . [is] in fact part of a long trail of cultural dislocations left behind by that abnormally large generation of Americans we call the baby boomers" (30).

4. Jay Howard and John Streck, *The Apostles of Rock* (Lexington: University Press of Kentucky, 1999); see also Mark Allen Powell, *The Encyclopedia of Contemporary Christian Music* (Peabody, Mass.: Hendrickson, 2002).

5. John Frame, *Contemporary Worship Music: A Biblical Defense* (Philipsburg, N.J.: P&R, 1997), 9.

6. Robb Redman, *The Great Worship Awakening: Singing a New Song in the Postmodern Church* (San Francisco: Jossey-Bass, 2002).

7. Ibid.; see also Barry Liesch, *The New Worship* (Grand Rapids, Mich.: Baker, 2001).

8. Cornelius Plantinga, Jr., and Sue Rozeboom, *Discerning the Spirits: A Guide to Thinking About Christian Worship Today* (Grand Rapids, Mich.: Eerdmans, 2003); see also G. A. Pritchard, *Willow Creek Seeker Services: Evaluating a New Way of Doing Church* (Grand Rapids, Mich.: Baker, 1996).

9. See note 5 above, Frame, *Contemporary Worship Music*, 9. CWM as defined by Frame and compared with traditional hymnody (1) is far more contemporary and popular in its literary and musical idioms, rather than traditional or classical; (2) consists mostly of one-stanza choruses as opposed to multi-stanza poetry; (3) uses texts that tend to be far simpler than those of traditional hymnody; (4) places far more emphasis on praise (as opposed to lament, confession of sin, teaching, personal testimony, or supplication), though other aspects of worship are also present.

10. Ibid.

11. See note 1 above, Barna, *Music and the Church*.

12. S. Gonzalez, "Who Would Have Imagined?" *Decision* (2003): 14.

13. Christian Song Writing Organization, "Christian Music and the Market," http://christian songwriting.org/files/newsbig-5.htm (accessed June 2005).

14. Cross Rhythms, "Best Selling Worship," http://www.crossrhythms.co.uk/news/shownews.php?article=1686; Cross Rhythms, "Christian Music Bounces Back," http://www.crossrhythms.co.uk/news/shownews.php?article=1618.

15. Jack Hayford, *Worship His Majesty: How Praising the King of Kings Will Change Your Life* (Ventura, Calif.: Gospel Light, 2000).

16. See note 7 above, Liesch, *The New Worship*, 13.

17. See note 3 above, Hamilton, "The Triumph of the Praise Songs."

18. Dan Lucarini and John Blanchard, *Why I Left the Contemporary Christian Music Movement* (Auburn, Mass.: Evangelical, 2002).

19. See note 2 above, Hustad, *Jubilate II*; see also note 7 above, Liesch, *The New Worship*.

20. See note 5 above, Frame, *Contemporary Worship Music*.

21. See note 7 above, Liesch, *The New Worship*, 21.

22. Ibid.; Marva Dawn, *Reaching Out without Dumbing Down: A Theology of Worship for the Turn-of-the-Century Culture* (Grand Rapids, Mich.: Eerdmans, 1995). This transition is evident in hymns as well. A cursory review of hymns from the eighteenth, nineteenth, and twentieth centuries demonstrates clear movement from first person plural to first person singular. Lyrics move from "us" responding to a transcendent God to "me" relating intimately to and even invoking a personal Savior.

23. Raymond T. Gawronski, "Why Orthodox Catholics Look to Zen," *New Oxford Review* 60 (Jul–Aug 1993): 14.

24. Karin Dovring, "Quantitative Semantics in 18th-century Sweden," *Public Opinion Quarterly* 18.4 (Win 1954–1955): 389–94. An orthodox Lutheran clergyman, Kumblaeus, subjected the volume to an early form of quantitative analysis to summarize the theological content of the songs and to compare it with approved Lutheran emphases. The result was inconclusive, with one side saying there were doctrinal problems with the *Songs* because of a disproportionate emphasis on certain topics, while the other side countered by pointing out a similar imbalance in the content of State-approved hymnals. The application of this analytic technique was imprecise and flawed by modern standards, but it "is of interest not only because it anticipated certain trends in modern content analysis, but also because it suggests a method of study which may be applied to other historical situations" (394).

25. Two popular twenty-first-century reflections of American hymns include Paul Westermeyer, *Let Justice Sing: Hymnody and Justice* (Collegeville, Minn.: Liturgical, 2004); see also Richard Mouw and Mark Noll, *Wonderful Words of Life: Hymns in American Protestant History and Theology* (Grand Rapids, Mich.: Eerdmans, 2004). Others include David W. Stowe, *How Sweet the Sound: Music in the Spiritual Lives of Americans* (Cambridge, Mass.: Harvard University Press, 2004); see also Mark Noll and Edith Blumhofer, *Singing the Lord's Song in a Strange Land: Hymnody in the History of North American Protestantism* (Tuscaloosa: University of Alabama Press, 2004).

26. Don Cusic, *The Sound of Light: The History of Gospel and Christian Music* (Milwaukee, Wis.: Hal Leonard, 2002). See also note 4 above, Powell, *The Encyclopedia of Contemporary Christian Music*; and Megan Livengood and Connie Ledoux Book, "Watering Down Christianity? An Examination of the Use of Theological Words in Christian Music," *Journal of Media and Religion* 3.2 (2004): 119–29. Livengood and Book were responding to a 1999 *Wall Street Journal* article that accused the CCM industry of watering down its lyrics. The content analysis revealed that the theological words in CCM have indeed become significantly less explicitly Christian.

27. Lou Carlozo, "The Latest Craze," *CCM* (January 16, 2006): http://www.ccmmagazine.com/features/654.aspx?Page=1.

28. See note 6 above, Redman, *The Great Worship Awakening*; see note 26 above, Cusic, *The Sound of Light*; Robert Webber, *Enter His Courts with Praise* (Peabody, Mass.: Hendrickson, 1997).

29. Bert Polman, "The Praise and Worship Hit Parade," *Reformed Worship* 20 (1991): 33–35; see also Daniel Franforter, *Stones for Bread: A Critique of Contemporary Worship* (Louisville, Ky.:

Westminster John Knox, 2001); see also note 22 above, Dawn, *Reaching Out Without Dumbing Down*; Emily Brink, ed., *Authentic Worship in a Changing Culture* (Grand Rapids, Mich.: CRC Publications, 1997).

30. Michael Hamilton, T. Dearborn, and S. Coil, eds., *The Triumph of Praise Songs: How Guitars Beat Out the Organ in the Worship Wars* (Grand Rapids, Mich.: Baker, 2004). Several works have explored how to "blend" CWM with more traditional worship music, while others have traced its historical development in the context of traditional worship music. Lester Ruth, "Lex Amandi, Lex Orandi: The Trinity in the Most Used Contemporary Christian Worship Songs" (lecture, Yale Institute of Sacred Music, New Haven, Conn., Feb 24–27, 2005). Ruth's Trinitarian analysis of 72 of the most-used CWM songs between 1995 and 2004 was the first large-scale quantitative attempt to address past oversights.

31. Epistle Jerome, *22.29.6 The Letters of St. Jerome*, trans. Charles C. Mierow (Westminster, Md.: Newman, 1962); Johannes Quasten and Walter J. Burghardt, eds., *Ancient Christian Writers: The Works of the Father in Translation 33* (London: Longmans, Green, 1963), 165.

32. Augustine, "De Doctrina Christiana [On Christian Instruction]," in *Writings of Saint Augustine*, trans. John J. Gavigan (New York: CIMA, 1947), 2:3–235.

33. Miriam U. Chrisman, *Lay Culture, Learned Culture: Books and Social Change in Strasbourg, 1480–1599* (New Haven, Conn.: Yale University Press, 1982).

34. Quentin J. Schultze, *High Tech Worship: Using Presentational Technologies Wisely* (Grand Rapids, Mich.: Baker, 2004); see also Tex Sample, *The Spectacle of Worship in a Wired World: Electronic Culture and the Gathered People of God* (Nashville: Abingdon, 1998).

35. Christian Copyright Licensing International, "CCLI Company Profile," http://www.ccli.com/ CCLI/CompanyProfile.cfm (accessed January 3, 2005). See also, Christian Copyright Licensing International, "Number of License Holders Worldwide," http://www.ccli.com/CCLI/ LicenseHolders.cfm (accessed December 12, 2004).

36. We purchased denominational data from CCLI in 2004. Beginning in 1989, CCLI reported the number of different denominations seeking music licenses. They reported denominational data again in 1996 and then again in 2003. In 1989, 130 churches licensed music from CCLI. In 1996, nearly all of the same denominations were still licensing music from CCLI, with significant increases in the number of churches overall. In 2003, 136 denominations were licensing music from CCLI. Once again, the average number of churches licensing music within each denomination increased slightly.

37. Keith Miller, "Categorizing Christian Rock: Five Philosophies Used by Christian Musicians," *Evangel Society* (2003), http://www.evangelsociety.org/miller/musicphilosophy.html (accessed January 25, 2006), posits a model of content analysis by listing five content-based categories by which Christian artists could be selected for play on Christian radio stations. He briefly defines each of the following and gives examples: Worship Music, Exhortational Music, "Roaring Lambs" Music, Positive Music, and Negative Music. (These seem to be arranged in descending order from worship to witness to "positive" music to "negative" music.)

Chapter 1: How Great Is Our God

1. James B. Torrance, *Worship, Community and the Triune God of Grace* (Downers Grove, Ill.: InterVarsity, 1996), 9; see also Matt Redman, *Facedown* (Ventura: Regal, 2004), 52.

2. John D. Witvliet, "The Opening of Worship—Trinity," *A More Profound Alleluia: Theology and Worship in Harmony*, ed. Leanne Van Dyk (Grand Rapids, Mich.: Eerdmans, 2005), 3.

3. Robin Parry, *Worshipping Trinity: Coming Back to the Heart of Worship* (Paternoster, UK: Milton Keynes, 2005), 8.

4. CCLI neither endorses nor denies any conclusions I have drawn from the use of CCLI-obtained information.

5. To be fair to CWM, those who use this phrase are speaking of a wider phenomenon. See note 1 above, Torrance, *Worship, Community and the Triune God of Grace*, 20. Susan White speaks of the danger of "Jesus-centered Unitarianism" in worship today. Susan White, "What Ever Happened to the Father? The Jesus Heresy in Modern Worship," *Worship Today*, available from http://www.gbod.org/worship/white.pdf; Internet (accessed January 14, 2005).

6. See note 3 above, Parry, *Worshipping Trinity*, 17–66. See how Parry explores the Trinitarian "geography" of the biblical story and Christian life; and (see note 2 above) Witvliet, "The Opening of Worship—Trinity," in *A More Profound Alleluia: Theology and Worship in Harmony*, 3–20 for the Trinitarian "grammar" of biblical remembrance in worship.

7. See note 3 above, Parry, *Worshipping Trinity*, 133, 141.

8. I found background data on 44 songs. Three books provided information on 35 of the 77 songs: Terry Lindsay, *The Sacrifice of Praise: Stories Behind the Greatest Praise and Worship Songs of All Time* (Brentwood, Tenn.: Integrity, 2002); see also Phil Christensen and Shari MacDonald, *Our God Reigns: The Stories Behind Your Favorite Praise and Worship Songs* (Grand Rapids, Mich.: Kregel, 2000) and their *Celebrate Jesus: The Stories Behind Your Favorite Praise and Worship Songs* (Grand Rapids, Mich.: Kregel, 2003). Issues of the magazine *Worship Leader* provided background information on 9 more songs.

9. Paul Baloche, Jimmy Owens, and Carol Owens, *God Songs: How to Write and Select Songs for Worship* (Lindale: leadworship.com, 2004), 48, 60.

10. Ibid., 80.

11. Graham Kendrick, "Worship in Spirit and in Truth," in *Composing Music for Worship*, ed. Stephen Darlington and Alan Kreider (Norwich: Canterbury, 2003), 97, 88.

12. See note 8 above, Christensen and MacDonald, *Our God Reigns*, 68.

13. Exceptions include Henry Smith (*Give Thanks*), Leonard Smith (*Our God Reigns*), David Ruis (*You're Worthy of My Praise*), Billy Foote (*You Are My King*), and pastor Jack Hayford (*Majesty*).

14. Robb Redman, *The Great Worship Awakening: Singing a New Song in the Postmodern Church* (San Francisco: Jossey-Bass, 2002), 55–67. The foremost companies include Integrity Music, WorshipTogether, the Vineyard Music Group, and Maranatha! Music.

15. Craig Dunnagan (Vice President, Music Publishing and Church Resources, Integrity Music), quoted in Baloche et al., *God Songs: How to Write and Select Songs for Worship*, 204.

16. See note 1 above, Redman, *Facedown*. He offers a caveat that these concerns do not apply equally to all CWM promoters, but even a little of this perspective is enough to marginalize Trinitarian concerns.

17. Darrell A. Harris (former owner of Star Song Records), in discussion with the author, July 2004.

18. Judson Cornwall, *Let Us Worship* (South Plainfield, N.J.: Bridge, 1983), 153–58, and see also David K. Blomgren et al., eds., *Restoring Praise and Worship to the Church* (Shippensburg, Pa.: Revival, 1999).

19. C. Michael Hawn, *Gather into One: Praying and Singing Globally* (Grand Rapids, Mich.: Eerdmans, 2003), 233.

20. Tex Sample, *The Spectacle of Worship in a Wired World: Electronic Culture and the Gathered People of God* (Nashville: Abingdon, 1998), 35. While no detailed study on this point has been undertaken to my knowledge, the emphasis on tempo (beat) in CWM selection hints at the accuracy of his suggestion.

21. Paul Baloche, for example, has songs based on 1 Peter 1:3-4 (*Praise Be to the God and Father*) and John 14:1-3 (*Let Not Your Heart Be Troubled*). Twila Paris has an adaptation of Charles Wesley's hymn contemplating Christ's ongoing priestly ministry before the Father, *Arise, My Soul, Arise*.

22. See note 11 above, Graham Kendrick, "Worship in Spirit and in Truth," 92, 10; David Di Sabatino, "Table Talk: An Interview with Graham Kendrick," *Worship Leader* 10.7 (Nov/Dec 2001):

30. For Redman, see note 1 above, *Facedown*; see note 3 above, Parry, *Worshipping Trinity*, xi; and see note 9 above, Baloche et al., *God Songs*, 215–16.

23. See note 1 above, Redman, *Facedown*, 52.

24. Robert E. Webber, "Is Our Worship Adequately Triune?" *Reformation and Revival Journal* 9.3 (Summer 2000): 121–32; see also Brian McLaren, "An Open Letter to Songwriters," *Worship Leader* 10.1 (Jan/Feb 2001): 44–45; see also Bert Waggoner, "Leading Trinitarian Worship," *Inside Worship* 52 (Feb 2004): 5–6.

25. Brian Doerksen, "Song Writing," in *Songwriting for Worship: Study Tools for the DVD* [CD], Equip Resources for Worship series (Anaheim, Calif.: Vineyard Music Global, 2004).

Chapter 2: I Could Sing of Your Love Forever

1. A. Arnold's personal Web log, "Red Fire Hydrant," http://theredfirehydrant.wearvirtue.com /blog/theology/jesus_is_my_boyfriend_whoaoh.html (accessed Sept 1, 2006); Church for Men, "Church for Men," www.churchformen.com (accessed Feb 28, 2006); see also David Murrow, *Why Men Hate Going to Church* (Nashville: Thomas Nelson, 2005).

2. Leila L. Bronner, *Stories of Biblical Mothers: Maternal Power in the Hebrew Bible* (New York: University Press of America, 2004).

3. C. S. Lewis, *The Four Loves* (New York: Harcourt, Brace, 1960). See also, Leon Morris, *Testaments of Love: A Study of Love in the Bible* (Grand Rapids, Mich.: Eerdmans, 1981).

4. Ann Swidler, *Talk of Love: How Culture Matters* (Chicago: University of Chicago Press, 2003), 129.

5. Stephen Mitchell, *Can Love Last? The Fate of Romance over Time* (New York: Norton, 2002), 27.

6. John Lofland and Lyn Lofland, *Analyzing Social Settings: A Guide to Qualitative Observation and Analysis*, 3rd ed. (Belmont, Calif.: Wadsworth, 1995).

7. The lyrics of *How Can We Name a Love* were revised in 1987, 1994: "Verse 1: How can we name a love that wakens heart and mind, indwelling all we know or think or do or seek or find? Within our daily world, in every human face, Love's echoes sound and god is found, hid in the commonplace. Verse 2: If we awoke to life upheld by loving care that asked no great reward but firm, assured, was simply there, we can, with parents' names, describe, and thus adore, love unconfined, our Father kind, our Mother strong and sure. Verse 3: When people share a task, and strength and skills unite in projects old or new, to make or do with shared delight, our Friend and Partner's will is better understood, that all should share, create, and care, and know that life is good. Verse 4: So in a hundred names, each day we all can meet a presence, sensed and shown at work, at home, or in the street. Yet names and titles all shine in a brighter sun: In Christ alone is love full grown and life and hope begun." Printed with permission. © 1975, 1995 Hope Publishing Company for the USA.

Chapter 3: I'm Desperate for You

1. Teresa Berger, *Women's Ways of Worship: Gender Analysis and Liturgical History* (Collegeville, Minn.: Liturgical, 1999).

2. Karl Barth, *Dogmatics in Outline* (New York: Harper and Bros., 1959).

3. Warner Sallman (painter), *Head of Christ*, 1941, available from www.warnersallman.com.

4. Richard and Frances Hook (painters), *Head of Christ*, 1941, available from www.online.nph.net/ images/products/235009.gif.

5. Frances Hook (painter), *Smiling Christ*, available from www.picturesofjesus4you.com/images/ smiling_christ_hook_l.jpg.

6. Ralph Kovac (painter), *Laughing Jesus*, available from www.laughingjesus.com.

7. Steve Sawyer (painter), *Undefeated*, available from www.art4god.com.

8. Be Mine, *Valentine*, EP compact disc, 2006.

9. Indiana Wesleyan University, *Factbook*, 2005–2006 edition.

10. David Skaggs and Anthony Adam, "Winning with Young Voters," in *Campaigns and Elections* (Washington, D.C.: The Pew Charitable Trusts, 2002).

Chapter 4: Let the Weak Say I Am Strong

1. Howard Snyder, *Liberating the Church: The Ecology of Church and Kingdom* (Downers Grove, Ill.: InterVarsity, 1983), 85.

2. Richard Foster, *Celebration of Discipline: The Path to Spiritual Growth*, 25th ed. (San Francisco: HarperCollins, 1978), 160.

3. John Yoder, *The Politics of Jesus* (Grand Rapids, Mich.: Eerdmans, 1972), 35.

4. Andy Crouch, "Salt-and-Pepper Politics: Choosing between Candidates Whose Consciences Are Too Clean," *Christianity Today* 48.10 (2004): 108.

5. Ruth Foster, "Dangerous Waters of Justice and Righteousness," *Christian Ethics Today*, available from http://www.christianethicstoday.com/Issue/024/Issue_024_October_1999.htm (accessed July 19, 2006); see also Brian Edgar, "Biblical Justice," *Evangelical Alliance*, http://www.evangelicalalliance .org.au/commissions/theological/articles/biblicaljustice.php (accessed July 19, 2006).

6. See note 4 above, Crouch, "Salt-and-Pepper Politics," 108.

7. Ibid.

8. Paul Westermeyer, *Let Justice Sing: Hymnody and Justice* (Collegeville, Minn.: Liturgical, 1998), 9.

9. Ibid., 25–26.

10. Ibid., 48.

11. See note 1 above, Snyder, *Liberating the Church*, 82.

12. See for example the discussion of early arguments in opposition to contemporary Christian music in Jay Howard and John Streck, *Apostles of Rock: The Splintered World of Contemporary Christian Music* (Lexington: University Press of Kentucky, 1999).

13. Charles Colson, "Slouching into Sloth," *Christianity Today* (2001): 120; see also Charles Colson and Anne Morse, "Soothing Ourselves to Death," *Christianity Today* (2006): 116.

14. Ronald Sider, ed., *For They Shall Be Fed: Scripture Readings and Prayers for a Just World* (Dallas: Word, 1997), x.

15. Jim Wallis, *God's Politics: Why the Right Gets It Wrong and the Left Doesn't Get It* (San Francisco: Harper, 2005), 212.

16. A. W. Tozer, *Whatever Happened to Worship?* (Camp Hill, Pa.: Christian Publications, 1985), 42.

17. See note 1 above, Snyder, *Liberating the Church*, 156.

18. Richard Foster, *Streams of Living Water: Celebrating the Great Traditions of Christian Faith* (San Francisco: Harper, 1998), 151.

19. See note 5 above, Edgar, "Biblical Justice."

20. Christian Copyright Licensing International, "CCLI's Global Site: Encouraging the Spirit of Worship," http://www.ccli.com (accessed May 22, 2006).

21. Mark Noll, *The Scandal of the Evangelical Mind* (Grand Rapids, Mich.: Eerdmans, 1994), 165.

22. Ibid., 54.

23. Shortly after the election George Barna credited the strong turnout of religiously motivated "values voters" with giving George W. Bush a second term in office. The survey revealed that while born-again believers constitute only 38% of the national population, they accounted for 53% of the voters. Born-again Christians supported Bush by a 62% to 38% margin. Evangelicals (a subcategory of the "born again" in Barna's research) chose Bush by an 85% to 15% margin. George Barna, "Born Again Christians Were a Significant Factor in President Bush's Re-Election," *The Barna Update*,

November 9, 2004, http://www.barna.org/FlexPage.aspx?Page=BarnaUpdateNarrow&Barna
UpdateID=174.

The American Religious Identification Survey, Barry Kosmin, Egon Mayer, and
Ariela Keysar, *American Religious Identification Survey* (2001), http://www.gc.cuny.
edu/faculty/research_briefs/aris/aris_index.htm (accessed July 31, 2006), showed 58% of Evangelical/
born-again respondents as preferring the Republican Party compared to only 12% preferring the
Democratic Party.

24. George Barna, "Born Again Adults Remain Firm in Opposition to Abortion and Gay
Marriage," *The Barna Update*, July 23, 2001, http://www.barna.org/FlexPage.aspx?Page=Barna
Update&BarnaUpdateID=94. See also George Barna, "The Year's Most Intriguing Findings from
Barna Research Studies," *The Barna Update*, December 12, 2000, http://www.barna.org/
FlexPage.aspx?Page=BarnaUpdate&BarnaUpdateID=103.

Chapter 5: Trading My Sorrows

1. C. S. Lewis, *The Problem of Pain* (New York: Macmillan, 1962), 26.

2. Michael Card, *A Sacred Sorrow: Reaching Out to God in the Lost Language of Lament* (Colorado
Springs: NavPress, 2005).

3. C. S. Lewis, *Reflections on the Psalms* (New York: Harcourt, Brace & World, 1958); see also
Walter Brueggemann, *Praying the Psalms* (Winona, Minn.: Saint Mary's Press, 1982), 20, on "disori-
entation" and "orientation" as the driving power of the Psalms.

4. Walter Brueggemann, *The Message of the Psalms: A Theological Commentary* (Minneapolis,
Minn.: Augsburg, 1984), 169, on getting a "fair deal" from God.

5. For a number of easily accessible websites that discuss definitions of pain and suffering, see the
following: http://www.answers.com/topic/suffering; http://www.answers.com/topic/pain-and-suffering;
http://dictionary.laborlawtalk.com/suffering; http://dictionary.laborlawtalk.com/pain; http://legal-
dictionary.thefreedictionary.com/pain+and+suffering.

6. This is a discussion that would merit further attention and could benefit greatly from the
involvement of theologians and pastors who are interested in how the musical expression of pain and
suffering plays a formative role in our corporate worship, regardless of whether they themselves are
musicians or not.

7. Older excellent words could be set to new music, but this is not always legally possible. If the
music is not conducive to congregational singing, good words will not redeem it.

8. A current example of this is Robin Mark's use of the hymn, *I Will Sing the Wondrous Story*, in
contemporary worship gatherings. Some North American hymnals print these hymn lyrics with the
tune written by Peter P. Bilhorn, 1865–1936, so this has become the "normal" tune for many churchgoers who have used these hymnals. To hear this tune (Tune 1), go to http://www.cyberhymnal.
org/htm/i/w/iwilsing.htm. However, Mark uses the alternate melody, known as HYFRYDOL
(Rowland H. Prichard, 1811–1887). This tune is often printed with the hymn lyrics of *Jesus, What a
Friend for Sinners* (words by J. Wilbur Chapman, 1859–1918). To hear this tune (Tune 2), go to
http://www.cyberhymnal.org/htm/a/s/asingtoj.htm. Mark's use of Tune 2 makes it sound fresh to those
more familiar with Tune 1, and Tune 2 is also more worship band–friendly (e.g., the chord structure
works well on guitar), as well as having a melody that falls on contemporary ears as more current. To
hear a sample of Robin Mark using Tune 2, go to http://dbmedia.crossrhythms.co.uk/audio/mp3/
236-4.mp3.

9. Contemporary worship songwriters with a gift for writing lyrics do not always have an equal gift
for writing a melody that is intuitively singable. An interesting possible future study would be, for
example, to compare the tunefulness or singability of melodies written by vocalists, pianists, and gui-
tarists to see if there is a discernible difference.

10. It is not possible here to demonstrate how the music and lyrics fit together in a meaningful way. This is something I would do in a seminar or workshop for worship teams and interested laypeople. It is best explored in a live setting with musical demonstration.

11. It should be noted here, however, that there are numerous songs that are not on the CCLI list that are excellent examples. One example would be Tim Hughes, *When the Tears Fall* [Tim Hughes © 2003 Thankyou Music], included on his recording, *When Silence Falls* [2004 Worship Together].

Chapter 6: We Have Come into His House

1. Harold Best, "Church Music Curriculum" (Proceedings of the 57th Annual Meeting. National Association of Schools of Music, Dallas, Texas, 1982), 137–38.

2. Barry Liesch, *The New Worship: Straight Talk on Music and the Church*, ext. ed. (Grand Rapids, Mich.: Baker, 2001), 161.

3. To support this model, David Pass presents a survey of 10 major theologians, including but not limited to Dulles, Gelineau, Wesley, and Moody. Pass, *Music and the Church: A Theology of Church Music*, 2nd ed. (South Africa: Password International, 2005), 75–80.

4. David Pass, *Music and the Church: A Theology of Church Music* (Nashville: Broadman, 1989), 128.

5. R. C. H. Lenski, *The Interpretation of the Acts of the Apostles* (Minneapolis, Minn.: Augsburg, 1934), 117.

6. Dietrich Bonhoeffer, *The Cost of Discipleship* (London: SCM, 1959), 224.

7. Ibid.

8. Karl Barth describes several ministries of the church: preaching, teaching, evangelism, mission, theology, and prophetic action. These activities can easily be subsumed under the *kerygmatic* mode of proclaiming the gospel. Barth, *Church Dogmatic* (Edinburgh: T & T Clark, 1962), 4.3:867, 870, 872, 874, 879, 895.

9. Gerhard Friedrich, *Theological Dictionary of the New Testament*, ed. G. Kittel (Grand Rapids, Mich.: Eerdmans, 1965), 3:703.

10. The fellowship described in Acts 2:42 denotes "the unanimity and unity brought about by the Spirit. The individual was completely upheld by the community." J. Schattenman, "Fellowship," in *New International Dictionary of New Testament Theology*, ed. C. Brown (Grand Rapids, Mich.: Zondervan, 1975), 1:642.

11. See note 2 above, Liesch, *The New Worship*, 167.

12. Craig Douglas Erickson, *Participating in Worship: History, Theory and Practice* (Louisville, Ky.: Westminster, 1989), 36–37.

13. Theodore Jennings, *Life as Worship* (Grand Rapids, Mich.: Eerdmans, 1982), 11. Note that *leitourgia* is also alluded to by the phrase "breaking of bread," especially for those in the traditional liturgical traditions where Communion is a sacramental act of corporate worship.

14. Joseph Gelineau, "Music and Singing in the Liturgy," in *The Study of Liturgy*, ed. C. Jones Wainwright and E. Yarnold (London: S.P.C.K., 1978), 443.

15. See note 3 above, Pass, *Music and the Church*, 76.

16. See note 6 above, Bonhoeffer, *The Cost of Discipleship*, 224.

17. Sally Morgenthaler, *Worship Evangelism: Inviting Unbelievers into the Presence of God* (Grand Rapids, Mich.: Zondervan, 1999).

18. Marva Dawn, *Reaching Out without Dumbing Down: A Theology of Worship for the Turn-of-the-Century Culture* (Grand Rapids, Mich.: Eerdmans, 1995).

19. In stage 1, there were 69/81 agreements (85%) on the number of thought-units in all 8 songs. So, for song 1, for example, coder 1 said there were 12 thought-units and coder 2 said 14 thought-units. In stage 2, coders determined individually into which category each thought-unit belonged. Of the 81 thought-units from stage 1, they had 76/81 agreements (93%).

20. See note 17 above, Morgenthaler, *Worship Evangelism*. See also James F. White, *Protestant Worship* (Louisville, Ky.: John Knox, 1989).

21. Keith Drury, *The Wonder of Worship: Why We Worship the Way We Do* (Indianapolis, Ind.: Wesleyan Publishing House, 2002), 232.

22. John C. LaRue, Jr., "Worship Music Trends," *Christianity Today*, August 2004, http://www.christianitytoday.com/yc/2004/004/7.64.html. In 2004, LaRue, vice president of Internet research and development at *Christianity Today* International, published a special report on the status of three different styles of worship services. In each of the studies (1993, 1996, 1999, 2001, and 2004), *Your Church* mailed approximately 1,000 surveys to a random selection of U.S. churches. Previous studies had an average response rate of 38%. The current study had a response rate of 16%, yielding a margin of error of 8%. ARIS and Barna Group, "Largest Denominational Families in the US, 2001," http://www.adherents.com/rel_USA.html#attendance.

23. We purchased denominational data from CCLI as part of this project. Approximately every 10 years, CCLI reports the number of denominations subscribing to its services. The list we purchased reported denominational totals for 1989, 1996, and 2003.

24. Between 1990 and 2000 socially conservative denominations grew faster than others, and mainline Protestant churches continued to decline. After the Mormons, the fastest-growing of the 17 large religious groups (those claiming more than a million adherents) were the Christian Churches/Churches of Christ and the Assemblies of God (the largest Pentecostal denomination). At the same time there was a steep decline in membership in the Presbyterian Church (USA), the United Church of Christ, and The United Methodist Church. Jane Lampman, "Charting America's Religious Landscape," *The Christian Science Monitor*, October 10, 2002, http://www.csmonitor.com/2002/1010/p12s01-lire.html.

25. John Hayes, "African-American Baptists," *New Georgia Encyclopedia*, July 14, 2006, http://www.georgiaencyclopedia.org/nge/Article.jsp?id=h-1543. "The sermon is the centerpiece of the worship service, and the minister's central task is to preach the Word, or Gospel message of Jesus Christ, which calls for a distinctly individual, inward response. In keeping with this requirement, Baptist churches receive an individual member only when that person has made a commitment of faith in his or her own right." See also Keith Drury, "Kinds of Worship Services," *Read My Mail*, February 2003, http://www.drurywriting.com/keith/Read_My_Mail_kinds_worship.htm. "By far the fastest growing and most popular format of worship today in North America is a charismatic style. Charismatic worship is designed for the worshipper to *experience* God—to come to church and meet God, feel His presence, hear from Him and 'connect' with the Holy Spirit and each other."

26. Hans Urs von Balthasar, "The Grandeur of the Liturgy," *Communio* 4.4 (Winter 1978): 347.

27. Joseph Gelineau, *The Liturgy Today and Tomorrow* (London: Darton, Longman & Todd, 1978), 51.

28. Monte Wilson, "Church-o-rama or Corporate Worship," in *The Compromised Church: The Present Evangelical Crisis*, ed. John H. Armstrong (Wheaton: Crossway, 1998). "I am saying that although the apostolic and primitive church emphasized worship as an act of obedience, we see it solely as an experience. Why? Because 'church is for me. Sunday worship is to be centered on *my* needs and desires. Never mind what the Father desires and commands. I am at the center. MY needs are paramount. Meet them or I'll go to church elsewhere.' The ego reigns supreme" (68).

29. See George Barna, *Revolution* (Wheaton, Ill.: Tyndale House, 2005).

30. John 1:14. "And the Word became flesh and lived among us."

31. Isaiah 6:1-5; 55:8-9; John 8:23.

Chapter 7: The Heart of Worship

1. David Barrett and T. M. Johnson, "Global Statistics," in *The New International Dictionary of Pentecostal and Charismatic Movements*, ed. by Stanley Burgess and E. M. Van Der Maas (Grand Rapids, Mich.: Zondervan, 2002), 284.

2. John Frame, *Contemporary Worship Music: A Biblical Defense* (Philipsburg, N.J.: P&R, 1997), 81. "CWM [Contemporary Worship Music] originated in a particular historical context of revival. It is not the product of someone's strategy to make worship more contemporary." See also note 5 on p. 9 where Frame explicity notes the charismatic movement as one of the "tributaries" of praise and worship songs. Other evangelical scholars who place the origins of praise and worship music in the charismatic movement include the following: Paul Basden, *The Worship Maze: Finding a Style to Fit Your Church* (Downers Grove, Ill.: InterVarsity, 1999), 76–87; Don Hustad, *Jubilate II* (Carol Stream, Ill.: Hope, 1993), 285; Don Hustad, *True Worship* (Wheaton: Harold Shaw, 1998), 43; Robb Redman, *The Great Worship Awakening* (San Francisco: Jossey-Bass, 2002), 48.

3. Peter Hocken, "Charismatic Movement," in *The New International Dictionary of Pentecostal and Charismatic Movements*, ed. Stanley Burgess and E. M. Van Der Maas (Grand Rapids, Mich.: Zondervan, 2002), 514–15.

4. Ibid.

5. Interested readers can find more information on these deceptively simple distinctions I have made in John Searle's work on the *background*, Pierre Bourdieu's *habitus*, and Margaret Archer's *practice*. John Searle, *The Construction of Social Reality* (London: Penguin, 1995); Pierre Bourdieu, *The Logic of Practice* (Stanford: Stanford University Press, 1990); Margaret Archer, *Being Human* (Cambridge: Cambridge University Press, 2000).

6. John D. Witvliet, "Conclusion: Assessing Continuity and Change in Late Medieval and Early Modern Christian Worship," in *Worship in Medieval and Early Modern Europe*, ed. Karin Maag and John D. Witvliet (Notre Dame, Ind.: University of Notre Dame Press, 2004), 336–38.

7. David Pass, *Music and the Church*, 2nd ed. (Johannesburg: PassWord, 2005), 117–23.

8. Harvey Cox, *Fire from Heaven* (London: Cassell, 1996), 81.

9. Alister McGrath, *The Twilight of Atheism* (London: Rider, 2004), 206.

10. Ibid., 212.

11. Ibid., 215.

12. James White, *Protestant Worship* (Louisville, Ky.: Westminster John Knox, 1989), 200.

13. Gordon Wakefield, ed., *A Dictionary of Christian Spirituality* (London: SCM, 1983), 307–13.

14. Patrick Miller, *They Cried Out to the Lord* (Minneapolis, Minn.: Fortress, 1994), 86–133.

15. Roland Allen, *And I Will Praise Him* (Grand Rapids, Mich.: Kregel, 1992), 73–89.

16. Bruce Waltke, "Psalms: Theology of," in *The New International Dictionary of Old Testament Theology and Exegesis*, ed. by Willem VanGemeren (Grand Rapids, Mich.: Zondervan, 1997), 4:1103–7.

17. Jürgen Moltmann, *The Trinity and the Kingdom of God* (London: SCM, 1981), 152–53.

18. See note 6 above, Witvliet, "Conclusion: Assessing Continuity and Change in Late Medieval and Early Modern Christian Worship," 337–38.

19. See note 12 above, White, *Protestant Worship*, 18.

20. Daniel Albrecht, *Rites in the Spirit* (Sheffield: Sheffield Academic Press, 1999), 25.

21. Ibid., 179–84.

22. Brian Childs, "Gratitude," in *Dictionary of Pastoral Care and Counseling*, ed. Rodney J. Hunter (Nashville: Abingdon, 1990), 470–71.

23. Jonathan Edwards, *The Religious Affections* (Edinburgh: Banner of Truth Trust, 1961), 23.

24. Ibid., 44.

25. See note 20 above, Albrecht, *Rites in the Spirit*, 156.

26. Joel Beeke, "Calvin on Piety," in *The Cambridge Companion to John Calvin*, ed. Donald K. McKim (Cambridge: Cambridge University Press, 2004), 139.

27. Wayne Grudem, *Bible Doctrine* (Downers Grove, Ill.: InterVarsity, 1999), 332.

28. Ibid., 326–31.

29. See note 26 above, Beeke, "Calvin on Piety," 130.

30. David Pass, *Principles of Christian Worship* (Johannesburg: PassWord, 2004), 2.

31. Jaroslav Pelikan, *Credo* (New Haven: Yale University Press, 2003), 309–18.

32. Robert F. Hayburn, *Papal Legislation on Sacred Music* (Collegeville, Minn.: Liturgical, 1979), 18.

33. Erik Routley, *Christian Hymns Observed* (London: Mowbray, 1982), 107.

Chapter 8: Praise the Name of Jesus

1. A fine narrative on texts of hymnody during the last 25 years can be found in Erik Routley, *A Panorama of Christian Hymnody*, ed. Paul A. Richardson (Chicago: GIA, 2005), 469–674.

2. Donald P. Hustad, "Let's Not Just Praise the Lord," *Christianity Today* 31 (Nov 6, 1987): 28–31; see also Robert Webber, "Enter His Courts with Praise," *Reformed Worship* 20 (June 1991): 9–12; Michael S. Hamilton, "The Triumph of the Praise Songs: How Guitars Beat out the Organ in the Worship Wars," *Christianity Today* 43 (July 12, 1999): 28–35; Cornelius Plantinga, Jr., "Theological Particularities of Recent Hymnody," *The Hymn* 52 (Oct 2001): 8–15.

3. Paul Westermeyer, *Let the People Sing: Hymn Tunes in Perspective* (Chicago: GIA, 2005), 4.

4. The best recent studies of hymn tunes are the Westermeyer book. See note 3 above, Westermeyer, *Let the People Sing*.

5. Robb Redman, "Songs from Praise and Worship Sources," *Sing! A New Creation: Leader's Edition* (Grand Rapids, Mich.: CRC, 2002), 420.

6. This is the famous phrase from the Roman Catholic Vatican II documents on worship that has been equally influential in Protestantism.

7. See the contrasting views of D. G. Hart in "Post-Modern Evangelical Worship," *Calvin Theological Journal* 30 (Nov 1995): 451–59; see also John M. Frame, *Contemporary Worship Music: A Biblical Defense* (Phillipsburg, N.J.: P&R, 1997).

8. Example 1 is from the printed score of Matt and Beth Redman's *Blessed Be Your Name*, © 2002, Thankyou Music. Example 2 is my notation of how congregations are likely to sing such a syncopated phrase.

9. Various Christians have objected to the romanticized lyrics of *Draw Me Close* and refuse to participate in the abstract worship of an unidentified "You" in *When I Look into Your Holiness*.

10. Peter Horrobin and Greg Leavers, *Complete Mission Praise* (London: Marshall Pickering, 1999); see also Hope Publishing Company, *Worship and Rejoice* (Carol Stream, Ill.: Hope, 2001). These are two modern (hardbound) hymnals that incorporate a variety of P-W songs amongst their eclectic collection of traditional, modern, and global Christian hymnody. It would be interesting to study the extent to which the four criteria I used in assigning some P-W songs to congregational use were also— *de facto*—operative in the minds of the editors of these two hymnals.

11. I discuss this "anthology" concept in "Forward Steps and Side-Steps in a Walk-Through of Christian Hymnody," in *Music in Christian Worship at the Service of the Liturgy*, ed. Charlotte Kroeker (Collegeville, Minn.: Liturgical, 2005), 62–72.

12. *In Christ Alone* is not on the list of 77 used in this volume, but is definitely on the global data lists of the CCLI agency for several years already, and most recently also appeared on the U.S. list for 2006.

Chapter 9: When the Music Fades

1. Jeremy Begbie, *Music in God's Purposes* (Edinburgh: Handsel, 1989), 6.

2. John Frame, *Contemporary Worship Music: A Biblical Defense* (Philipsburg, N.J.: P&R, 1997), 108.

3. Terri B. McLean, *New Harmonies: Choosing Contemporary Music for Worship* (Bethesda, Md.: Alban Institute, 1998), 41.

4. John D. Witvliet, *Worship Seeking Understanding: Windows into Christian Practice* (Grand Rapids, Mich.: Baker, 2003), 263.

5. Personal discussion with Keith Getty, August 4, 2006, Chagrin Falls, Cleveland, Ohio. Keith Getty is the co-composer of *In Christ Alone*, which is currently ranked number 1 in the British CCLI list. Getty points to classic ballads, folk melodies, show tunes like *You'll Never Walk Alone*, and the finest hymn tunes as evidence that the common people need, first and foremost, a great melody.

6. Tommy Walker, *Songs from Heaven* (Ventura, Calif.: Regal, 2005), 49.

7. The melody of his modern folk piece *Here I Am, Lord* (not in the 77) has captured thousands around the world. It is challenging to discover why that capturing process occurs in so many similarly good melodies.

8. Alan Walker, *An Anatomy of Musical Criticism* (New York: Chilton, 1968).

9. Fred E. Maus, *The New Grove Dictionary of Music and Musicians*, 2nd ed., vol. 6 (New York: Macmillan, 2001).

10. Sally Morgenthaler, *Worship Evangelism: Inviting Unbelievers into the Presence of God* (Grand Rapids, Mich.: Zondervan, 1995), 220.

11. See note 3 above, McLean, *New Harmonies*, 42.

12. Don E. Collins, *Sound Decisions: Evaluating Contemporary Music for Lutheran Worship* (Minneapolis, Minn.: Augsburg Fortress, 1997), 13.

13. Leonard B. Meyer, *Music, the Arts, and Ideas* (Chicago: The University of Chicago Press, 1994).

14. Alice Parker, *The Anatomy of Melody: Exploring the Single Line of Song* (Chicago: GIA, 2006), 129.

15. See note 10 above, Sally Morgenthaler, *Worship Evangelism*, 220.

16. In defense of Smith's song there is a fair degree of variety within the basic ideas, there is a contrasting upward-moving chorus melody, and the main elements return in an appropriate, nonformulaic way.

17. John D. Witvliet, "Beyond Style," in *The Conviction of Things Not Seen: Worship and Ministry in the 21st Century*, ed. Todd Johnson (Grand Rapids, Mich.: Brazos, 2002).

18. C. S. Lewis, "On Church Music," in *Christian Reflections* (Grand Rapids, Mich.: Eerdmans, 2003), 96.

19. See note 2 above, Frame, *Contemporary Worship Music*, 127.

Chapter 10: When I Survey the Wondrous Cross

1. Barry Liesch, *The New Worship: Straight Talk on Music and the Church* (Grand Rapids, Mich.: Baker, 2001), 9.

2. Marva Dawn, *Reaching Out without Dumbing Down: A Theology of Worship for the Turn-of-the-Century Culture* (Grand Rapids, Mich.: Eerdmans, 1995), 167.

3. Greg Scheer, unpublished manuscript, 2006, "Praise and Worship from Jesus People to Gen X," 5. Greg Scheer is Minister of Worship at Church of the Servant in Grand Rapids and Music Associate at the Calvin Institute of Christian Worship. His manuscript is scheduled to appear in *New Songs of Celebration Render: Streams of 21st-Century Congregational Song*, ed. C. Michael Hawn (GIA), forthcoming.

4. Margaret Brady, *An Investigation of the Use of Contemporary Congregational Music in Undergraduate Sacred Music Programs* (DeKalb: Northern Illinois University Press, 2002), 58–59.

5. Katherine Charlton, *Rock Music Styles: A History* (New York: McGraw Hill, 2003), xii.

6. CCLI lists the chorus of *Turn Your Eyes upon Jesus* as having been copyrighted in 1989, when it is actually the chorus of a hymn written in 1922. *Joy to the World*, a Christmas carol from the 1700s, was also removed from the list.

7. Michael Campbell, *And the Beat Goes On: An Introduction to Popular Music in America, 1840 to Today* (Belmont, Calif.: Schirmer, 1996), 319.

8. Rhythm in popular music is the interaction of the beat with different emphases, such as the back beat emphasizing beat 2 and 4 in a 4-beat count. Melody is a group of pitches moving to create the melodic line, heard as the most important voice. Melodic lines that move in stepwise patterns are called scales. There are eight steps or degrees to each major scale. Harmony is a group of pitches heard in both voices and instruments as a simultaneous event. Instrumentation refers to the voices and instruments chosen for the song. Texture is the amount of sounds layered together, as in thin texture for few voices and thick texture for many voices. Form is the organization of sections of music, such as verse and chorus, or sections that are labeled in order of appearance, such as ABA.

9. See note 7 above, Campbell, *And the Beat Goes On*, 212.

10. Ibid., 212–13.

11. Ibid., 217–18, 232–53.

12. Ibid., 113, 153, 248, 261.

13. James Goff, *Close Harmony: A History of Southern Gospel* (Chapel Hill: University of North Carolina Press, 2002), 9.

14. Thomas Bergler, "'I Found My Thrill': The Youth for Christ Movement and American Congregational Singing, 1940–1970," in *Wonderful Words of Life: Hymns in American Protestant History and Theology*, ed. Richard Mouw and Mark Noll (Grand Rapids, Mich.: Eerdmans, 2004), 123.

15. See note 7 above, Campbell, *And the Beat Goes On*, 239.

16. See note 3 above, Scheer, "Praise and Worship from Jesus People to Gen X," 5.

17. Donald Hustad, *Jubilate II: Church Music in Worship Renewal* (Carol Stream, Ill.: Hope, 1993), 462.

18. See note 7 above, Campbell, *And the Beat Goes On*, 213, 287–88.

19. See note 3 above, Scheer, "Praise and Worship from Jesus People to Gen X," 5–6.

20. See note 7 above, Campbell, *And the Beat Goes On*, 242.

21. Robert E. Webber, ed., *The Complete Library of Christian Worship: Music and the Arts in Christian Worship* (Peabody, Mass.: Hendrickson, 1994), 4:76.

22. Michael Campbell, *Rock and Roll: An Introduction* (New York: Schirmer, 1999), 339–42, 347, 355–57.

23. See note 21 above, Webber, *The Complete Library of Christian Worship*, 270–77.

24. See note 3 above, Scheer, "Praise and Worship from Jesus People to Gen X," 16.

25. Ibid., 17.

26. Michael Campbell, in discussion with the author.

27. Eddie Gibbs and Ryan Bolger, *Emerging Churches: Creating Christian Community in Postmodern Cultures* (Grand Rapids, Mich.: Baker Academic, 2005), 20–21.

28. After ten years of ministry this service was discontinued in 2006.

29. See note 3 above, Scheer, "Praise and Worship from Jesus People to Gen X," 23.

30. Terry York, "Add One Hymn: Recipe for CCM and 'Modern Worship' Congregational Song," *The Hymn: A Journal of Congregational Song* 55.3 (July 2004): 32.

31. Worship Together.com, "Membership," http://www.worshiptogether.com/Membership (accessed Aug 5, 2006).

32. Peter Van der Merwe, *Origins of the Popular Style: The Antecedents of Twentieth-Century Popular Music* (Oxford: Clarendon, 1989), 4.

33. Harold E. Best, *Music Through the Eyes of Faith* (San Francisco: Harper, 1993), 93.

Conclusion: Discipleship and the Future of Contemporary Worship Music

1. I have explored this metaphor at greater length in John D. Witvliet, *Worship Seeking Understanding* (Grand Rapids, Mich.: Baker Academic, 2003), chapter 9.

2. Michael Hawn, *Gather into One: Praying and Singing Globally* (Grand Rapids, Mich.: Eerdmans, 2003), 234–40. By cyclical forms, Hawn refers to forms of music that return to repeated refrains, sometimes with subtle variations. By linear forms, he refers to texts that unfold over time, texts that move somewhere, perhaps by telling a story or outlining an idea.

3. For more on this, see Paul Ryan, "Consider Those 'In Between' Words: Spoken Transitions in Worship," *Reformed Worship* 79 (March 2006): 18–19, also available online at www.reformedworship. org. See also Joan Huyser-Honig, "The 'In Between' Words: How to Keep Fellow Worshippers Tuned in" (Calvin Institute of Christian Worship, 2006) accessed from http://www.calvin.edu/worship/stories/inbetween.php.

4. See the description in Barry Liesch, *New Music for Worship: Straight Talk on Music and the Church* (Grand Rapids, Mich.: Baker, 1996), chapters 3–4.

5. Ron Rienstra, *Planning Contemporary Worship*, vol. 2 (Grand Rapids, Mich.: Faith Alive, 2003, 2006). See also Joan Huyser-Honig, "Planning Contemporary Worship Services" (Calvin Institute of Christian Worship, 2006) accessed from http://www.calvin.edu/worship/stories/contemp_wrshp.php.

6. See, for example, Geoffrey Wainwright, *Doxology: The Praise of God in Worship, Doctrine, and Life* (New York: Oxford University Press, 1980), for a study of worship-related topics in light of each tradition theme and topic in Christian systematic theology. For work in the free church tradition, see Christopher J. Ellis, *Gathering: A Theology and Spirituality of Worship in Free Church Tradition* (London: SCM, 2004).

7. The very notion of genuinely corporate worship may be very difficult for anyone in the postmodern West to genuinely appreciate. One example that illustrates the difference is that of the creed in worship. A creed in worship will nearly always involve different words than any individual testimony would express. For the creed expresses the faith not merely of an individual but of the church. The point of speaking a creed in unison is (a) that the faith of the church is so much larger and richer than any individual's faith, and (b) that each of us as individuals has much to learn by taking the creeds as our mentors. For more on this, see, for example, Ron Byars, "Creed/Ecclesiology" in *Worship and Theology in Harmony*, ed. Leanne Van Dyk (Grand Rapids, Mich.: Eerdmans, 2004), 86–92.

8. Matt Redman, *The Unquenchable Worshipper* (Ventura, Calif.: Regal, 2001), 27–28; see also Matt Redman, *Blessed Be Your Name: Worshipping God on the Road Marked with Suffering* (Ventura, Calif.: Regal, 2005); Matt Redman, *Inside out Worship: Insights for Passionate and Purposeful Worship* (Ventura, Calif.: Regal, 2005); Louie Giglio, *The Air I Breathe: Worship As a Way of Life* (Sisters, Ore.: Multnomah, 2003); David A. Crowder, *Praise Habit: Finding God in Sunsets and Sushi* (Colorado Springs: NavPress, 2005); Darlene Zschech, *Extravagant Worship* (Minneapolis, Minn.: Bethany House, 2001); Gerrit Gustafson, *The Adventure of Worship* (Grand Rapids, Mich.: Chosen, 2006); David M. Edwards, *Worship Three Sixty-Five: The Power of a Worshipping Life* (Nashville: Broadman and Holman, 2006).

9. This is a goal of Robin Parry, *Worshipping Trinity: Coming Back to the Heart of Worship* (Cumbria, Calif.: Paternoster, 2005). Similarly, Gerrit Scott Dawson offers a compelling case for recovery of our awareness of the priestly work of the ascended Jesus as we worship, in Gerrit Scott Dawson, *Jesus*

Ascended: The Meaning of Christ's Continuing Incarnation (Philipsburg, N.J.: P&R, 2004). Reggie Kidd helps worshipers reconceive of music as "Christ's Song in Our Worship" in Reggie Kidd, *With One Voice* (Grand Rapids, Mich.: Baker, 2005).

10. Robb Redman, *The Great Worship Awakening: Singing a New Song in the Postmodern Church* (San Francisco: Jossey-Bass, 2002).

11. Beyond these are many other volumes critical of CWM, but they are not primarily historical in nature.

12. Paul F. Bradshaw and Lawrence A. Hoffman, eds., *The Changing Face of Jewish and Christian Worship in North America* (Notre Dame, Ind.: University of Notre Dame Press, 1991); see also Lawrence A. Hoffman and Janet R. Walton, *Sacred Sound and Social Change: Liturgical Music in Jewish and Christian Experience* (Notre Dame, Ind.: University of Notre Dame Press, 1992).

13. For starters, see Edith L. Blumhofer and Mark A. Noll, *Singing the Lord's Song in a Strange Land: Hymnody in the History of North American Protestantism* (Tuscaloosa: University of Alabama Press, 2004); see also David W. Stowe, *How Sweet the Sound: Music in the Spiritual Lives of Americans* (Cambridge, Mass.: Harvard University Press, 2004); Stephen A. Marini, *Sacred Song in America: Religion, Music, and Public Culture* (Chicago: University of Illinois Press, 2003).

14. Indeed, one of the reasons that CWM has felt so new and unprecedented is that our working knowledge of liturgical history is primarily that of formal, approved liturgical texts and intellectual analyses. The publication of several recent social histories is a promising start on rounding out our sense of history. See also Susan J. White, *A History of Women in Christian Worship* (Cleveland: Pilgrim, 2003); Martin Stringer, *A Sociological History of Christian Worship* (Cambridge: Cambridge University Press, 2005); Frank Senn, *The People's Work: A Social History of the Liturgy* (Minneapolis, Minn.: Fortress, 2006); Tex Sample, *White Soul: Country Music, the Church and Working Americans* (Nashville: Abingdon, 1996).

15. For an example of more journalistic accounts, see Randall Balmer, *Mine Eyes Have Seen the Glory*, 4th ed. (New York: Oxford University Press, 2006). For a sample history-oriented academic monograph, see also Howard Dorgan, *Giving Glory to God in Appalachia: Worship Practices of Six Baptist Subdenominations* (Knoxville: University of Tennessee Press, 1987). For a sample sociology-oriented academic monograph, see also Timothy J. Nelson, *Every Time I Feel the Spirit: Religious Experience and Ritual in an African American Church* (New York: New York University Press, 2005).

16. Brenda Eatman Aghahowa, *Praising in Black and White: Unity and Diversity in Christian Worship* (Cleveland: United Church Press, 1996); see also Melva Wilson Costen, *In Spirit and in Truth: The Music of African American Worship* (Louisville, Ky.: Westminster, 2004); James Abbington, ed., *Readings in African American Church Music and Worship* (Chicago: GIA, 2001).

17. See, for example, Efrem Smith and Phil Jackson, *The Hip-Hop Church: Connecting with the Movement Shaping Our Culture* (Downers Grove, Ill.: InterVarsity, 2005).

18. See, for example, Karen J. Chai, "Competing for the Second Generation: English-Language Ministry at a Korean Protestant Church," in *Gatherings in Diaspora: Religious Communities and the New Immigration*, ed. R. Stephen Warner and Judith G. Wittner (Philadelphia: Temple University Press, 1998). See also Su Yon Pak and others, *Singing the Lord's Song in a New Land: Korean American Practices of Faith* (Louisville: Westminster, 2005).

19. Justo L. González, ed., *¡Alabadle! Hispanic Christian Worship* (Nashville: Abingdon, 1996).

20. Gerardo Marti, *A Mosaic of Believers: Diversity and Innovation in Multicultural Church* (Bloomington: Indiana University Press, 2005).

21. Robert Wuthnow, *All in Sync: How Music and Art Are Revitalizing American Religion* (Berkeley: University of California Press, 2004); see also Mark Chavez, *Congregations in America* (Cambridge, Mass.: Harvard University Press, 2004); Nancy Tatom Ammerman, *Pillars of Faith: American Congregations and Their Partners* (Berkeley: University of California Press, 2005).

22. Mary E. McGann, *A Precious Fountain: Music in the Worship of an African American Catholic Community* (Collegeville, Minn.: Liturgical Press, 2004). See note 20 above, Marti, *A Mosaic of Believers*; see also note 15, Nelson, *Every Time I Feel the Spirit*.

23. Thomas Edward Frank, *The Soul of the Congregation: An Invitation to Congregational Reflection* (Nashville: Abingdon, 2000).

24. Pete Ward, *Selling Worship: How What We Sing Has Changed the Church* (Cumbria, Calif.: Paternoster, 2005).

25. Michael Card, *A Sacred Sorrow: Reaching Out to God with the Lost Language of Lament* (Colorado Springs: NavPress, 2005).

26. See, for example, Camilo José Vergara, *How the Other Half Worships* (New Brunswick, N.J.: Rutgers University Press, 2005).

27. Quentin Schultze, *High-Tech Worship?* (Grand Rapids, Mich.: Baker, 2004); see also Richard Gaillardetz, *Transforming Our Days: Spirituality, Community, and Liturgy in a Technological Culture* (New York: Crossroad, 2000); Shane Hipps, *The Hidden Power of Electronic Culture: How Media Shapes Faith, the Gospel, and Church* (Grand Rapids, Mich.: Zondervan, 2005); Tex Sample, *Powerful Persuasion: Multimedia Witness in Christian Worship* (Nashville: Abingdon, 2005).

28. Quentin Schultze, *Habits of the High-Tech Heart: Living Virtuously in the Information Age* (Grand Rapids, Mich.: Baker Academic, 2002).

29. See, for example, William Willimon, *Worship and Pastoral Care* (Nashville: Abingdon, 1979).

30. See, for example, Brett Webb Mitchell, *Dancing with Disabilities: Opening the Church to All God's Children* (Cleveland: United Church Press, 1996).

31. Kathy Smith, *Stilling the Storm: Worship and Congregational Leadership in Difficult Times* (Herndon, Va.: Alban Institute, 2006).

32. Peter Bush and Christine O'Reilly, *Where 20 or 30 Are Gathered: Leading Worship in the Small Church* (Herndon, Va.: Alban Institute, 2006).

33. Cornelius Plantinga and Sue A. Rozeboom, *Discerning the Spirits: A Guide to Thinking about Christian Worship Today* (Grand Rapids, Mich.: Eerdmans, 2003), chapter 3.

34. See the musical issues that run through Michael Hawn, *One Bread, One Body: Exploring Cultural Diversity in Worship* (Bethesda, Md.: Alban Institute, 2003).

35. Nancy Tatom Ammerman and others, *Studying Congregations* (Nashville: Abingdon, 1998).

36. See, for example, E. Byron Anderson, *Worship and Christian Identity: Practicing Ourselves* (Collegeville, Minn.: Liturgical Press, 2003); see also Debra Dean Murphy, *Teaching That Transforms: Worship as the Heart of Christian Education* (Grand Rapids, Mich.: Brazos, 2004); Don E. Saliers, "Liturgy Teaching Us to Pray: Christian Liturgy and Grateful Lives of Prayer," in *Liturgy and Spirituality in Context: Perspectives on Prayer and Culture*, ed. by Eleanor Bernstein, C.S.J. (Collegeville, Minn.: Liturgical, 1990).

37. See, for example, Dallas Willard, *The Spirit of the Disciplines: Understanding How God Changes Lives* (San Francisco: Harper Collins, 1988); Debra Rienstra, *So Much More: An Invitation to Christian Spirituality* (San Francisco: Jossey-Bass, 2005).

38. See, for example, Joyce Ann Mercer, *Welcoming Children: A Practical Theology of Childhood* (St. Louis: Chalice, 2005).

39. I would suggest that narrative specificity is a very important part of faithful worship. People who worship a God who acts in history should ground their worship with vivid and specific gratitude for the variety of ways God has acted. My sense is that CWM has made worship a more "present tense" in orientation, rather than helping worshipers sense their participation over time in the grand narrative of God's work from creation to new creation. This is closely tied to the use of certain musical forms. See my discussion above, and for more extended discussion see note 1 above, Witvliet, *Worship Seeking Understanding*, chapter 1. I hasten to add, however, that there is nothing to prevent CWM

songwriters from doing more with narrative forms and specific historical references. In fact, I would suggest that this is a significant area for future development.

40. See, for example, Jon Middendorf, *Worship-Centered Youth Ministry: A Compass for Guiding Youth into God's Story* (Kansas City, Mo.: Beacon Hill, 2000).

41. Mark Yaconelli, *Contemplative Youth Ministry: Practicing the Presence of Jesus* (Grand Rapids, Mich.: Zondervan, 2006); see also Carol E. Lytch, *Choosing Church: What Makes a Difference for Teens* (Louisville: Westminster, 2004); Kenda Creasy Dean, *Practicing Passion: Youth and the Quest for a Passionate Church* (Grand Rapids, Mich.: Eerdmans, 2004).

42. For a sampling of works on methodology in liturgical study, see Paul F. Bradshaw, *The Search for the Origins of Christian Worship: Sources and Methods for the Study of Early Liturgy* (New York: Oxford University Press, 1992); Anton Baumstark, *Comparative Liturgy* (London: Mowbray, 1958); James F. White, *Protestant Worship* (Louisville, Ky.: Westminster, 1992); Joyce Ann Zimmerman, *Liturgy and Hermeneutics* (Collegeville, Minn.: Liturgical, 1999); Mary E. McGann, *Exploring Music as Worship and Theology: Research in Liturgical Practice* (Collegeville, Minn.: Liturgical, 2002); Edward Foley, *Ritual Music: Studies in Liturgical Musicology* (Beltsville, Md.: Pastoral, 1995); Helen Cameron et al., *Studying Local Churches: A Handbook* (London: SCM, 2005).

43. See Greg Scheer's review of recently released Psalm-based CDs at http://www.calvin.edu/worship/Psalms.

44. Debra Rienstra, "Language in Worship" (forthcoming). On the craft of composition, see Stephen Darlington and Alan Krieder, eds., *Composing Music for Worship* (Norwich: Canterbury, 2003).

45. I think here of the careful refinement process that Keith Getty gives to his songwriting. See http://www.calvin.edu/worship/stories/getty.php.

46. See Austin Lovelace, *The Anatomy of Hymnody* (Chicago: GIA, 1965) for a very accessible guide to the craft of text writing. In many cases, his approaches for analyzing hymntexts would open up new and creative ways to understand CWM, and many inspire new approaches to the craft of text-writing for CWM songwriters.

47. I am also well aware that nearly limitless choice can, counterintuitively, reduce the range of options we research. Like psychologists who have studied how the seemingly limitless choices in our supermarkets actually reduce the range of options buyers seriously look into, we may discover that our Internet-based information culture has actually stymied thoughtful research into multiple musical options for most congregations.

48. I have been tangentially involved in the development of a forthcoming songbook for worship that will attempt to present songs in biblical order, starting with a volume on the New Testament that will present songs in biblical order from Matthew to Revelation. It has been a challenging process, to say the least. While we have over 50 settings of grand vision of worship for Revelation 4 and 5, we have almost no songs on the CCLI list for vast stretches of the Gospels and large portions of Paul's letters—including some of the most lyrical parts of them. *Singing Scripture* (Grand Rapids, Mich.: Faith Alive Publications, forthcoming). Another example of this kind of book is *Hymns for the Gospels* (Chicago: GIA, 2001).

49. For more on this helpful metaphor, see Thomas G. Long, *Testimony* (San Francisco: Jossey-Bass, 2004), 47.

50. For more on worship and the fruit of the Spirit, see Philip Kenneson, *Life on the Vine: Cultivating the Fruit of the Spirit in Christian Community* (Downers Grove, Ill.: InterVarsity, 1999).

SONG INDEX

Top 77 CWM songs as reported by CCLI between 1989 and 2005 (in alphabetical order)